EFFECTIVE CRISIS MANAGEMEI

Also available from Cassell:

Cannon: *Marketing – Principles and Practice*, 5th edition

Denvir, Ferguson and Walker: *Creating New Clients*

Evans: *Supervisory Management*, 5th edition

Forsyth: *Career Skills*

Mendelsohn: *The Guide to Franchising*, 6th edition

Pettinger: *Managing the Flexible Workforce*

Effective Crisis Management

Worldwide Principles and Practice

Mike Seymour and
Simon Moore

CASSELL

London and New York

Cassell

Wellington House   370 Lexington Avenue
125 Strand   New York
London WC2R 0BB   NY 10017-6550

First published 2000

British Library Cataloguing-in-Publication Data
A catalogue record for this book is available from the British Library.

ISBN 0-304-70328-1 (hardback)
     0-304-70329-X (paperback)

Typeset by ensystems Ltd, Saffron Walden, Essex
Printed in Great Britain by Cromwell Press Ltd, Trowbridge, Wiltshire

Contents

Acknowledgements

WE WOULD LIKE TO acknowledge the help, advice and support we received from our wives Sandra and Lindy, plus Erik Austin, Bentley College, Andrea Cochran, Gisela Damm, Michelle DiMatteo, Adam Moore, Sandra den Otter, Bruce MacNaughton, Javed Siddiqi, Patricia L. Williams, and their students and families. We are also grateful to those who gave permission to quote their work. May we also apologize to those we have been unable to reach or whose material we may unwittingly have used. If ever we are contacted by any such person, we will gladly give due acknowledgement.

The names of people and organizations used in the Bluepage story are fictitious and not intended to resemble any person or organization.

To Lindy, Adam and Anna

Preface

CRISES HAPPEN MORE than we imagine. They are not always easy to see unless they affect our own lives. Perhaps we are so glutted with media-driven scandals that we no longer notice them. The *Daily Yomiuri* would probably mean nothing to most people outside Japan. In fact, it is an English-language newspaper, serious and well written. I happened to glance over a copy during a recent trip to Tokyo. On page one, alongside stories about an earthquake, a North Korean submarine and the state of US–China relations, is a report informing us that 166.1 billion yen in interest is owed by ten oil companies to the Japan National Oil Corporation, 'that the public corporation will almost certainly fail to recover, according to documents obtained by the *Yomiuri Shimbun* on Monday'. The two largest defaulters are named. The numbers involved certainly look enormous. 'In addition', the report continues, '68 oil development firms received loans for mining areas that are still not paid off.' The account concludes: 'This shows that the public corporation is handing out loans without a clear vision.'[1]

A crisis, surely. For whom? Certainly for the two companies actually named; also the remaining eight defaulters, and then the 68 companies who have not paid off their loans. Most of all, a crisis for the Japan National Oil Corporation, which has launched an investigation with the International Trade and Industry Ministry.

Who cares? Probably not you or I. But others do care very much. The shareholders care. Suppliers care. Lenders care. Employees care, clearly, since a confidential document has been leaked by an employee to a journalist. This, then, is news of a crisis, emerging in the bottom right-hand front page of a respected Japanese newspaper, that could lead to massive restructuring in the oil industry and wound the reputation of a public body with an international profile. It is a crisis, and an intense effort will be needed by many organizations to overcome their difficulties. Some companies may lie low, keep quiet and try to get away with it. Others will not. They will have an international audience demanding answers: analysts, fund managers, venture capitalists, investors, customers. The quality of those answers will be critical to their survival.

We are not finished with the *Daily Yomiuri* yet. Right at the bottom of page one is a preview for a story on the following page. 'A researcher says that substances suspected to be environmental hormones in cup noodle containers are dissolved into soup.' Noodle soup restaurants are a cheap, popular and fast way to eat in Japan. Page two carries the full story. Substances from the polystyrene cups, which have been detected in the soup by a government scientist, may have the ability to 'disrupt' the body's 'reproductive functions'.[2] In Japan, this is a big story and in fact there have been immediate responses from the two industry associations representing convenience foods and styrene. Both organizations say that their own tests have found no effects on laboratory animals, and they describe the tests in detail. A communications plan is clearly in place, which is not surprising, given the size of the industry and the potential for this issue to wear businesses down by attrition and the gradual accumulation of evidence. Is it a good communications plan? It is hard to say at this stage, but the details of the association's tests are less likely to stick in the public memory than the headline. Perhaps something more is needed.

It does not take much imagination to see that for every media outlet in every country there are dozens of corporate crises unrolling at any moment. Some of these crises are extremely localized – perhaps a neighbourhood protest against a new building development; others may be national, or international, and involve the coordination of people and resources over large areas of space and multiple time zones.

A crisis defies all the usual rules of business management. At its height, it produces a situation of total flux, when, as the ancient Greek philosopher Heraclitus famously put it: 'You cannot step twice into the same river, for other waters are continually flowing on.'[3] Developments may surge one after the other with giddying speed, and the troubled company will feel sorely tempted towards a policy of silence, or of simply reacting to events.

This need not happen. It is far better to agree with Heraclitus that there is no distinction between good and bad days, and that 'every day is like every other'.[4] A crisis is not black and white; or a single stroke of ill-fortune. It is an event that exploits an existing gap between you and your public. A crisis is not simply a bad day at the office. It is a time when you will have to display greater flexibility and sensitivity than is normal in order to deal with the challenges – and the chances – that it presents.

Notes

1   'Y166.1 bil. in interest owed to public corp'. *Daily Yomiuri*, 30 June 1998.
2   'Environmental hormones found dissolving into cup noodles'. *Daily Yomiuri*, 30 June 1998.
3   Wheelwright, P. *Heraclitus*. New York: Atheneum, 1964, p. 29.
4   *ibid.*, p. 84.

Introduction

NOT EVERY CRISIS kills. A crisis can threaten reputation without threatening lives. Nevertheless, the basic problem remains the same – a series of hard questions. What happened? Who did it? What is your company going to say? How much did you know in advance? What are you doing about it? The advent of a crisis forces you to confront these questions, and the outside world will be impatient to hear answers.

You are more likely to experience a crisis than the person who last held your job. It will happen when an event gate-crashes your business so violently that the usual systems cannot cope. Talented people who are used to unravelling the daily headaches of working life will be blinded by the harsh glare when the roof is torn off and the outside floods in. They are not in control. They – you – are in a crisis.

Many of the conditions for your crisis were in place long before the event that triggered it. The event itself is not necessarily the problem. You could act with speed and decision to correct whatever has happened, but still not recover.

Your crisis is more likely now that the world is more demanding about what you do. This is because the information revolution and the global economy work in opposite ways. On one hand a company has new opportunities for market growth and intelligence-gathering; on the other, the outside world is taking a greater interest in a business's operations, products, employment record, environmental or safety reputation. High-tech allows companies to filter into new markets, and audiences in those new markets to filter back into the companies, exporting concerns as easily as firms export their products. The most sophisticated management teams have problems appreciating how readily borders are ignored or jumped by media and other key audiences.

In fact, your crisis will demonstrate how people unknown to you, perhaps living thousands of miles away, can make use of the same communication tools as you to push a company to the brink. What drives them on? From a standing start, their passion, indignation, suffering or motivation, however ill-informed, have the potential to ignite a crisis that blows up in your face. The flying sparks are the antithesis of business expectations: volatility, irrationality, rumour, cynicism, lack of facts, lack of *interest* in facts, fear and – most frustrating of all – a bloody-minded refusal to listen to what you, the company's executive, have to say.

And it is what you have to say, and how you say it, that will shape the crisis. Even the most international of corporations has trouble accepting that it must talk differently when a crisis strikes. You will find yourself communicating about once-marginal aspects of your operations, and about subjects that only yesterday seemed so obscure as to be scarcely worth noting. You will be pulled in different directions; expected to prove your concern, not merely with deeds but, harder still, with words. Perhaps some audiences will want you publicly to display emotion when you need to be in control of yourself; perhaps you will feel pressure to be more open about your company's actions, when legal advice is to clam up and concede nothing. You may find yourself dealing with a community, culture or powerful interest group whose priorities are utterly alien to anything you have previously experienced, but who have the strength to make or break you in their part of the world, and in your own. How do you respond if your crisis occurs overseas? After the crash of Japan Airlines Flight 123 in August 1985, the ground mechanic committed ritual suicide. The same act of atonement will hardly be expected of you, but it is entirely possible that you may feel pressured to take unfamiliar positions filled with awkward legal implications in your own country.

In a crisis, communication technology may turn against you. The media, the internet, the telephone all thunder down the information highway to besiege the company. They too are swept along by the pace of events, and by this drastic departure from everyday routine. Strangely, they are not enemies, although it may not feel that way. Other spectators will also gather to watch the crisis, joining those who feel they have in some manner been damaged by your company. Those other audiences must be tackled in different ways because they affect the current of public opinion: that nebulous, imprecise, unfair arbiter of your crisis. You can be swept along in the current, or you can attempt to navigate and direct the flow of comment in ways that are helpful, informative and accurate.

Given the number of high-profile international corporate disasters in recent years, from oil spills and tampering scares to human rights violations and deadly product failures, it is surprising how little attention is paid in business or education to the role of crisis communication. One explanation is that crises turn the usual approach to problem-solving on its head. Instead of fixing whatever went wrong, and then announcing it, you must make communications an equal priority, and fit the solution of the problem into the other critical issues you will be forced to talk about. Corporations and business schools are concerned with planning and managing, not dealing with the flux created when plans smash on the ground and managers cannot concentrate on the systems that in normal circumstances move the company forward. You are encouraged to think logically; you are excellent at dealing with facts, and the novel tension between a structured, controlled approach and one that addresses rapid and senseless swings in attitude based on half-facts or, infuriatingly, half-truths will be hard enough to handle without the added minute-by-minute distractions that also threaten to tear the rudder from your hands.

A crisis can take on a life of its own and propel participants in unexpected directions. You may be forced to decide if a crisis in one market requires a response in another, and how extensive that response should be. There may not be much time to decide. The first few hours of a crisis will not be long enough to find answers, but those hours may seal the company's fate. A company's reputation, equity and even survival may hinge on its communications. For that reason if for no other, it is essential to overcome the disruptions that a crisis can cause, to understand the absolute worst that can happen, and know what can be done before, during and after the crisis.

Effective crisis communication, especially on a worldwide scale, demands patience, decision, stamina, nerve, insight, sensitivity and the courage to turn and face the light at a time when most human beings and corporations want to look away. You will feel a tremendous temptation to escape the clamour, to tune out the deafening noise that, like a neighbour's car alarm, makes it hard to concentrate on the job in hand.

Crisis communication, the subject of this book, is an effective discipline born out of hard experience. It has helped organizations across the globe in their time of trial, and becomes more effective with each new crisis. It has consistently been identified as a growth area in the communication business, and a number of able practitioners are on hand for troubled companies to consult. More research into the subject is being undertaken by academics, who are slowly enriching the field with their contributions. This is all to the good: best practice rests firmly upon best theory.

Many subjects have something to contribute to effective crisis communication: psychology, risk assessment, history, media relations, multiculturalism, to name a few; but they must all be useful to the man or woman – to you – sitting in an office, late on a Friday afternoon. You have just put down the telephone, transfixed by the scale of the problem. What will you do next? This book provides some answers.

A crisis can sweep over working lives and devour every second. You must be prepared. This book is about what to expect and what to do in a crisis. It also conveys the sheer size of a modern crisis, because no solution can work unless the obstacles are understood: obstacles to coordination, to fact-gathering, to action itself. Some of these obstacles are structural, others are emotional. In a crisis more than any other situation, the structural and emotional run hand in hand; one has a profound affect on the other, and both demand total attention.

You cannot always expect life to go back to how it was before the crisis, but this is no bad thing. The Chinese character for crisis combines the words 'danger' and 'opportunity'. In a business crisis, the former theme receives most attention; but the opportunities of a crisis must not be neglected. A well-handled crisis should not be defined by mere survival, but by seizing opportunities to rebuild, educate and even to enhance.

This book is divided into two parts. Part I sets out the environment of a crisis, where perhaps the opening question is: how do I know if I am in a crisis or not? Some crises burst in rudely, but others roll slowly from issue to issue until the necessary momentum is generated. There are ways to minimize surprise, to read the early warning signals when they start to flash red. What does it feel like in a crisis, emotionally and tactically? This, perhaps, is the hardest thing for any exploration of crisis – written or oral – to convey, especially when the focus is on solutions. Yet it is that feeling, shared by all the participants, that blocks effective action. In order to be mastered, it must be understood.

You must communicate as soon as the crisis strikes, and as it spreads. In Part I we explain the conditions that you will find in these challenging arenas. Other questions will be tackled. What special factors foment an international crisis? How will the media and other participants in the crisis deploy the technology at their disposal? Who, for that matter, are the other participants – the people who apparently want to make life hard for your company? They are less monolithic and possibly less antagonistic than you might think. What are their concerns, how do they organize, what can we as crisis communicators learn from the way they go about their business?

Even though a crisis operates at many levels and is often difficult to reduce to precise numbers, it must also be quantified. Investors have always reacted as quickly as the media to fear of a crisis. The *Titanic*'s parent company, IMM, suffered a $2.6 million drop in share value over 15–16 April 1912, the two days after the sinking. This was 'a number not too different' from IMM's net loss for the disaster.[1] There is always a cost to the besieged company and this, in the last analysis, is what the crisis leaves behind – the fiscal and personal wreckage, followed by an operational and communications clean-up whose scale depends on the size of the damage. The areas where your crisis costs are most likely to fall will be reviewed.

Part II presents solutions to crisis. Effective crisis communication is a means for retrieving control, on a worldwide scale if required. Must a crisis be decided by what is said about you, or by what you choose to say about yourself? At the heart of a successful programme is the ability to communicate the problem on your own terms rather than on terms set by others. At the very least, the public debate must fairly incorporate your legitimate priorities. The management and coordination of your communications should aim towards that objective. Part II explains how to reach it, and in doing so deals with other problems: can normal company activities be conducted in a crisis? Is it possible to divide the crisis from your everyday operations? They can, and it is, and the essential operational recommendations are included here. Your crisis response should be a coordinated effort, strengthened by input from other fields. We will see how crisis managers use rumour management, information technology and internal communication, and mesh their tools into a tight, coherent strategy that rests on carefully crafted messages.

The best sort of crisis is of course one that never happens; but the next best is one you have anticipated and prepared for. Crisis preparedness, the subject of the last chapter, is planning against disaster. A good preparedness plan must have the capacity to read those early warning signals, to trigger information gathering and management systems, to define the problem and analyse options for action at multinational and local levels – in other words to 'think global, act local'. The process may bring other issues into sharp focus, including your existing record of openness and the transparency of your operations.

Along with many real examples drawn from events, research and a decade of global crisis experience, we also relate, in stages, one particular crisis. It shows how the ideas presented here can be applied in practice; how pitfalls and opportunities – once far off, now yawning beneath your feet – can be anticipated and mastered even in the tumult of events; and most of all, it demonstrates that effective crisis communication can help you to meet the challenge, to rise above disaster and to build, with confidence, for a better future.

Note

1   Khanna, A. 'The Titanic: the untold story'. *Financial Analysts Journal*, vol. 54, no. 5, September/October 1998, 16–18.

Part I

When the crisis strikes

Case study: Bluepage

The person who ruined the company edged her walking frame down the garden path toward her front door, as the car drove off. Alice Hill did not really want to be so old and clumsy. She had been waiting to die for so long that she was beginning to wonder if God had forgotten to write her name on his final muster-roll. Ninety-six seemed a perfectly satisfactory age to reach, and it was enough. Alice Hill did not like to be less mobile than she had been a year ago; twice in the last four months she had suffered falls that left carpet burn, tearing and huge purple bruises on her near-translucent skin. That was what had prompted her family into action. They weren't particularly well-off, but the investment was worth it to her daughters and grandchildren. It was quite marvellous really. To them she was important: the hub of a growing circle of relatives from her own children to great-grandchildren. She was their symbol: they wanted her to live, and preferably to live independently.

It had been raining that day, and Mrs Hill knew to be careful of the wet leaves on the path. This new frame really was manoeuvrable, with a handy tray in front for her glasses. Although she wasn't quite used to its lightness yet, with no help she had reached the end of the road this morning where her grandson's car was waiting. Now she was on her way back along the forty feet to the front door, quite alone, because her driver wasn't able to wait and she had insisted he leave.

Everything took so long, though. Click went the frame, then the soft brushing of her feet as she dragged them after it. Mrs Hill was concentrating on getting used to the walker, and so when it hit the depression left by the missing brick in the path (her son-in-law had promised to fill it in when he had a moment), she at first thought that the thin metal had actually snapped beneath her. Then she went down, trying as she did so to land on the grass rather than the path. Most of her did, but not all. Frame, glasses, Mrs Hill and blood mixed up together on the lawn and part of the rockery. Her head bleeding, and lapsing into unconsciousness, Alice Hill remembered her family's investment, and their love, and felt for the button at her neck.

Jennifer returned to her office and roused the computer out of its torpor. She did not have much time but that was not an unfamiliar position to her. Besides, she had built up a good relationship with the people who mattered to her company. They would give her a little latitude if necessary but she doubted that she would need it. It was typical that she was the last in the long chain of activities that Bluepage placed between a decision and eventually being able to talk about it. Her colleagues were ultra-cautious, a philosophy drummed into them by the founder of the company, who seemed to have an uncanny understanding about the kind of reassurance his audiences would need. Their new advertisements summed up the approach perfectly: the graceful fingers circling the device, the tastefully arranged legs stretched on the ground, one slightly crossing the other and both bent elegantly at the knee; the inset photograph of a worried but confident couple, barely middle-aged, able to put off the decisions about sending their mother to a nursing home for a few more years. The slogan: 'Trust Bluepage'.

The founder had found the right market at the right time: guilty baby boomers juggling their expenses. A dramatic rise in the number of elderly people was forecast in the media, almost every day it seemed, so that the issue was always nicely front and centre of people's consciousness. Bluepage offered easy, affordable instalment plans. For Jennifer, who handled the company's public relations marketing, her large and anxious audiences were a dream come true: Bluepage was not just a company flogging its wares to trade press; it genuinely felt itself to be, in part, a social service. At least, the Mission Statement said as much. With careful word-smithing, Jennifer could present new products and special offers to fit neatly into the concerns of the family and mature reader magazines that were her main targets; from Christmas ('a time of caring') to summer ('who's looking after them when you're away?') and round again.

If there had been one blip on her horizon, it had been Year 2000. A tiny blip, however. Her audiences were not, as a whole, particularly interested in computer circuitry and the concern was more prevalent within the company. It was good to know, mind you, that the problem didn't exist at Bluepage. The demonstration that morning had been quite conclusive. It was worth a release: Bluepage, alone in the business, had this issue in hand. A small announcement would not do any harm, and it would help head off any questions as the new millennium approached: questions from customers, and from investors, who had been pushing the stock upward as the company opened new offices in The Netherlands and was (an open secret) eyeing the vast markets of North America. Jennifer typed a draft headline: 'Bluepage leads with safety into the millennium'.

Mrs Hill was found next morning by the milkman. The high brick walls had hidden her from the view of neighbours and the street, and she had few visitors. The milkman ran next door and phoned for an ambulance. At the hospital they fished in her pocket and found a card with emergency numbers written down. Her family was very organized that way.

'Pretty tough woman', the doctor told them. Alice Hill was showing the marks of severe exposure. She had been outside too long, but would be OK. 'If someone had found her earlier I doubt whether she'd even need to be in hospital.' He spoke mildly, but the family felt the sting of guilt. In the hospital café, there was a bad-tempered conversation.

'If you weren't in a hurry all the time, this wouldn't have happened.'

'No, not now, John', whispered Mrs Hill's eldest daughter. Her husband, however, was implacable.

'Next stop a home, if she comes out of this. She had independence. Now it's gone.'

'Well, it was bound to happen one day', Mrs Hill's daughter said, half to herself. Her eyes brimmed suddenly with tears. 'We've been lucky, really.'

But John, a short, rotund man contemplating his own retirement, had not been listening.

'This didn't need to happen. You heard the doctor.' He glared at David, their son. 'All because you couldn't keep off those computers. You had to get back to them, didn't you? Couldn't just see her safely to the door, could you?'

David went home early that afternoon. He didn't feel like work. Instead, he sat down at his desk and flicked on his computer which whirred obediently into life.

Jennifer finished the release, had it quickly approved (the Marketing Director was very pleased with her work) and sent it off to her usual contacts at family and senior citizen media outlets. It was much quieter here than her previous work at a large consultancy, but that was exactly what she was looking for: room to breathe. Now she could leave early. A weekend stretched before her without fear of calls from clients, account managers or harried journalists. The forecast was sun and scattered clouds. She began making plans for Saturday, and had got as far as a leisurely breakfast when her secretary came in holding a sheet of paper.

'Look what I found, Jen', she said. 'We're famous.'

Jennifer took the paper. It was a printout from a chatroom. 'Have you been skiving off again?', she asked sarcastically. They both visited websites connected with health and the elderly from time to time, to keep track of gossip and news: their customers were not generally computer-conscious, but some of the age concern interest groups had interesting sites.

'It came up on the search engine. Hard to believe that there's a chatroom for senior citizens, but then again why not?'

Jennifer looked at the address. 'Never heard of it.' She read the comment. 'What does he mean, the alarm didn't work? Of course they work', she added emphatically, remembering the test that morning.

'Well, you know the sorts of things people like to do on the web – start rumours, make things up.'

'Who's going to see this?', Jennifer wondered out loud. 'None of our media, that's for certain. None of our customers, that's even more certain.' She stuck a post-it note on the paper and scribbled on it. 'Send it to customer services. I wish this person had left a number to call. It might be a hoax. Still, it's got to be looked into.' But at least

it's nothing to do with me, she thought to herself. Friday afternoon was beckoning. Jennifer hurried into her coat and left the office at 4.30 p.m.

The note would not reach customer services until after the weekend.

At 4.45 p.m. Mark Kempner, a middle-aged accountant, visited the same chatroom and almost immediately found the message about Mrs Hill's fall. He read it, printed it and dialled a number. He read the message out, very carefully, had a brief conversation and hung up. On his mantelpiece was a photograph of his late mother.

At 4.50 p.m. the phone rang at the desk of Mary Sutcliffe, a journalist for a popular and middlebrow tabloid newspaper.

'Mary – this is Max Jackson at Age Watch.'

'Hello Max.' They had known each other for quite a while. Mary covered social and family issues for the newspaper's weekend editions. If money was not an issue, she would have preferred working at Age Watch itself. She admired their work: the long hours spent talking to politicians, local authorities, consumer protection agencies and the media about the plight of the elderly. The grind of fund-raising. The occasional reward of a newspaper quotation or radio interview. From her perspective, the human interest stories they generated were very welcome indeed. She couldn't think of one of her readers who was not old or who didn't have parents. If Age Watch got a little publicity in return, so much the better.

'I think there's a problem that your readers should know about.' Max paused for effect. 'An urgent, life-threatening problem.' Within an hour, Sutcliffe had gathered together all the material for an excellent story.

Word of Mrs Hill's fall continued to spread. Although the computers at Bluepage were all off by 6 p.m. as everyone hurried home for the weekend, out in interspace the chatroom pulsed into unaccustomed activity. One by one, new stories began to appear. Soon, telephones were ringing at other offices and other homes.

Saturday breakfast was one of Jennifer's weekly luxuries. She lived in a flat in west London, and liked to nip out early to the patisserie, choose a few croissants and pastries, and consume them with orange juice and a large cappuccino.

When she got back, the light on her answering machine was flashing.

'Jen? It's Michael Bates.' What does he want, she thought with a surge of irritation. Her Marketing Director was not known for bothering people out of hours. 'We have a problem. Call me at home. Oh – did you send that Year 2000 release?' 'Of course I bloody did', Jennifer said to herself, as she dialled Michael's number. 'Why bother me about that?'

Michael's five-year-old daughter picked up the phone, and was persuaded to fetch her daddy.

'Jennifer – glad you're in. Look, sorry to bother you now. Have you heard the

news this morning? No? We've got a problem.' Jennifer felt sick, and her mouth went dry. What had she done?

'Some people are claiming that their parents died because our alarm didn't work. That's basically it. I've called Frank.' Frank Asser was the Bluepage lawyer. 'He wants a meeting at the office at ten. I'd like you there.' He continued hurriedly: 'So, did you send that release?'

After Jennifer hung up, she went shakily into the kitchen and stared at the pretty pink box she had taken from the patisserie. Then she put it in the fridge, still feeling sick, went back to the telephone and dialled her office voicemail.

'You have forty new messages.' She hung up. The phone rang almost immediately.

'Jennifer Stone? This is Sam Green of the Herald. Holly Barnes of Mature & Wise told me your name. So', he continued with disarming cheerfulness, 'how do you feel about killing all those old people?'

1 The crisis: what it is, why it happens, and what it teaches us

What is a crisis?

Storms swept southern Ontario in the first two weeks of 1999 and dumped about four feet of snow on the city of Toronto along with record low temperatures. Mayor Lastman asked the army to help clean up and commuters struggled with massive snowdrifts, closed offices and transport cancellations. Nowhere was the situation worse than at Toronto's Pearson International Airport. Passengers flooded the terminals looking for aeroplanes to board. Canadian Airlines took the decision to cancel flights quickly, leaving its customers in no doubt as to the situation. Its bigger competitor, Air Canada, did not, out of consideration for the large number of travellers returning home after the holidays. Many of its customers waited for days, sleeping at the terminal while the airline tried to make up its mind. Thousands of desperate and upset passengers besieged the check-in desks for information, but the airline did not have enough staff to cope. Television cameras arrived to capture the anger and chaos. The airline eventually apologized for the breakdown, tried to shift some of the responsibility to the airport authority, and finally, under a blizzard of hostile national coverage, conceded that its communications had been seriously at fault.

This is how most companies imagine a crisis: as an 'Act of God', an event beyond their control that catches them by surprise. A UK survey by Infoplan in 1997 found 90 per cent of the top 500 companies believed themselves prepared for such crises as natural disasters, product failures, health or safety alerts, blackmail and terrorism.[1]

While most of these anticipated crises are external threats, a high proportion depend on internal factors. Harassment, discrimination, decisions to recall, personal scandals, lawsuits and product failures are examples of problems that can emerge from within the organization. The Institute for Crisis Management (ICM), an Indiana-based firm, concluded that 'smouldering' crises were at present more common than 'sudden' ones. They analysed over 59,000 news stories on business crises and identified the fastest-growing crisis categories between 1995 and 1996. These appear to be related to 'internal' issues:

- white-collar crime[2]
- class actions
- sexual harassment
- casualty accidents

Crisis categories can be sliced and diced in all sorts of ways: is the crisis a recall of a meat product, or does the underlying public fear of tainted food make health scares the real issue? Different crises require different messages and can involve different audiences. While it is vital to be aware of one's external vulnerabilities, it is equally vital to realize that whatever the crisis and whatever the industry sector, an organization must meet the crisis by relying upon its internal culture. A forward-thinking company must be ready to handle issues, particularly those driven by external trends – health concerns, scientific debate, media fashion, interest group focus – which contribute to long-running problems such as BSE/CJD for the meat industry or Electro-Magnetic Emissions (EME) for the telecommunications sector. In business terms, the outcome of a crisis – the disruption of normal patterns of corporate activity by a sudden or overpowering and initially uncontrollable event – lies in the hands of the company rather than an 'Act of God'.

Why do crises happen?

A crisis 'happens' in two ways: first, by actually catching a company unprepared; second, by exploiting surprise and weaknesses in the company's culture to dig itself in.

Crises generally assume one of the following guises:

- The Cobra – the 'sudden' crisis. Disaster hits, taking a company completely by surprise, and plunging it straight into crisis.
- The Python – the 'slow-burning' crisis, or 'crisis creep'. A crisis can steal up and gradually crush you, issue by issue.

The Cobra: examples of surprise

Turned over by the Elk Test

A motoring magazine in Sweden staged a safety 'Elk Test' for the new Mercedes 'A-Class' car in late 1997. Daimler-Benz[3] fully expected the test would generate positive coverage for its 'Baby Benz', an attempt to move the company closer to the mass market. The Elk Test is a Swedish invention in which the test driver swerves sharply back and forth to replicate avoiding one of the large unpredictable beasts who wander onto Scandinavian roads. Unfortunately, the A-Class turned over and landed on its roof while trying to miss an imaginary elk at just 37 mph. A couple of the journalists present had the wit to call two television stations. Then they called for an ambulance. Cameras were on the scene in minutes to film the driver, another journalist, being retrieved from the crumpled car. A reporter then hurried off to break the bad news to Daimler-Benz's Swedish office. Caught by surprise, but confident about the 8 million kilometres of road testing that they had already conducted, the company's world headquarters in Stuttgart reacted by blaming the make of tyre. Within a week, though, German magazines were printing pictures of the crash,[4] while Daimler-Benz launched a 300 million Deutschmark ($177m, 153m Euros[5]) refit of tyres and electronic stabilizing systems amid cancelled orders and mocking media coverage around the world.

The Elk Test struck Daimler-Benz unexpectedly. *Time* magazine speculated that 'unpalatable facts about the A-Class's stability may have been deflected or minimized somewhere in middle management – what engineers call the "mud level" of the corporate table of organization'.[6]

Aeroplane disaster: an effective response

One of the earliest and biggest corporate crises of the postwar era was also sudden and, unlike many subsequent crises, well handled. It struck in February 1958 at Munich when a British European Airways (BEA) Elizabethan aeroplane made a third attempt to take off in a blizzard, overshot the runway, struck a house at the end of the tarmac with one wing, and ploughed into a shed. Half of those on board died in the subsequent fire. BEA was faced with a massive crisis communications problem, and no professional advice on how to go about it because no advisors as yet existed.

Of course it was hardly the first aeroplane disaster. Only the previous March a BEA flight in the UK had smashed into a block of houses during a take-off attempt and killed 22 people. This latest incident, though, fused together several elements that now regularly convert disasters into crises. One element is the contradictory, combustible brew that is created when demand for an unfamiliar product – in the 1950s mass commercial flight – generates fear about its safety from the very people who want to use it. The second element, the one that actually blazed the Munich air tragedy across the front pages of the international media, was of the involvement of celebrities – the deaths of half the Manchester United football team, the world-famous 'Busby Babes', which in 1958 was the best football team in Europe.

When crises strike suddenly, every decision must be made quickly, without knowing its full ramifications. Event comes crowding in on event with the potential for emotion to overpower the best of corporate intentions. BEA for instance had to deal with the worldwide shock of the crash itself, and a prolonged aftermath, embodied in a dramatic fight for survival by the team's captain, Duncan Edwards. Journalists flocked to the airport and hospital in Munich, and to Manchester and London in the UK. There were intrusive photographs of grieving and anxious relatives, including Edwards' fiancée Molly Leach leaving for Germany, 'her eyes red rimmed and looking tired'.[7] Edwards became the focus of the tragedy. His two-week struggle for life was followed closely in the newspapers, with daily reports in some cases, and his death drew blanket coverage.

The Munich air crash is one of the best remembered disasters of the postwar period, but more for the young, famous and talented lives that were taken than for the conduct of the company that theoretically was responsible for their safety. The day that Edwards' death was headline news, a small but telling article also made one or two front pages, reporting that the Chairman of BEA, Lord Douglas, had flown to Moscow that day for talks on a new London–Moscow direct air service to be operated with Aeroflot. 'Lord Douglas said he believed the new service would start by September 1.'[8] Might this sign of business as usual seem a little insensitive at a time of nationwide mourning? Apparently not. No public criticism or complaint about Lord Douglas appeared in the media. There was in fact little criticism of BEA at any time, despite questions about the decisions taken by the pilot and BEA ground crew. 'BEA have also been magnificent', wrote the *Manchester Evening News* reporter in Munich after Edwards died. 'They spared no expense and no effort to see that Edwards lacked nothing.'[9] This sentence was printed as a separate paragraph in his story, in bold text. The personalizing of a crisis through a sport focus such as the 1958 Munich crash – or, for that matter, the 1972 Munich Olympic hostage-taking tragedy – will be considered at other points in these pages because it dramatically exposes one of the most important principles of crisis communication: the need to communicate in understandable, human terms to large, demanding and usually non-technical audiences.

That Munich is remembered as a sporting rather than a sporting *and* corporate tragedy was neither inevitable nor an accident. It was in part because of the way BEA publicly responded to the pressures the crisis generated, which were further complicated by international and political dimensions as politicians, ministries and crash investigators in two countries sought to coordinate their activities under the eyes of the world's media and each other.

Faced with a corporate crisis, we are tempted to behave as if faced with a personal crisis: by freezing with shock, by denying that a crisis is in progress or by concentrating on mundane tasks in the hope that the problem will go away. It takes discipline to raise one's head to face the anticipated hail of criticisms, judgements and allegations. Some corporations, like some people, are better at it than others. BEA instantly demonstrated its concern for the bereaved and for the victims of the Munich tragedy, flying relatives out to Munich and identifying itself publicly with the international sense of grief. On the day that 21 bodies were flown back to the UK in a special BEA plane, a ceremony was held in which the company took a central and much reported part. Grey-uniformed German police formed up in a square around a 'gleaming silver Viscount' at Munich Airport. Police carried the wreaths of the British Consul General and the Munich City Corporation. There were twenty floral tributes in all, reported the *Manchester Evening News*, including a large wreath from BEA. Mr Roger Rother, BEA's airport superintendent at Munich, placed them aboard the plane, which had fuselage windows screened. A silent group stood watching – airport mechanics, waitresses and cleaners, as well as official mourners. Many were in tears. A BEA officer signalled to the pilot and Mr Rother saluted as the Viscount moved slowly down the taxiway.[10] The 'Airport Tribute' was widely reported in the media, since journalists were admitted to the event.

This was an impressively open display of sincerity, especially given the unusual degree of attention focused on BEA at the time. BEA's effective response takes on an extra dimension when we remember in parenthesis that one crisis may involve more than one organization. If BEA avoided criticism, what about the company that made the Elizabethan's engines, or the Ministry of Aviation, or the German airport authorities, or the pilots? The engine manufacturers, Bristols, suffered a steep drop in shares until it was confirmed that their product was not responsible. Then the competence of Munich Airport drew heavy criticism. Finally, blame devolved onto the head of the luckless chief pilot, Captain Thain, who lost his pilot's licence, became a chicken farmer and spent the next decade engaged in a public relations campaign to restore his reputation. To take a more recent example, the controversial failure of the National Aeronautics and Space Administration (NASA) 1990 Hubble telescope created a crisis for NASA *and* Hubble's contractor, Perkin-Elmer, which had apparently ground the mirror incorrectly. This demand for a guilty party is often a reflexive part of any crisis. The reflex is based on a belief – bred over time by crises depicted through the media – that all situations must be resolved in black-and-white terms. Consequently there will be a strong desire to identify victims and villains – with young families, cheated consumers, an anxious and scared public ranged against an apparently monolithic, heartless corporation or uncaring management.

Somehow, a reasoned, cool perspective on affairs must shoehorn its way into this frenetic segment of the crisis cycle. Otherwise rationality is only likely to prevail after the frenzy has subsided, which may come too late to salvage the person or company exposed to attack. In the crisis at Munich, the real cause – the hitherto unknown dragging effect of slush during take-off – did not emerge for seven years: far too late for Captain Thain. Similarly, during the more recent crisis presented to Perrier in 1990 by its benzene-contaminated water, discovery of the simple cause – inoperative filters – did not help salvage the company's future as an independent organization; this demonstrates, if nothing else, that businesses have taken many years to absorb the main lesson of Munich: what actually happens is usually less important than how you explain what happened and what you do, through operations and communications, to demonstrate your commitment and concern.

The Python: examples of 'crisis creep'

A stealth crisis is a known problem whose full damage potential has been insufficiently appreciated or even ignored. An issue may slowly but surely gather momentum until its coils close around a company with irresistible force. The Python is harder to escape than the Cobra: the company may have spent too long denying that a problem exists, and the culture of denial (of which more later) may be well entrenched, leading to ethical lapses. A 'crisis' is easier to ignore if it creeps forward, often over several years, lacks the universal dramas of sudden death, injury or criminal activity, and seeps instead from an issue that may be of tangential relevance to what the company exists to do, but is of deep interest to society at large – gender discrimination, racial prejudice, sexual harassment or a sudden health scare. It can be, as Intel discovered when it failed to react to the minute flaw in its Pentium chip, a relatively obscure fault in a product gradually magnified out of proportion by the media or eagle-eyed consumers.

That said, there are lessons to be learnt from ignoring an issue until it is too late.

Dalkon Shield: tardy communication on weak foundations

Crisis communication does not exist to hide misdemeanours, or to suppress tragedies. It cannot and should not save a product that is wantonly dangerous or unsafe through malicious or criminal activity. Crisis communication cannot justify misdeeds, although it can provide discipline to the crisis process so that the temptation to act unethically because of unbearable public pressure is constrained.

If a company acts unethically and refuses to take responsibility for its actions, no amount of communication can rescue it from public condemnation. The infamous Dalkon Shield, an intra-uterine device (IUD) manufactured by A. H. Robins, was launched in 1970. As a health journal later reminded readers, the shield's 'multifilament tailstring that extended into the vagina became a vehicle for bacteria'. In consequence, 'About 235,000 American women suffered injuries, most of which involved life-threatening pelvic cancer, infertility, complete hysterectomy, and/or chronic pelvic pain'.[11] Several women died.

A. H. Robins stopped selling the product in June 1974, although for a long time the company continued to claim its shield was 'safe and effective' when properly used and that reintroduction of the device was being made 'difficult, if not impossible' because of 'unfavorable publicity'.[12] In 1980, six years after the decision to discontinue sales, A. H. Robins contacted family practitioners and distributed a press release: 'We now recommend removal of this IUD from any of your patients who continue to use it, even though they may not be experiencing any pelvic symptoms.'[13] Public opinion, meanwhile, had run ahead of the company's communications. Spurred by women's health groups and growing revelations about cover-ups and lax research into the shield's safety, a series of long and punishing lawsuits eventually led A. H. Robins to seek debt protection by filing for bankruptcy. This crisis over a single product, drawn out over several years, slowly squeezed the life out of a large American corporation.

A. H. Robins failed to see that an awareness of ethical standards must come first. Without that, there can be no open communication between a company and its public. Ethics must be closely intertwined with communication: a company cannot communicate itself out of a crisis if it remains trapped in a moral vacuum by reason of its own mistakes, fear, inertia, obstinacy or arrogance. The vast majority of companies have little reason to dread building truth into their communications, and every reason to fear the consequences of denial through insecurity or over-caution.

Brent Spar: learning effective communication the hard way

A famous crisis emerged from Royal Dutch Shell's decision in 1995 to dump its ageing Brent Spar oil platform in the North Sea. This was a carefully weighed decision taken after four years of studies, thirty of which were independent, and endorsements from academics and other experts, all of whom agreed after thirteen options were reviewed that sinking the platform in 6000 fathoms of water was environmentally safer than land disposal (an option which carried serious hazards), and a quarter of the cost.

This prolonged effort, which included consultations with fishermen and environmentalists, ended with approval and granting of licences by the UK government. Just four months later, the operation lay in ruins. In that time Shell had been thoroughly outwitted by Greenpeace, which knew how to press the buttons that activate the media and key stakeholders in a crisis. Petrol station forecourts in Germany were firebombed, a boycott launched, and the Brent Spar was occupied by protesters who defied Shell's efforts to evict them using high-pressure water jets. These incidents were splashed across newspapers and television. In the end, every EU government but two had turned against the company. At the time of writing the Brent Spar now lies in a Norwegian fjord waiting to be dismantled and disposed of on land, representing a disturbing precedent for the oil industry as a whole, since roughly 70 more ageing rigs in the North Sea will soon need to be decommissioned.

Shell's managers, originally confident that they had taken a thorough approach to a sensitive issue, had not anticipated how dramatically the situation could overheat under the glare of environmental group action. The company later looked back on its Brent Spar experience in an insightful and refreshingly frank corporate publication. The lessons Shell learned are applicable to all companies facing an issue with the potential to become a crisis. Managers at Shell concluded that:

- The Company should have consulted a wider range of stakeholder groups.
- It failed to appreciate the need for genuine two-way dialogue.
- It should have considered people's emotional reactions as well as operational issues.
- It should have realized that the general public would be interested in its activities.
- It needed to adjust its messages for different cultures without sacrificing the truth.

- It needed to educate its key audiences, particularly the media, *before* the crisis occurred.[14]

Communicating on issues and risks – the sensitive task of dealing with a latent or slowly advancing crisis *before* it breaks in full force – requires a distinct approach which is explored in Chapter 6.

Are we in a crisis yet? The vulnerabilities of company culture

Why *do* so many companies continue to freeze, go off course, in those first moments when the crisis strikes? Let us look at some of the reasons, starting with the pre-conditions that will ferment into your crisis, and moving on to those first astonishing moments when the crisis strikes.

We are heading for a crisis if we . . .

(i) *get too comfortable about risks*

A paradoxical cause of crisis is that a company is used to dealing with its risks. Familiarity breeds acceptance, if not contempt. The first-ever study of the feelings and perceptions of North Sea offshore workers found the majority generally felt safe about their daily jobs, which involved high-risk operations conducted in the most hazardous conditions imaginable. Nevertheless, only 50 per cent of respondents felt safe on the helicopter journeys to and from their platforms.[15] People do not, cannot and will not accept risks with which they are unfamiliar. Your company's understanding of its own product or service allows it to live with the risks it carries. On the day that something goes badly wrong, though, it is hard to convert that complex web of technical understanding into a convincing public explanation. In this way, the checks and quality controls that usually cushion you from disaster can contribute to the public sense that the risk is unfamiliar, and suddenly become obstacles to recovery.

(ii) *start with the wrong perspective*

Faced with the enormity of crisis, the first sensible instinct on all sides is to gain some sort of perspective on the damage done. Without perspective it is hard to structure a response let alone mend whatever damage has occurred. The trouble is that companies do not approach the crisis from the same perspective as those who are affected by it and, equally critically, those who worry that the same thing might happen to them. Although we have fears – fear of serious illness, of dying, of losing our life savings, of buying toys that may harm our children – most of us do not expect to live in a risk-free environment. Instead, we attempt to incorporate our fears into daily life. Significantly for crisis communications, research into risk by psychologists suggests that its 'presentation format is important'.[16]

> The precise manner in which risks are expressed can have a major impact on perceptions and behaviour. For example, an action increasing one's annual chances of death from 1 in 10,000 to 1.3 in 10,000 would probably be seen as much more risky if it were described, instead, as producing a 30 per cent increase in annual mortality risk.[17]

Regular international flyers board an aeroplane even though they may be aware that the flight has a fraction of a percentage chance of crashing to the ground; some British men continue to enjoy large amounts of fatty food knowing they have a mere five in 10,000 chance of succumbing to colon cancer. These unconscious equations, manifested in the age-old belief that 'it' will happen to somebody else, helps an individual accept a limited degree of risk in his or her life until the worst actually does happen: either personally, or in another way that feels uncomfortably close to home and swiftly converts the statistical protection into flesh and blood. Technology has enlarged this trend; 'home ownership' of crises via television news can have the effect of inflaming concerns among a particular group of people (particularly if the crisis chimes with a strongly held personal belief or fear) or reducing disaster to 'interest' pieces. Tidal waves in Bangladesh might feel too far away in distance and daily experience to motivate a viewer in Barcelona.

When a personal connection is made, the protective equation warps into an impulse that many companies find hard to connect with. Suddenly, it is not one in 10,000 succumbing to bowel cancer, but one whole person, whose relatives are on television blaming the product that they feel is responsible. The equation distils from the anonymous comfort of tiny fractions into the chilling reality of powerful whole numbers.

That at least, is how your audience will react. Will your company respect that reaction in the language of its crisis communications? It may require changes in corporate thinking that are hard to effect unless experienced crisis advisers are available or a well-rehearsed crisis communication plan is in position. But without those changes, the gap in perception may be too vast to close and your company may be pushed into a corner, and branded as uncaring or incompetent.

(iii) *fail to respect the emotions of our audiences*

In a crisis you must, more than in any other business situation, put yourself into the shoes of your audience, see the problem from their perspective, and shift your communication to accommodate the disturbing emotions they now feel. That emotion must play a role in crisis communication is often hard to explain to troubled companies, and harder still for them to accept.

When companies used to correcting operational problems are faced with an emotional problem by external audiences, it is tempting either to dismiss the issue or to offer bland reassurances that all is well. Such approaches view the concern as hysteria or, like A. H. Robins, as a by-product of unfavourable publicity. There is no understanding of the powerful equation described above, in which the logic of emotion becomes: 'very small risk = *some* risk'.

Failure to strike the correct emotional chord in crisis communication can have a powerful impact. When seventeen-year-old Shannon Moseley was killed in a fiery truck crash driving a Sierra pickup truck, his parents sued General Motors (GM) whose lawyers, to quote the headline from *Automotive News*, 'didn't quench $105 million fire lit by GM's arrogance and denial'. The jury debated the safety issue for two and a half days, but a lawyer who tracked the proceedings recorded: 'Running through all these deliberations for many of the jurors was a fierce anger at GM management.' The former GM chairman Robert Stempel came in for particular criticism over questions he would not answer, and 'GM engineer Kashmerick's tale of a shredding party reinforced the sense of wrongdoing and irresponsibility at the company.' The guilty verdict was 'only a matter of time'.[18] In this way, the technical debate over the safety or otherwise of the pickup's petrol tank was influenced by bad communication decisions of the company in the aftermath of the accident, and the impact of those decisions on the public.

Even after it was found liable in the lawsuit brought by Shannon Moseley's parents, GM continued to ignore the chasm between corporate and public attitudes that had contributed so much to its defeat. 'It is a crushing blow that you've delivered us', said GM's lawyer. 'We accept it.'[19]

> But as Bartlit was giving GM's *mea culpa* to the jury inside the courtroom, outside in the corridor a GM flack [employee] was distributing a defiant press release rejecting the jurors' determination that the pickup was defective and accusing them of being swayed by emotion.[20]

Needless to say, when the Moseleys' lawyer 'stepped forward to make his case for damages, he had the [GM] press release in his hand'.[21]

The trial was covered live by *Court TV* and NBC news, and had attracted a lot of media interest; all of which makes GM's approach even harder to understand. Questionable behaviour and mishandled communications – particularly GM's inability to alter its message by responding sensitively to public emotions – cramped its communications into defensive and non-credible denials, injured its reputation, its product and, more specifically, helped to decide the outcome of the case. A strategic role for crisis communication is essential to bridge the perception gap between a corporation and its public audiences.

General Motors might argue that its responsibility was to maintain public confidence in its product. After all, the consumer at large would scarcely be likely to follow the details of a single case. Long after the trial, GM's confident attitude might be all that anyone would recall. Seen from this standpoint, GM's vociferous denials of responsibility may make strategic sense. After all, crisis communication must be more concerned with public opinion than legal outcomes – the latter is the task of lawyers. At the same time, a credible response to crisis can only work over time if it is set in context with the events themselves. Proclamations of innocence or loud reassurances are unlikely to be remembered favourably unless they respect the spirit of the occasion. In this case, a young man had been killed and that needed to be balanced alongside GM's natural urge to defend itself if its message was to have any lasting credibility. The manufacturer's message was inevitably going to be compared with those issued by the bereaved parents, their lawyer, and ultimately the jury's verdict. Looking back on the Brent Spar crisis, Shell's Public Affairs Manager commented:

> There is the need to ensure that you are really listening and that you are appreciating and responding to peoples fears and emotions. We should have done more of that before we started. Once we had started, we never, to my knowledge, actually said, 'look, we understand why people have a problem with this . . .' So we never sympathized, showed any empathy before we tried to explain.[22]

A wiser, more humane and strategically beneficial approach by GM would have been to show greater public sensitivity towards the tragedy as a complement to their main message that the product was sound and safe, if that was truly felt to be the case.

(iv) *try to 'lose' the problem*

Ironically, your crisis may develop because of a failure to live up to your own image. In our highly competitive age, companies like to present themselves as sharply honed tools on the cutting edge of their particular activity, be it sports shoes or silicon chips. If they are big enough, companies also like to present themselves as secure, reliable and trustworthy places for customers, employees, investors and communities: that is, any of the audiences that matter to them in the normal course of affairs.

It is a truism to say that the pressures of commerce today, the demands for quick returns or innovative products, have led to a radical restructuring of business practice. Companies are faster moving, team-orientated; they are often quick at reaching decisions, or at capitalizing on the talents of employees and marketing new products to impatient and distracted consumers.

All the more astonishing, then, that – in contrast to widespread claims about their reputation for speed, for taking the initiative, and aggressive expansion – so many companies display precisely the opposite tendency in a crisis, the one occasion when these qualities, above all others, are desperately required.

One of the challenges of crisis communication is convincing executives that they are actually in a crisis and need to make fast changes to their internal organization and their usual means of communication. Denial is a natural human trait, and not surprisingly, it is tempting for harassed managers to cling to the procedures of everyday problem-solving. Denial is often the first response to a crisis, and may be expressed as: Caution, Committees and Covering oneself. If for instance the company is large, contains many departments or is spread over a number of sites, there is a strong possibility that communication blockages may occur as a person or group tries to muffle the cry of alarm, or shrinks from communicating a clear message for fear of running into legal difficulties, or 'loses' the crisis in lengthy internal debates thus ensuring that responsibility does not devolve onto his or her head alone.

However accurate the claims of the leanest, meanest, most predatory corporation may be, the fact is that it necessarily remains locked into normal rhythms of business. The structures work well in peacetime, but in a crisis they are severely tested and occasionally useless. Wartime conditions prevail: big decisions with a lot riding on them must be made in a drastically shorter time than usual. The usual corporate 'decision tree' will of course be available, but in all likelihood it will be too rigid and deep-rooted to supply the flexibility needed when the crisis strikes.

The larger the company, the greater the challenge to produce swift and accurate decision-making. In a company with branch operations at home or abroad, or with subsidiary companies, the initial confusion may revolve around mixed public messages or a defensive desire to pass responsibility to another part of the organization.

(v) *individuals or teams try going it alone*

At the opposite extreme, the Chief Executive Officer (CEO) may try to take personal charge of all crisis operations. This is a fine principle, but often risky in practice. It is also, incidentally, another helpful sign of approaching trouble, for if the CEO is used to being in total control, he or she will know there is a crisis when outside events erode his or her power. Outsiders who seem ill-informed or malicious may make infuriating public comments that affect the reputation of the company. It is a frustrating situation if you are used to leading – you may even complain or grumble, and find your protests turned against you. A crisis has broken out when the mess becomes too big for chief executives to clear up alone.

(vi) *ignore the warning signs*

We have touched on two species of crisis, the sudden cobra and the slower python, and observed that the most sudden crises are easier to see: a crash, devastating fire, or unexpected accidents using your products. Such events may indeed be totally unanticipated but there is no mistaking them once they intrude into the normal run of company affairs. In contrast, it has also been seen with Dalkon Shield that even life-threatening crises can 'emerge' rather than explode on the scene. An irritating issue can slowly move centre-stage; a product is laced with a degree of risk if it is ignored or insufficiently explained.

Companies do not always see a need for special measures, and ignore the dangers even in the most explosive circumstances. Others, such as Shell, fail to track the accumulation of mundane, often technical matters until an event arrives that catapults the whole tortuous affair into disaster. As Chrysler lurched towards a massive and very public financial crisis in the late 1970s, the incoming Chief Executive, Lee Iacocca, found all the ingredients of an organization locked in denial: 'All through the company, people were scared and despondent. Nobody was doing anything right.' The company had buried its head in the sand. 'There was no real committee setup, no cement in the organizational chart, no system of meetings to get people talking to each other.' Chrysler fragmented into 'a bunch of mini-empires, with nobody giving a damn about what anyone else was doing'.[23] You know you are facing a potential crisis when there is a problem for which nobody is prepared to accept responsibility. Albert Speer recounted a related tendency in Hitler's Berlin bunker, as defeat drew closer:

> the apparatus of command continued to run mechanically. Apparently there was still some momentum here which went on operating even when the motor was running down.[24]

This is a common characteristic: denial by burying yourself in routine. Managers at every level in Manville Corporation, the asbestos manufacturer, 'were unwilling or unable to believe in the long-term consequences of exposure to their product', wrote Bill Sells, who for more than 30 years was an executive with Johns-Manville and the Manville Corporation. Sells declared that the 'blunder was not the manufacture and sale of a dangerous product', since other companies produced more dangerous substances, such as 'deadly chemicals, explosives [and] poisons'. Instead, Manville executives 'denied, or at least failed to acknowledge, the depth and persistence of management accountability'. Sells argued that if Manville had responded to the dangers with 'extensive medical research, assiduous communication, insistent warnings, and a rigorous dust-reduction program, it could have saved lives and would probably have saved the stockholders, the industry, and for that matter, the product'.[25]

Lessons learnt from international crises

Crises can seem so pointless in hindsight: not because of abuses or accidents that must inevitably land in the public arena, but because of the capacity for misplaced public relations to worsen and widen some problems. Through bitter experience, companies learn valuable lessons about what to do and say. As noted earlier, doing and saying are intimately connected in a crisis, and are often one and the same to external audiences.

Mitsubishi Motor Manufacturing Company (MMMC) learnt several useful lessons in April 1996 when, in an announcement that attracted much media interest, the US Equal Employment Opportunity Commission (EEOC) filed its largest ever lawsuit on behalf of 700 female Mitsubishi employees (out of a total of 900 women at the factory concerned). A further 29 women filed a private suit. Allegations were made about sexist remarks, molestation, and walls and equipment carrying crude drawings of couples engaged in sex or women spreading their legs. Oddly, the Mitsubishi plant involved was located in the city of Normal, Illinois.

The company's response was given by Gary Shultz, a lawyer, MMMC vice president and general counsel for the Normal plant. His remarks set the tone for the opening phase of the crisis and were made in a telephone interview with Associated Press. 'If we are surprised and horrified by anything, it's the manner that this has been brought to the public's attention', he said. 'A public spectacle has been made of claims made against this company.'[26] Mr Shultz probably felt under pressure: the EEOC had said that each employee could collect up to $300,000 in damages; and the effect on Normal itself (population 6000) as journalists descended was also going to tell.

For these reasons, perhaps, the company's first communication response appeared to be laden with testosterone. MMMC accused the Clinton administration of playing politics. It installed telephones so that workers could call Washington politicians and denounce the charges and began 'seeking access to personal records' of the 29 women who filed the private suit, 'including gynecological data and information on their divorces', and even abortion records.[27] Back in Normal, some local businesses, politicians and residents shunned the women, an action that, to outside observers, looked as if it had been taken through fear of losing trade, jobs or the plant itself.

MMMC's blitzkrieg included a mass protest outside the EEOC offices in Chicago. Over half of the factory's 4000 employees were given a 'day off' and bussed 120 miles to Chicago in the company of their employers and local dignitaries including the Mayor of Bloomington, Normal's adjacent city.

Mitsubishi's approach appears to have been inspired partly by a previous EEOC attack on 'Hooters', a restaurant chain famed for the skimpiness of the waitresses' attire. Hooters retaliated against the EEOC with a high-profile and humorous publicity campaign. In the crisis in Normal, though, MMMC's effort backfired. As one newspaper reported: 'The rally was seen as a staged attempt to intimidate the Equal Employment Opportunity Commission.'[28] 'Television comedians mocked the company, and congresswomen lined up to condemn it.'[29] Jesse Jackson's Rainbow Coalition and the National Organization for Women (NOW) launched a boycott. NOW began organizing pickets of Mitsubishi dealers in 30 cities across America. The boycott even spread to Chrysler, which was facing a similar lawsuit with the EEOC. 'We're looking in all directions . . . including shareholders in the company, lenders to the company', warned NOW's President, Patricia Ireland.[30] A protest rally was planned at the company's annual shareholder meeting in Tokyo. One prominent midwestern newspaper described Mitsubishi's tactics as 'desperate moves'. It observed: 'job security has become a Faustian bargain: sell out co-workers or be prepared to walk'.[31]

The media put Corporate Japan under the microscope, and reported on abuses of female employees by Japanese executives.

Mitsubishi was forced to change its position. Gary Shultz, its erstwhile representative, dropped from public view. In Tokyo, the President of the company stepped down after only ten months in office, 'a move widely seen as a demotion' partially related to the problems Mitsubishi created for itself in America.[32] The *Financial Times* of London reported that the company had 'signalled an end to its vigorous campaign against the Equal Opportunities Commission's suit'. Mitsubishi's chairman stated: 'We want to settle the sexual harassment case as soon as possible.'[33] Lynn Martin, a former Labor Secretary and Illinois congresswoman, was appointed by the company to conduct a thorough review of its workplace policies. Jesse Jackson and Patricia Ireland were invited to tour the Normal factory and met with Tsuneo Ohinouye, MMMC's Chief Executive in America.[34]

Mitsubishi is a crisis that got needlessly out of control, largely through misjudged communications, before and after the troubles entered the legal stage. A year earlier in *Public Relations Quarterly*, author and consultant James Lukaszewski had warned readers about using confrontational public relations in support of legal battles:

- Wars are very messy, very expensive and your side will take the heaviest casualties.
- If you hire only warriors as lawyers, you'll always be at war.
- Wars have a way of never ending.[35]

How could Mitsubishi have got it so wrong? We might feel sure that we at least would not make the same mistakes. This, however, would be taking advantage of hindsight. What lessons can we learn? What does it tell us about the nature of crises and the temptations of decision-making under pressure? What does it say about the resources we will need to surmount a communication crisis? Lastly, why did the process of decision-making misfire?

The nature of crises

- **Cultural differences must be managed, not ignored.** An international crisis magnifies cultural as well as managerial obstacles. It did not seem to have occurred to executives in Tokyo that what was considered 'normal', or at least not unusual, in Japan might be less acceptable – if not illegal – behaviour elsewhere. For international companies, differences between societies must be thought through as a necessary part of crisis preparation. This requires substantial input from other nationalities. In the case of Japanese companies, Alex Kerr, a long-time resident of the country, has observed: 'While foreign influence is welcomed, the cardinal rule is never to delegate responsibility to foreigners themselves.'[36] William Holstein, world editor for *Business Week*, co-wrote a commentary criticizing Mitsubishi's handling of the problem. He pointed out that Japanese companies in America are often tightly controlled from Japan, which makes it difficult to hire good local employees.[37]

- **Crises proliferate into other issues and other regions**. Within a few weeks of the MMMC lawsuit announcement, the media were also picking apart tensions in the local community, alleging that the United Auto Workers union had refused to act on complaints from women at the plant, exploring the issue of sexual harassment in Japan itself, approaching third-party experts for opinions which – because they are perceived to be independent – appear more credible in the public eye. The whole business of weaving together fact, interpretation and opinion into a point of view that becomes the 'truth' is intensified, while other problems are unexpectedly thrown into relief. Almost immediately, pressure groups like NOW were capitalizing on the company's weakness to draw attention to themselves and to issues they cared about. Very quickly, MMMC was associated with a range of other sins in addition to the harassment in Illinois.

- **Everyone will want to talk.** Mitsubishi's problems were worsened by the number of people wanting to communicate. This is symptomatic of any crisis, and in Mitsubishi's case the crisis was heightened by anonymous interviews with and statements from the company's own employees that undermined its own position. This trend can be traced in part to the enormity of the issue and low morale among the workforce, but any organization in trouble can expect to deal with a certain amount of internal leakage. Mitsubishi, it was asserted in *Business Week*, 'frightened plant employees by telling them their jobs would be in jeopardy if they broke ranks with the company on the issue'.[38] The fact that the company failed to establish credible relations with employees as well as the media made it more likely that the latter would swarm over the former in search of the truth. The same credibility failure made it harder for the company to counter damaging comments from disaffected employees. In a crisis, proper decision-making and effective communications at all levels are mutually dependent. The fate of one decides the fate of the other.

Needs in a crisis

- **Match your decision-makers to the scale of the crisis.** Decisions about communication must be precisely aligned to the scale of the controversy. Mitsubishi's spokespeople were in the wrong place to influence the controversy, which began locally, swiftly became national and finished in the company's Tokyo boardroom. The issue rippled outwards with nothing credible standing in its path. There was insufficient appreciation that a nationwide problem would require a nationwide effort. With a national crisis in the making, a nationally coordinated communication strategy should have been developed by Mitsubishi, with close contact between Normal, a national crisis team and Tokyo. Instead, the initial communication was left to a small team of men based near the plant. A purely parish-pump approach brought global problems.

- **Fluid management and expert help.** Crises cannot be managed on the cheap, or on the wing. Outside consultants with a wider perspective on the crisis are a necessity. It was reported in one newspaper that Gary Shultz ran a two-person law firm in Bloomington before his appointment with MMMC, and lacked a background in professional crisis communication.[39] The company was also handicapped by its internal lines of communication. Apparently Tokyo did not see a need to change its ways, or keep constituent companies abreast of developments. Dozens of companies around the world bore the Mitsubishi name. Pressure from that quarter finally encouraged changes in the parent company's communication, and in its senior management. Traditionally, according to Holstein, 'the vast majority of these companies still insist that all important decisions flow back to Tokyo'.[40] Only when the crisis built up a good head of steam did Mitsubishi's companies realise that a new managerial approach was needed.

Because of the scandal at the manufacturing plant, Mitsubishi's salespeople in America found themselves at the receiving end of a dealership boycott and demonstrations, but because they were regarded internally (if not externally by the public) as a separate operation there was little coordination between Mitsubishi Manufacturing and Mitsubishi Sales. Messages and resources do not appear to have been pooled, and no use was apparently made of their sales and marketing PR agency, a nationwide organization whose input on the problem might have been critical at an early stage. Isolated at the top were executives at Mitsubishi's global headquarters in

Japan; a country where, writes Alex Kerr: 'Well-established rhythms and politenesses shield you from most unpleasantness. Japan can be a kind of "lotus land", where one floats peacefully away on the placid surface of things.'[41] In the distance, management from corporate ivory towers is likely to carry no real understanding and achieve minimal effect on the ground where the crisis is raging out of control.

Summary

- Crises manifest themselves:

    Like a cobra. Disaster hits, takes a company completely by surprise, and plunges it straight into crisis. Examples include the unexpected impact of the A-Class car 'Elk Test' on Daimler-Benz, which initially exploited several shortcomings in the company's 'decision-tree'.

    Like a python. A crisis steals up and gradually crushes you, issue by issue – known as 'crisis creep'. A. H. Robins did not respond effectively to nearly a decade of controversy over the Dalkon Shield, and eventually filed for bankruptcy. Royal Dutch Shell, reviewing the Brent Spar crisis, concluded that several important components of a longer-term communication strategy should have been in place to include:

    > Consultation with a wider range of interest groups.
    > Greater understanding of the need for two-way dialogue.
    > An understanding of the impact of emotion on the debate.
    > A realization that the public would be interested in its operations.
    > The need to review messages to meet the needs of different
    >   cultures.
    > The need for education of key audiences ahead of the crisis.

- Decision-makers at all levels are dependent on the effectiveness of their company's communications. In a crisis, the chain of decision-making must change to recognize this fact. This principle is exemplified by the inadequate links between operations and communications made by Mitsubishi's Tokyo headquarters during its sexual harassment crisis in the USA.

- Companies are vulnerable to crisis if they:

    > Get too comfortable about risks.
    > Start with the wrong perspective.
    > Fail to respect the emotions of their audiences.
    > Try to 'lose' the problem.
    > Individuals or teams try going it alone.
    > Ignore the warning signs.

- Crises demonstrate that:
    Cultural differences must be managed, not ignored.
    Crises proliferate into other issues and other regions.
    Everyone will want to talk.
- In a crisis companies must:
    Match their decision-makers to the scale of the crisis.
    Change operational structures.
    Coordinate between every affected area of the company.

Notes

1   *The 1997 Review of Crisis and Risk Management.* London: Infoplan International.
2   'Crisis outlook for 1997'. *Institute for Crisis Management.* http://www.crisisexperts.com/1997outlook.html
3   Merged as DaimlerChrysler in November 1998.
4   'A-Class disaster'. *Sunday Times*, 16 November 1997.
5   All exchange rates cited in these pages are as of 23 January 1999.
6   'Tilting at elks'. *Time*, 8 December 1997.
7   *Manchester Evening News*, Friday 7 February 1958.
8   *ibid.*
9   *ibid.*
10 *ibid.*
11 'Dalkon Shield not to be remarketed.' *Facts on File*, 25 October 1975.
12 *ibid.*
13 A. H. Robins Press Release on PR Newswire. Thursday 25 September 1980. Richmond, Virginia.
14 Hunt, P. Public Affairs Manager, Shell UK. (1997) *Brent Spar: A Drop in the Ocean?* Business in the Community Occasional Paper 5. London: Shell, p. 1.
15 'North Sea workers voice fears on helicopter safety'. *Glasgow Herald*, 3 February 1995.
16 Slovic, P., Fischoff, B. and Lichtenstein, S., 'Facts versus fears: understanding perceived risk'. *Judgement and Decision Making* (1986). Cambridge: Cambridge University Press, pp. 478–9. Also cited in Moore, Simon. *An Invitation to Public Relations.* London: Cassell, 1996, p. 60.
17 *ibid.*
18 *Automotive News*, 10 May 1993.
19 *ibid.*
20 *ibid.*
21 *ibid.*
22 Hunt, P. *op. cit.*

23   Iacocca, L. (with William Novak). *Iacocca: An Autobiography*. London: Sidgwick & Jackson, 1985, pp. 152–5.

24   Speer, A. *Inside the Third Reich*. London: Sphere, 1971, p. 630.

25   Sells, W. 'What asbestos taught me about managing risk.' *Harvard Business Review*, March–April 1994, p. 76.

26   'Hundreds harassed at Mitsubishi, suit claims.' Associated Press report. *The Record*, 10 April 1996.

27   'Pitting worker against worker.' *Des Moines Register*, 26 April 1996.

28   'Mitsubishi retools its PR strategy: firm came out swinging over harassment case, gave itself black eye.' *St. Louis Post-Dispatch*, 28 May 1996.

29   *ibid.*

30   'Protest spreads to Chrysler.' *Automotive News*, 27 May 1996.

31   'Pitting worker against worker.' *Des Moines Register*, 26 April 1996.

32   'Companies and finance: Mitsubishi Motors chief quits after 10 months.' *Financial Times*, 27 April 1996.

33   *ibid.*

34   'Protest spreads to Chrysler.' *Automotive News*, 27 May 1996.

35   Lukaszewski, James E. 'Managing litigation visibility: how to avoid lousy trial publicity.' *Public Relations Quarterly*, 22 March 1995.

36   Kerr, Alex. *Lost Japan*, Melbourne: Lonely Planet, p. 231.

37   Holstein, W. J. 'Mitsubishi and the cement ceiling.' *Business Week*, 13 May 1996.

38   *ibid.*

39   'Mitsubishi retools its PR strategy: firm came out swinging over harassment case, gave itself black eye.' *St Louis Post-Dispatch*, 28 May 1996.

40   Holstein, W. J. *op. cit.*

41   Kerr, Alex. *op. cit.*, p. 106.

2 The crisis unfolds

IT IS IMPORTANT TO UNDERSTAND how a crisis unfolds, the main challenges it raises and the damage it can do. These are the themes of this chapter. It is possible to detect a pattern of events in the apparent chaos of a crisis, and to talk about the crisis *life-cycle* through which a stricken company must pass – perhaps suddenly and violently, or in a slow lingering manner. Here, we look at the obstacles to decision-making that are thrown up: the initial surprise and hesitation, the tension between information availability and the need to communicate. Other problems are also tackled: the issue of 'openness', and the real agendas of your critics. We finish the chapter with a survey of the damage that a corporate crisis can trail in its wake, and an account of one company's journey through the crisis cycle.

The crisis life-cycle

Stage one: the storm breaks

Whether sudden or gradual, once the crisis breaks the 'personality' of the company will be uncovered for all to see – or at least for all who *matter* to see.

The position you take as the crisis breaks is critical. A crisis is often contained or lost by first actions and the tone of the initial messages relayed to the outside world.

- You will be in a fishbowl and the media and other audiences will be looking in.
- Your early messages will carry an impact that is hard for others to forget or for you to change.
- You will feel that control is slipping out of your hands. Other people will shape public perceptions, and will communicate in the vacuum that may be left by your company's reluctance to respond.
- There will be a lack of solid detail about the crisis. It will be hard to

provide information demanded by the media, analysts and others. But you will need to say something.

- Consequently, you will be tempted to resort to a short-term focus, to panic and to speculate.
- For a period of time, everyone loses perspective on the crisis.

DuPont passed through these phases when it did not immediately withdraw its Benlate 50 DF fungicide after it was first linked to children born in the late 1980s and early 1990s with eye defects – or no eyes at all. Instead, the company stuck aggressively to its initial position that Benlate was safe while lawsuits were filed by families around the world. In 1995 alone DuPont faced more than 200 court cases. Shops in Auckland, New Zealand, voluntarily withdrew Benlate after the country was shocked by television footage of eyeless children born to three women who had used the product for the city's Parks Department. One American judge offered to cut DuPont's fine from $115 million to $14 million if it published a full-page newspaper apology for withholding evidence. After paying out many hundreds of millions of dollars in fines and legal fees, and incurring much ill-will for continually insisting that there was nothing wrong if Benlate was used properly, DuPont withdrew the product from garden use at the end of 1996, saying it had done so for commercial reasons.[1]

Some companies have the foresight to take control at the outset. The crash of Japan Airlines (JAL) Flight 123 into mountains in Japan on 12 August 1985, killing 520 people, prompted an instant response from the chairman. He at once journeyed to the crash site to meet bereaved relatives who had been flown out at the company's expense. As they disembarked he stood at the foot of the steps, bowing low to express his shame. The company spent $1.5 million dollars on two memorial services and established a scholarship fund for children whose parents died in the tragedy.

From the outset JAL had moved to swiftly inform the families of the victims. In contrast, in 1988 one relative of a victim on Pan Am's Flight 103 over Lockerbie, Scotland, did not learn officially of her husband's death until six weeks after the crash. Pan Am did fly family members to Scotland, and demonstrated concern. But, asks Dr Marion Pinsdorf in a telling analysis, 'did CEO Thomas Plaskett appear? Apologize? Attend memorial services? Atone for responsibility? No, no, no, no.' Of course both airlines surely cared, but Japan Airlines was *seen* by fellow-countrymen and women to care, and management was *seen* to be human.[2]

Stage two: the storm rages

After the crisis strikes, it can spread with startling speed, usually while your company is still off-balance and unsure what to do. First, the crisis enters the bloodstream of your organization. Misinformation, gossip, nagging grievances and rumours are part and parcel of corporate life at the best of times. A crisis can magnify these characteristics until they impede the regular activity of the company. The rapid flow of events and media attacks – and the comments of family, friends and neighbours – affect employee morale, which further stimulates the crisis atmosphere. A shop-floor representative at Mercedes described how the Elk Test affected workers. 'First they were shocked. Then came anger toward management for having let it happen.'[3]

Your crisis will also create unexpected and unfamiliar communication problems. Hostile individuals and interest groups may express their opinions in imaginative, headline-grabbing ways, apparently with the aim of making a bad situation much worse. Such was the case when Shell struggled to evict Greenpeace demonstrators from the Brent Spar platform, under the eyes of the world's media. 'We had rescued Greenpeace's people from the water several times, under increasingly desperate and hazardous conditions. There were real fears that someone could be killed.'[4] In a crisis, you will have difficulty constructing a response that matches the heated atmosphere of the occasion.

As the crisis spreads and intensifies on the second stage of a crisis life-cycle, a number of developments are likely:

- Other stakeholders are pulled into the vortex: customers, stockholders, banks, employees, analysts. They may initially draw their information, which will shape their perceptions, opinions and conclusions, from the media.
- Speculation and rumours begin to develop in the absence of hard facts.
- Third parties – regulators, politicians, scientists and other experts – add their weight to the climate of opinion.
- Corporate management may come under intense scrutiny from all these internal and external groups – and more.

At this stage it is vital to grasp the hierarchy of your communications. While the media are your noisiest audience, their needs are essentially short-term when set against the other communication challenges with which senior management are now wrestling. It is helpful to view that challenge on five levels:

- corporate – good internal communications are essential to company morale, confidence and coherence.
- local – around the plant, headquarters or affected facility.
- regional – if the disaster occurs in a district with a strong and distinct identity from other parts of the country.
- national – communicating to audiences *within* individual markets.
- international – across and bridging continents.

At this stage, with the problem up and running hard and fast, crisis management presents three distinct challenges for a company:

- to define and to resolve the problem.
- to coordinate and control all communications.
- to manage the rest of the business.

Stage three: the storm passes

A crisis fits Winston Churchill's description of a military offensive as something that loses force as it proceeds: 'It was like throwing a bucket of water on the floor. It first rushed forward, then soaked forward, and finally stopped altogether until another bucket could be brought.'[5] The first stage is always a surprise; the second stage can be difficult. But as the situation subsides, you become less driven by sudden and violent shifts and changes in the crisis, and are presented with more opportunities to explain what happened and, preferably, how it will never happen again.

But rebuilding consists of more than providing explanations:

- **Creating positive perceptions.** There are opportunities in a crisis to build positive perceptions of your company or product that last beyond the crisis period. During the Tylenol scare in 1982, Johnson and Johnson (J&J) recalled the product, established a toll-free hotline for questions, and provided refunds or exchanges. We shall examine elsewhere how J&J's response to cyanide in its Tylenol became an early model for crisis managers to follow (see page 121).[6]
- **Internal rebuilding.** Having learnt its lessons, a crisis-hit company should embark on a long-term programme that tackles the management issues and communication problems that exacerbated the crisis.

In Shell's case, several internal and external communication needs were identified after the Brent Spar débâcle. They are worth noting here:

The need to use new technologies, such as the internet, in communicating effectively.

The need to *simplify* corporate messages when dealing with the media.

The need to *manage* strategic decisions in an environment where even a stable legal framework cannot protect the company from unforeseen political consequences.[7]

Problems and challenges in crisis decision-making

The problem of surprise and hesitation

The degree of intensity reached by a crisis – personal, corporate or political – hinges in part on what is said in the earliest stages, and for many organizations the surprise of a breaking crisis can breed a dangerous delay. After the Deputy Prime Minister Sir Geoffrey Howe left Margaret Thatcher's Conservative cabinet, his powerful resignation speech to Parliament precipitated a massive political crisis which triggered the 1990 leadership election, and the Prime Minister's defeat. In his autobiography, Sir Geoffrey recollected his speech and its immediate aftermath:

> The reaction as I sat down was quite unlike anything that I had ever before experienced. No 'hear hears' from my own side. But no hubbub from the other side either – just bemused silence. And then a mounting babel of noise, as Members began talking to each other, in astonished reaction, on their way to the exits.[8]

That initial stunned pause, so vividly described here, characterizes an ill-prepared organization hesitating in the first moments of a crisis, until the 'mounting babel' of media and audience noise smothers its messages. Even well-handled crises are not immune from faltering starts. A spokesman for Daimler-Benz – which eventually recovered well from the Elk Test disaster – stated in the first hours after the crash that 'the company did not think it was necessary to issue a statement'.[9] Executives changed their minds in time, after viewing magazine coverage and watching video footage of the incident that one automotive analyst warned 'could become a major image problem'.[10] Foodmaker, owners of the American burger chain Jack In The Box, also recovered with a series of responsible and effectively communicated initiatives when they sold burgers contaminated with a fatal strain of *e.coli* in 1993. But the company stumbled at first by not immediately shutting restaurants or demonstrating it was teaching employees how to handle food hygienically, and was criticized for its heavy-handed approaches to victims (see page 127, page 151 and page 196).

Whether a crisis strikes suddenly, like the Elk Test, or crushes a company as slowly as growing concern about health risks crushed the asbestos industry, hesitation is common as surprised companies blink in the unaccustomed glare of unwanted lights and scrutiny. Yet in those first moments of surprise lies the best opportunity for a credible corporate response that takes a clear lead and helps to limit the damage.

The problem of stress

An executive working for a large infant food company locked into a salmonella crisis received a call from a journalist who asked: 'How many babies have you killed today?'[11] The stresses and strains that a crisis inflicts are considerable, though they can only be fully appreciated in the midst of events.

In Britain, it has been estimated that as much as half of sickness absence is 'due to work-related stress and depression, costing an estimated $11 billion in lost revenue each year'.[12] In the USA the figure is put at $20 billion.[13] Even though workplace stress is commonplace, a study by the UK counselling charity, the Samaritans, found that there was little communication about the topic: 'A taboo persists. Stress and depression is compounded by fear, confusion and shame.'[14]

Yet it would be irresponsible not to face the fact that a corporate crisis overheats the usual causes of stress until the lid blows off the corporation and many people in it. In *Managing Stress*, the author and medical journalist Mark Greener notes that stress is created by changes to the familiar environment; anything that causes change, causes stress. Usually, people can deal with the pressure; some even need it in order to perform well. Stress becomes dangerous when the demands for coping with it outstrip resources, strength and time.[15] As we have already seen, crises amply fulfil these conditions. They change the familiar working environment and place huge demands on resources, strength and time. 'The ensuing maelstrom was unbelievable', wrote journalist Joe Klein after he was unmasked as 'Anonymous', author of the racy, insider presidential novel, *Primary Colors*. You will be caught unawares, forced to communicate with all the back-up you might like, and say things that you thought you would never be called upon to say. You may be held personally accountable by outside audiences while feeling the hot breath of lawyers, anxious shareholders, employees and other impatient stakeholders in your company. Under the gun, managers will experience corporate and personal stress at extreme levels. When Klein finally drew breath, it was to reflect on facing the same media scrutiny that in normal times he applied on others: 'It is impossible to think straight. It is very easy to screw up, and it is unrelenting.'[16]

The peculiarities of crisis stress have been felt by thousands of able executives at all levels. During the first hours of a major crisis in the North Sea the CEO of an international company, which was directly implicated by the serious accident, gathered together his team bolstered by outside experts. When presented with a list of the questions most likely to be raised by the media, the CEO caught the eye of those asking him to consider the first draft of 'Q&Rs' – the questions he would in all likelihood have to deal with, and the responses he should consider. Then he glanced at the sheet of paper, angrily muttering to his startled team that no-one could ask such questions. He then dropped to his knees and disappeared under the table, angrily informing his startled consultants about a need for more telephone points in the room.

Crisis stress is not confined to crawling about under boardroom tables. There is a wide menu of symptoms to suffer and analyses for the sufferer to choose: anxiety attacks, apathy, sweating, twitching and fear; the well-known Type A–Type B division (and all their variants) much used in medical studies, which finds that a very competitive, impatient, aggressive and restless Type A tends to suffer more than the unhurried, relaxed and more passive Type B.[17]

Few executives have talked openly about how they actually *felt* during a crisis. However, Lee Iacocca has described what happened to him in 1979 during Chrysler's financial troubles, one of which was an obsessive infiltration of the crisis into his home life:

> I started waking up in the middle of the night. My mind never got settled. I was working constantly. There were times when I wondered about my sanity, about whether I could keep it all together. You can run sprints only so long before you're out of breath.[18]

Albert Speer, who had the gargantuan task of managing Nazi war industry, described his different reaction to 'excessive intellectual strain' as the bomb-shattered German economy staggered towards final collapse:

> I could observe in myself how my mind went on working mechanically, while at the same time my ability to absorb fresh impressions diminished and I made decisions in an apathetic way.[19]

Corporate crises, of course, are crises in part because they create such personal pressure. A counter to stress and fatigue – and the dangerous impact they can have on judgement – is the imposition of a tight schedule of activity. During a crisis, it is essential to allow decision-makers frequent breaks between meetings (see page 102). A good crisis plan (and there are some very good ones) cannot eradicate stress, but can at least recognize and make use of it. Psychiatrists believe that executive stress is moderated by a sense of control.[20] Channelled by the discipline of preparedness, stress can help to produce messages and actions that control the crisis. In this way it becomes an asset. 'Stress can save jobs. It can force positive changes. It can compel the development of new products.'[21] One retired company chairman has suggested:

- Communication eliminates frustration.
- It is better to light a candle than curse the darkness. Ordinary people will produce extraordinary results if they are informed.[22]

Managing the information deficit

Stress is eased by communication, and communication is eased by information. One of the frustrations often heard during crises, from all parties, concerns lack of real information.

Most companies in crisis will not be in possession of all the facts, and to begin with your company will be hampered by the tension of finding that you have nothing to say to audiences hungry for information. Although you may work hard to provide information as quickly as possible, the vacuum will inevitably fill with expert opinion and speculation. You may feel as if you are losing control of the situation. You will find that the amount of actual knowledge you possess is outstripped by the volume and variety of information that is demanded of you. Worse, you may be unable to reach the people who can supply you with the vital information for operational and communication decisions. 'Even the most rudimentary questions were impossible for them to answer', Iacocca wrote of the management team he inherited at Chrysler. 'But never mind the answers: these guys didn't even know the questions!'[23]

Normal fact-gathering mechanisms may be inadequate in your crisis. There is the danger that a suspicious or defensive employee may tell you what they think you prefer to hear, rather than what is actually happening. There is the danger that you are so busy fielding incoming calls that you cannot give your fullest attention to any information you have gathered in. There is the danger that valuable data reaches you too slowly to be of any use because the public debate has moved too far ahead.

Information starvation has an undoubted impact on a crisis. This was dramatically seen when TWA was publicly attacked by the popular mayor of New York, Rudolph Giuliani, as 'totally callous and incompetent'[24] for its delay in issuing a passenger list after the crash of Flight 800 over Long Island, New York, on 17 July 1996. TWA also failed to anticipate and handle the needs that must accompany the provision of information. Once the crash became known, a toll-free number was released for relatives, but this particular audience did not play by the airline's rules: 'People weren't going to stay home and call on the phone', said the mayor, who lost a friend in the disaster. 'They were going to get in their cars and come to the airport. I know New Yorkers. And I was right.'[25] About 60 people gathered at John F. Kennedy airport that night, but they were given no information by the airline. The TWA executive on the spot even went home at 2 a.m. because he was tired. Furious, Giuliani distributed an unofficial list himself, warning that it was unconfirmed. The next day the mayor went on CBS TV's 'This Morning' show to continue his attack in a heated exchange with a TWA spokesperson that one newspaper called 'extraordinary'.[26] 'What happened here is outrageous', he said. 'All night upper-level management was missing.' The airline representative, participating by telephone, was told: 'You have unnecessarily caused pain to these families.'[27]

Relatives of the victims, and the media, also faulted TWA's tardy information flow, and the way it was communicated. The airline itself admitted that its response team did not start notifying families of victims until 8 a.m., some 11 hours after the crash. [28] The toll-free number caused trouble. One man who had seen off his wife and daughter was up all night trying to call the number, but did not get through until 6 a.m., and was put on hold for half an hour. 'All they did was take my name and phone number, and tell me when they release the passenger list, they'll call me', he said. 'I don't know what to expect. I don't have a clue.'[29] The airline finally called him at 4.30 p.m. By now, much of the airline and travel industry was highly critical. 'There are companies that prepare for these things and there are companies that are less than prepared. TWA has, unfortunately, been less than fully responsive', commented the head of a large travel agency.[30]

But is lack of information always the issue? A 1996 poll of 1313 executives in Singapore, the USA, Hong Kong, Britain and Australia suggested substantial numbers were suffering stress from an information glut.[31] Modern information technology and communication systems create their own pressures, before and during a crisis – the pressure upon harassed executives to be selective, to correctly and quickly analyse, critique, anticipate and distil into successful messages. TWA is a small airline. It had to produce an accurate and verifiable passenger list with only a small crisis team working under intense pressure. The airline, acting responsibly, released the list when it felt certain of its accuracy. Perhaps TWA did its best, but what the airline and the industry should have had in place, regardless of the availability of the facts, were mechanisms to ensure open, frequent, accessible and *human* contact with grieving friends and relatives. The quantity of information available in a crisis, even a crisis that involves loss of life, ranks *alongside* the quality of the communications machinery that you have in place.

However much information is available, and in the early moments of some crises there may be very little, the challenge is not necessarily the amount of material to hand, but the use that is made of it, and whether your company's resources meet the communication needs of your audiences. As TWA discovered, the needs go far beyond a simple desire for information. In order to be effective, crisis communication cannot depend on information alone. Only up-to-date, clear and accurate communications will suffice, with messages being tailored to meet the particular needs of each audience.

The challenge of being open

Sir Geoffrey Howe described the events that followed the shooting of three members of an IRA 'active-service unit' by SAS soldiers in Gibraltar in March 1988. The British Government's official announcement triggered a public storm, and led to a trial in which the SAS men were acquitted. The announcement had to be frantically changed when it was discovered that the IRA car did not even contain a bomb, as the SAS had supposed. The next day a second car, with the bomb, was found parked on the Spanish side of the border, but by then it was too late: the perception had been formed. The 'Death on the Rock' crisis was well underway. 'Once again, and for psychologically understandable reasons', Sir Geoffrey said, 'we had thought too little about the right way of publicizing a secret. We thus appeared to be incompetent as well as inaccurate. It is small wonder that we were suspected too of deliberate (even if quite pointless) deceit.'[32]

Being open is one of the axioms of crisis management. Openness tells people you are trustworthy and honest. Research and experience indicates that a brisk 'no comment' will suggest that you and your company have something to hide. It may also suggest that you do not care, or are not competent to deal with the problem that you have created.

These perceptions compound the problems for companies. It is hard enough personally to face heavy criticism, while legal fears may also discourage you from saying things that may need to be said, and said quickly.

Does it not make sense to be able to provide honest, factual information to any audience that requires it? To forestall or contain confrontation by talking with a community about the environmental implications of your operations? To explain in accessible terms the health and safety drawbacks of your necessary but risky product?

Many communication consultants will advise reluctant companies to be open. The same consultants balance this advice with consideration of the risks of openness if not communicated with care and sensitivity. In rare circumstances, being open can even spark a crisis. When that happens, clarifications and apologies lack substance because it is felt that the truth has already been told.

The pitfalls of openness

The real problem is: how can a praiseworthy desire for openness be part of a managed approach to crisis planning? An answer can be found by examining two instances of the misuse and careful use of openness by companies facing crises.

One of the most celebrated cases of misdirected openness occurred in April 1991. Gerald Ratner, flamboyant head of the profitable British jewellery chain of the same name, was used to appraising his mass-marketed products in blunt terms. In 1988, for example, a fascinated journalist asked Ratner how one of his best-selling Christmas gifts, 'a lead crystal sherry decanter with six matching, egg-cup shaped glasses on a silver plated tray', could be sold for only £14.99 (US$22.50, 19 Euros). 'Because it's crap', explained Gerald. His cousin Victor quickly intervened to say that the true reason was careful buying by the company. Gerald's explanation did not attract comment, and for three more years Ratners expanded the business of selling cheap jewellery, by careful buying, efficient use of human resources, and cost-cutting production. The *Financial Times* reported: 'In the pursuit of ever cheaper products Ratner has worked with suppliers to produce hollow gold jewellery without seams, thus shaving a few more pence from the price.'[33]

In 1991, Gerald Ratner again publicly described his jewellery as crap, this time in an address to the Annual Dinner of the Institute of Directors (IoD). Perhaps he remembered his earlier, uneventful, uses of the word when he sat down to prepare his remarks. Ratner must have felt particularly confident that evening: his global chain of 2400 stores had just taken pre-tax profits of £112 million ($185m, 159m Euros), bucking the market trend.

Ratner's 25-minute speech explained his formula for beating the recession: sell low quality at low prices. His explanation was delivered with customary panache. For example:

> We also do cut glass sherry decanters complete with six glasses on a silver-plated tray that your butler can serve you drinks on, all for £4.95. People say how can you sell this for such a low price? I say because it is total crap.[34]

After describing how his untraditional, garish shops with loud music infallibly drew the sort of customer he was looking for, Ratner went on to describe his products as being in 'the worst possible taste'.[35] He made fun of a line of earrings which had 'very little to do with quality'. Ratner declared: 'We even sell a pair of earrings for under a pound, which is cheaper than a prawn sandwich from Marks & Spencer but I have to say the earrings won't probably last as long.'

Afterwards, Ratner sat down with a journalist, who warned him about the likely impact of his remarks. 'Do you really think tomorrow's press will be that bad?' Ratner replied, as realization faintly began to dawn. 'I only said it as a joke.'[36] The IoD had thoroughly enjoyed his speech, as had several journalists. In fact, the first coverage had already appeared from the Press Association: 'SUCCESS BASED ON "TOTAL CRAP" ADMITS BIGGEST JEWELLER.'

Ratner's 'openness' was now a major problem rather than an amusing and refreshing exercise in honesty. The difference between 'crap' in 1988 and 1991 was not really the word itself. Nor was it, as one journalist proposed, that Ratner had 'made the fatal error of translating a private joke into a public statement'.[37] What inflated his old joke into a crisis was the medium chosen for its delivery. Ratner, commented Ivan Fallon: 'has done it a thousand times, but he didn't do it in the Royal Albert Hall before the massed ranks of Britain's directors'.[38] The tabloid press, the preferred reading matter among Ratner's regular clientele, tore into the speech. Britain's biggest tabloid, the *Sun*, printed a photograph of a woman crying over her wedding ring: 'I hate to think of people saying "Michele got her ring from Ratners, it must be crap".' The *Daily Mirror*'s headline was 'You 22 Carat Mugs'. Journalists staked out Ratner's family and trailed him when he was not at home. The *Sun* followed up its first story with a feature article on Ratner's lifestyle, 'The House that Crap Built'. 'Retailers have an old saying that you will never lose money by underestimating public taste', mused *The Economist*. 'But should you gloat about it?'[39]

A columnist for the *Daily Telegraph*, the venerable quality newspaper, remarked: 'My advice would be to descend into the tabloid lions' den and apologise. The speech should go like this: "I'm sorry, I am proud of my shops, proud of my staff and proud of my customers." The words may be uncomfortable but they might just exorcise the whole thing.'[40] Ratner tried to laugh it off: 'It's the motorway accident syndrome,' he averred. 'Everyone slows down to have a look.'[41] A poster was proposed by a Ratners shop manager: 'What we mean by CRAP: Cheap, Reliable, Affordable Prices.' An advertising campaign was hastily assembled and ran full-page in the tabloids the following week, featuring endorsements of Ratners products by soccer star Paul Gascoigne and soap-opera personalities. However, as media criticism continued, Ratner veered toward the approach recommended by the *Daily Telegraph*: offering public apologies via a notice pinned up in his stores and via the *Sun*, where he was photographed holding a toy pistol to his head.

These efforts notwithstanding, two months after the speech sales were down 11 per cent. Ratners no longer proudly bucked the negative market trend. Its shares fell as the stock market average rose. The scent of 'total crap' lingered in the public's consciousness. Within a year, the company had changed its name to Signet and Ratner himself had resigned. His crisis may have been started by the media, but the outcome was decided by his customers, who felt that they had heard the truth about the company from the chairman's own lips.

Openness is not a virtue in itself. It is not certain that full disclosure will be always be received in the spirit it was offered. The people who are interested in your information will have communication needs of their own, and will hear and interpret what you have to say in light of their needs, perceptions, prejudices and agendas.

Strategic openness

Openness is ethical and strategically important. If you do not tell your story in full, others will do so for you. There is ample space available on cable, satellite and network television, on the radio (particularly local and regional stations), in print and in the burgeoning world of online magazines and chatrooms. This growth in demand has led to a sensitive problem for corporations: just how open are they expected to be? One easy answer is to be completely open using whatever platforms are available, but Gerald Ratner showed how this can backfire.

In crisis communication, openness is not an end in itself. It is a powerful weapon, well able to injure the well-intentioned user, and all those with a stake in his or her success. Like any powerful weapon, it must be used properly. The CEO of a large oil company once received a letter from a popular environmental interest group about pollutants they claimed were leaking into a river that ran past its refineries. The company was told that several corporations had been identified as a threat to the river and unless they shut down operations they would find themselves on the receiving end of a major and highly public protest campaign. The oil company's first indignant reaction was that the letter amounted to blackmail, and that the interest group did not understand or care about the business of the company.

Early corporate opinion favoured either telling the interest group to mind its own business, or not replying at all. These options were motivated by considerations other than simple indignation. How could an autonomous company, run by professionals in their field, working within statutory regulations, adjust operations to the demands of third parties with no investment in or commercial knowledge of the oil industry, or the wider commercial and political environment in which the business existed? The idea of submitting a multinational corporation to a single-issue interest group would set an appalling precedent. The company could be exposed to every sort of demand; and the rest of the industry would hardly thank them for that. What would be the effect of such an action on investor confidence? The board would justly come under attack for surrendering its authority. Meanwhile, hanging over the company was the possibility of a public protest undermining the refinery and the company's reputation on a local, and possibly national, scale.

The fact was that the river was much cleaner than the interest group claimed. The company had invested heavily in filtration and other systems that cut back drastically on leaks and waste run-off. It had gone to great lengths to clean its operations, with a good deal of success. Realization of this fact in the end encouraged the company to take another course of action. It ignored the rude, hectoring tone of the letter it had received and answered by describing its own concern for the river's environment and the steps it was taking. The company also invited the interest group's representatives to visit the refinery for themselves, to view the operations and ask questions.

This response – an open invitation – is particularly noteworthy when we remember the temptations of a defensive or hesitant reaction to crises. It was courageous, and demonstrated the company's confidence in its own procedures.

What does this indicate about openness?

- **It can be used strategically.** By inviting the interest group to view its operations, the company showed it was committed to a solution and interested in talking *with*, and not *at*, its potential opponents. It is useful to note that the interest group declined the invitation, but did not carry out its protest. The publicity attached to refusing the company's offer would have been damaging in this case, while acceptance may have 'compromised' the group's mission in the eyes of some of its supporters.

• **Choose your communication vehicle with care.** The more lead time you have on a crisis, the better it is to reach out to potential pressure points and incorporate them into your communication. The oil company could easily have interpreted openness as an urgent need to announce their achievements in the media. While there is nothing ethically unsound about that, that particular version of openness could have acted as a red rag to the interest group, and given them a valid opportunity to publicly raise their side of the issue.

Companies must be open in a crisis, remembering that openness is a tool as well as a virtue. Being open is not about grabbing at chances to have your say or to let off steam: it is also about choosing messages and communication vehicles that build understanding and supply objective information and substantive comment. Used properly, a readiness to communicate openly can provide a company with an essential weapon in the crisis management armoury.

The problem of your 'opponents'

Your critics: victims, interest groups and the media

In your crisis, you will be exposed to criticism. Possibly your crisis will not unfold on the same scale as the TWA crash or Brent Spar, but criticism is part of any crisis, and critics add their own input to events, distracting you from what you may feel to be the only real issue: 'fixing' the problem. The media will also be a source of frustration. Rumours, personal attacks, speculation and misplaced accusations will abound. You will feel anger towards them, as members of the 118-strong International Olympic Committee (IOC) doubtless did in December 1998, after revelations that they received bribes and favours from Salt Lake City's committee competing to host the winter Games. As the scandal widened to envelop other cities and the entire Olympic movement, a columnist in one respected Canadian news magazine described the IOC as 'self-aggrandising geezers', 'nobodies', 'elderly toffs . . . shamelessly hauling their bandy-legged bodies from first-class flights to shiny black limos to five-star hotels'.[42] Deserved or not, abuse is the common currency of crisis. Companies find arguments misrepresented, remarks misquoted, selective editing, flaming headlines and damaging pictures. Individuals may suffer underhand tactics: the captain of the car ferry *Herald of Free Enterprise*, which capsized at Zeebrugge in March 1987, later had microphones placed in his car.

The natural reaction to anyone putting you under such pressure is to regard them as enemies. For that reason alone, it is worth looking at your critics and the media in more depth, since they are likely to be the most energetic of your many audiences in a crisis. In Part II communication strategies with all key audiences are examined in detail. For now though, as the crisis unfolds, it is useful to examine our attitudes towards our 'opponents', because those attitudes form major obstacles to effective crisis communication.

What drives their communications?

While it is true that crises can serve wider motives for the media and interest groups – such as building circulation, subscriptions, networking, keeping a particular issue alive – it is no less true that they are capitalizing on wider social changes that many companies fail to incorporate in their own crisis communications.

- **Global education.** In markets around the world, educational standards are rising every year. The result of increased levels of knowledge is an accompanying rise in awareness. The effect on business is apparent in markets around the world, and takes the form of five factors:
  1. *Increased cynicism.* Wherever we operate, it is easy to agree that the general public are becoming less passive about what companies do or say. These reactions are not limited to any particular sector or industry. It would appear that the direct effect of increased knowledge and ready information is that established organizations and large operations are viewed suspiciously by large sections of the public.
  2. *Demands for ever higher standards.* Looking back over the last ten to fifteen years, it can be seen how public interest and pressure has focused on the ways companies operate. This trend can be found in all industries, but particularly in the manufacturing and industrial sectors. It may be tempting to treat it as both unwelcome or temporary, but it is probable that the demands for ever-increasing

standards will continue. The public will not give up in their pursuit of higher operating and standards.

3. *Public demands for increased transparency.* The third intrusive factor, which flows from increased education, is that the general public seems to want to know more and more about the way business is conducted. Gone are the days when the company chairman stood up annually to deliver the trading statement for the year. Nowadays, more detailed information is expected about management and operations at all levels of business. This is an uncomfortable trend because instead of relatively easy conversations with analysts and journalists specializing in your particular industry, you are suddenly required to answer questions, often difficult and hostile, from people who clearly do not comprehend or like business, or the complicated nature of your operations.

4. *Increased focus on health, safety and the environment.* Looking back over the same period of fifteen years, we have seen a growing awareness among the general public about health, safety and environmental matters. At the same time we have heard industries tell us that they have been concentrating on those important areas for decades. In crises, companies find it frustrating to be dragged over old, familiar ground. But is that frustration justified? While you may feel under constant criticism in areas where you have invested heavily in management time, technology and finance, the world outside has moved on. Today the general public has emotional concerns, which are evident in fears and phobias about illnesses and risks that were unknown a few years ago. Consequently they want answers and reassurances from you and any industry that may contribute to this medical risk or that scientific threat; to their health; their family's future; their local population and their environment.

5. *Public demands for choice.* The public has become used to richness bred on belief in the right to choose. This is part and parcel of free enterprise, but in a crisis it takes on an added importance. The person in the street savours the power to choose: to buy or not to buy, to decide on a whim to boycott your product. Can we ignore these rights or the communications factors which may weigh in his or her decision?

The media

The media shape attitudes and influence prejudices in a crisis. This unavoidable fact means there is no point in carrying a brief for or against the media. It is simplistic to criticize the media on the basis of questionable editorial decisions or the outrageous activities of particular journalists. Instead it needs to be remembered that:

- the speed and spread of modern communications means news is available with bewildering immediacy;
- the media play a critical role in education and the cultivation of public awareness discussed earlier. A large proportion of the population in Europe and the USA gain all new information from the media, once they have completed formal education.

It is also important to accept that, like any other business, the media are driven by business imperatives. Media outlets need to retain and attract readers, listeners, viewers and advertisers. The product in which every journalist and editor trades is the story. It must be realized that a story is subject to the same constraints as any other commodity – it has to sell. When you have a problem, or are perceived to have one, your view of the 'facts' is likely to differ from how an editor will see the essential dramatic ingredients needed for a 'good' story. Your message needs to respect those ingredients, without losing its integrity, if it is to be effective.

Lastly, we need to appreciate the limited time and space available to the media as they scramble to be first with the news, while attracting and maintaining interest and attention. The advent of 24-hour news has, broadly, rendered deadlines dead. At the same time, readers, listeners and viewers expect a wide range of information in every copy of their newspaper or in each newscast. They have also come to expect each successive report to include 'new' facts and different angles.

Interest groups

Nike's CEO Phil Knight has complained about opponents of his overseas labour practices. 'Essentially, those critics will hang around restaurants, outside factories, in the pubs, to get those anecdotes, to tell how dreadful this whole globalisation process is in general, and how evil Nike is in specifics.'[43] You may, like Knight, be angry about the people attacking your company. Activists, victims, lawyers or politicians will be swarming over your organization in search of information. You have never had to deal with them before and you are discovering that trying to control them, especially on an international scale, is like trying to stop water leaking from a soaking sponge.

Your feelings are especially complicated when your critics are the victims of your crisis: the injured, the down-sized, the bereaved, the bankrupt. Although you try hard to sympathize with them, because you too are human, you are also a company officer with professional responsibilities. What do you, in your stressed, crisis-fighting mode, suspect they want from you? Money? Legal action? The right to level any accusations that they like about you? Show their emotion at your expense? The right to hate your company publicly? To stir people up against you in spite of your attempts to show goodwill?

Furthermore, you will be curiously hampered by your own business experience. Your technical language – the very terminology that lets a company deal confidently with its risks – is alien to your critics and the media, and confirms what they already suspected: that you do not care, understand, or listen.

For these reasons it is instructive, first, to step back and understand how critical interest groups see themselves; second, to understand how they communicate.

How interest groups see themselves

- **Defending the citizen.** Throughout this book, the terms 'activists', 'pressure groups', or even 'NGOs' (non-government organizations) are not used. We believe that the terms 'interest groups' or 'citizens' groups' better describe what these organizations hope to achieve. It is excellent 'positioning' because the aims and goals of any group, when so described, are shown to be universal – defending the interests of everyone. We are all citizens and thus interest groups believe they exist to defend and reassure us. It is important to appreciate the positioning because of the credibility that the media and general public attach to interest groups. Over time many groups have moved from the extreme fringe to the respectable centre by managing to change popular perceptions of what they do. In the process, the less imaginative corporations they targeted were pushed in the opposite direction.

- **As professionals.** The larger groups are now well managed and motivated by good business principles. Membership means finance, which provides the life blood for future campaigning and action. Successful high-profile campaigns bring in more members, and success depends critically on an ability to communicate through the media and down a range of other routes. Greenpeace spent over a million dollars (860,000 Euros) on its campaign against the Brent Spar rig, according to the PR head of Greenpeace International.[44] When company managers are tempted to stay silent in the face of interest group activity, this decision needs to be balanced against the realization that they will be facing skilled communicators calling on the most up-to-date techniques.

How do your critics communicate?

- **By using universal terms and targeting them against a variety of issues.** It is as simple as, for instance, victims inviting us to share their terrible grief; or as complex as interest groups achieving change by showing how often technical matters raise global concerns like the environment, human or animal rights, worker exploitation. Shell realized as much about Greenpeace. 'They are very skilled communicators. In fact their distinctive competence is actually communications and their product is the environment.'[45]
- **By using emotion as a key.** The ability of interest groups to stir deep emotions cannot be dismissed as histrionics. Phil Knight saw how cleverly this *modus operandi* was employed against Nike.

  > Nike has taken the emotion off the athletic field, and sold its products that way. And there is really no emotion quite as strong as that emotion out on the athletic field. And now our critics have found it in their interests, to kind of flip that emotion around, and use it to criticize us, and increase their own fundraising.[46]

- **By concentrating on a few key issues rather than the full facts.** The crisis itself is secondary to the message that must be delivered. Shell found itself 'on the receiving end of highly selective and misleading use of information to whip up public concern. It was very cleverly orchestrated.'[47] Greenpeace invested heavily to ensure that it was their pictures that appeared on the TV screens in every home. Their success may be gauged by the TV footage at the height of the crisis. In the last five days, before Shell reversed its disposal plans for the Brent Spar platform, over 70 per cent of the footage screened in the UK was shot by and packaged to national TV stations by Greenpeace.
- **By growing more international every year.** All the major interest groups are ready to cooperate across geographical borders and do so regularly during campaigns. This internationalization includes a willingness to seek common agendas in areas of interest. Companies in crisis could face a diverse collection of interest groups targeting it for a variety of issues. This trend is seen in the way that Friends of the

Earth, Greenpeace and People for Ethical Treatment of Animals (PETA) lead campaigns in cooperation with a range of related activist and political interests.

A final word about your 'opponents.' Yes, some politicians are certainly publicity hungry, some reporters are only interested in scapegoats or scandals, and some critics are unreasonable. In the last analysis, they are driven by different motives than you, so why waste precious words and time arguing when you could be putting out messages of your own? Your unfolding crisis is, *at worst*, a contest between alternate messages. It should not degenerate into a trial, with your company in the dock and your critics leading the prosecution.

How can a crisis hurt you?

The damage created by a crisis depends on the nature of the problem, the public perception of your company before you entered the crisis and the success of your crisis communication strategy – which must be intimately tied to operational decision-making.

The crisis will create strategic damage, reduce profits and impose new costs on your company.

Strategic damage

The strategic damage can be severe and is felt in different ways.

(i) *damage to growth*

Depressed shares, loss of investor confidence, lost customers and hurt profits affect a company's expansion plans and its competitive position. Executives are forced to invest in recovery rather than growth. To some degree these things happen regardless of the company's response to the crisis. 'We believed that we could recover from it in a relatively quick time,' one Foodmaker executive recalled of the *e.coli* burger deaths in 1993, but the time needed 'was greater and longer than anyone had expected'.[48] They were not helped when Standard & Poor's lowered its rating of Foodmaker's debt, which raised the possibility of higher interest rates for future borrowing.

Occasionally the crisis alone is responsible. In November 1992, undercover cameras of ABC's 'Prime Time Live' exposed several abuses practised by employees at the US grocery chain, Food Lion. Cameras caught workers 'bathing stale chicken parts in barbecue sauce and selling the concoction as gourmet chicken'. Food Lion responded to this unwelcome intrusion by slapping a $100 million suit on ABC to get control of the tapes. Three years later, this was followed by another suit brought against trade unions trying to organize at company facilities. The effect of both actions was to focus additional attention towards Food Lion's employment practices, in addition to dredging up the original food-handling controversy. By October 1995, the company issued a statement that it was time to move forward again. 'We're done cutting back', said Tom Smith, president and chief executive. 'It's time to grow.' 'The eye of the hurricane has passed', he added. Setting aside the merits or demerits of Food Lion's response to the original crises, what destruction had been left behind? Sales declined sharply in some markets and earnings plunged. Shares dropped from a dollar a share in 1993 to 37 cents a share. The result was that Food Lion's expansion plans were delayed while rivals such as Wal-Mart were growing or moving into the grocery business. According to *Bloomberg Business News*, 'Food Lion Inc. has belied its name in the last few years: It has been cowering rather than roaring.'[49]

In 1996 the successful American health-food company Odwalla reacted to news that *e.coli*-laden apples were going into its juices by quickly stopping production and removing from store shelves all products made with apple juice. This did not prevent shares from losing almost a third of their value, despite record sales. One analyst commented that expansion would not resume until Odwalla discovered the reason for the contamination, took steps to prevent it happening again and suffered 'through a couple of quarters of lower sales'.[50]

Other crises might worsen an already deteriorating situation. From the middle of 1997, when its Asian labour issue attained crisis velocity, Nike was dealing with other broadsides, including slumping sales (a disease also suffered by Nike's competitors), new products that did not meet expectations, including a line of shoes whose symbol offended Islamic groups (see page 69). The welter of bad news had a serious impact on the cohesion of its workforce, leading to the resignations of several senior executives. This was especially important to Nike since, as a local Oregon newspaper reminded its readers: 'One of Nike's great strengths historically has been its ability to retain the hearts and minds of its top managers.'[51] In February and March 1998, 1600 employees were laid off. Phil Knight found himself dealing with an unfamiliar set of problems: the problems of failure. 'In an emotional company meeting in April', Knight reportedly 'apologized to Nike staffers for the turmoil and vowed to lead the company back'.[52] The Asian crisis had played a large part in Nike's misfortunes.

(ii) *Damage to corporate reputation*

The cost to reputation cannot easily be quantified, but the damage appears in several ways. First, in the bond of trust between the company and customers – the heart of any business. In the case of food and drink products, for instance, the ultimate trust lies with consumers. When a product problem becomes public knowledge, the bonds of trust are stressed as confidence sinks. If crisis management by the company does not bolster confidence and restore trust, as was the case when Perrier appeared to react tardily to the scare over benzene carcinogens in its mineral water, the results can be fatal. Ultimately the product or even the business may perish or, as happened with Perrier, be taken over (see page 149).

Second, damage to public reputation can be expressed in massive internal changes. On occasion, the shock is so great that a corporation must change in practically every aspect of its external and internal culture: operations, communications, management. The *Financial Times* noted that: 'The fiasco over the planned sinking of the obsolete Brent Spar oil storage platform in the Atlantic Ocean produced such disarray within the group that it shook Shell's management structure to its foundations.'[53]

Third, a damaged reputation may expose your company to further crises. Brent Spar weakened Shell in the eyes of the media and several European governments during the ill-starred effort to sink the rig. This encouraged interest groups to launch further attacks, for example using Shell to publicize the plight of democracy in Nigeria by attacking its environmental misdeeds and its quiescent attitude when the military government executed civil rights campaigners in 1995. Nelson Mandela led calls for Shell to pull out of a new venture in Nigeria, and a worldwide boycott was launched (ineffectively) by a patchwork of organizations including Anita Roddick's Body Shop.

Damage to reputation is partly the sum of the harm a crisis inflicts on specific areas of company activity. It is also something less tangible – a threat to the idea a company likes to have about itself regardless of profit or production. Phil Knight explained in a public appearance:

> I truthfully don't think that there has been a material impact on Nike sales by, [sic] 'Well, I'm not going to buy Nike shoes because of what's going on in their factories' . . . I've said before I think there are other factors that have caused those sales to decrease. But obviously this is an important issue to us, mainly because of how it affects our reputation, and that's important to us, and it's important to us as a company and as to a brand. And it's one of the reasons we address this issue.[54]

(iii) *damage to personal reputation*

Your crisis could involve personal reputation. Robert Allen, CEO of the US telecommunications giant AT&T, cut 40,000 people from the company's payroll as part of a plan to compete with the surge in smaller, cheaper rivals. A 1995 proxy statement to shareholders then revealed that Allen had received stock options that increased his total pay package from $6.7 million to $16 million. Executives pointed out that Mr Allen's actual pay was in reality much less, because he and other top managers could not cash in their options for at least four years. Their remarks were undone when Allen himself reacted with what was regarded as 'a long and testy message' to company employees, in which he announced that he had 'actually taken a 20 per cent cut in cash compensation'.[55]

This defensive response was badly received. The CEO seemed more interested in his money than the feelings of those laid off. The pay package, declared one newspaper, 'is likely to antagonize many workers and increase bad publicity that has already infuriated the usually unflappable chief executive'. Having made that the basis of its story, the media, as is common in crisis, proceeded to generate the very outcome it predicted. Personal criticism was levelled at Allen's performance: 'Why do you want to retain him – he's an average performer', observed an expert in corporate compensation. 'He's not even a face card, he's a seven in the deck.' There were leaks from within. 'The question is, at a time when AT&T is going through this wrenching transition, is this fair?', whispered one anonymous AT&T executive. 'He's comparing himself with other CEOs, but the question for corporate America is whether you can get loyalty out of men down the line with that kind of logic.' Allen reacted personally, lashing out at 'relentless' and 'inaccurate' news coverage and his job cuts. Meanwhile the crisis at AT&T spread to a general assessment of his patchy record, even by critics within the company. Allen's control over the message vanished as the media went wherever they could to get the information they needed. 'At least some AT&T employees were quick to disagree' with his business decisions, 'though privately, asserting that at least part of AT&T's problems stemmed from calamitous misjudgments in buying NCR and fumbling a long litany of attempts to introduce innovative new consumer electronic products.'[56] The focus moved, and the controversy spread from criticism of one person to attacks on the reputation of a large company. An attack on personal reputation spreads beyond the subject and into other areas, creating a 'mosaic' of other mistakes that are traced back to the doorstep of the chosen 'victim'.

Financial damage

The costs of crisis are wide-ranging and difficult to calculate. This section draws upon the manufacturing and retail sectors for examples where major costs could be incurred. In many cases it is impossible to anticipate accurately the full financial impact. What is clear is that being prepared may help to minimize the loss of income and reputation at a time of crisis.

(i) *pulling the product*

In manufacturing and retail companies, costs can be confidently forecast and quickly calculated for the operational actions of pulling products from the marketplace. For example:

- product recall and pickup
- stock replacement
- transportation.

DuPont took an after-tax charge of $47 million in the third quarter of 1996 to cover crop damage claims and legal expenses related to the recall, officially undertaken for 'commercial reasons', of Benlate 50 DF fungicide, the subject of several controversial lawsuits (see page 32). Net income for the quarter was $898 million, up from $769 million in the third quarter of 1995. Without that charge, earnings per share would have been eight cents higher. On top of the $47 million were further recall charges of $63 and $110 million respectively for the nine months ended 30 September 1995 and 30 September 1996.[57]

Less easily calculated, but costly in time and effort, are quality assurance checks and special investigations. A serious contamination will demand that every quality assurance or quality control measure is called upon to unearth the cause and likely extent of the product's problem. Regrettably, this detective work is usually long and complex.

Checks against product specifications are often invalid if poisons or toxic materials have been used to lace food or drink products. When on-shelf contamination or spiking is involved, analysis may have to start from the most basic chemical research.

(ii) *clean-up costs*

Once a problem has been identified, measures are needed to ensure it does not recur, at least before the eyes of distrustful customers. It will be necessary to change operational procedures or tighten quality and environmental controls to reduce the risks. Afterwards, major customers may insist on inspecting new systems and procedures.

You might have to re-package the product to reassure the public that they are buying 'safer', 'improved' or 'new' products. Re-packaging is costly, especially if it is necessary to conduct design and production stages at an accelerated pace.

(iii) *production, sales and marketing costs*

Operational costs can be worked out in advance. In a manufacturing company management could benefit from calculating outline figures as part of a practise recall exercise. On top of this, though, are hidden costs which can never be forecast before or fully assessed after a serious product contamination takes place.

For instance, production losses always takes place at a time of crisis for any of the following reasons:

- Precautionary destruction of product when the cause and extent of the problem has not been fully defined.
- A requirement to stop production lines to check for faults, add new equipment or set up new procedures.
- Damage to sales, which can be immediate, as a product or company name hits the headlines.

Consumers might grow cautious despite messages from either the company or medical experts. Until public confidence is won back, levels of sales can plummet. The long-term management of reputation must be addressed beyond the immediate event that sparked the crisis. After a poison scare surrounding Big Ben pies, a popular Australian dish for over a century, some food industry sources estimated that the owner, George Weston Foods Ltd, spent at least A$12 million (US $8m, 8.4m Euros) trying to reposition the brand over a year, before the business was sold in 1994.[58]

When a serious contamination issue is running, advertising or promotion programmes may have to be put on hold or even cancelled. Cancellation or postponement is always expensive and wasteful of the preparatory work, but management will not be seen to be acting responsibly in a crisis if it continues normal marketing activity.

(iv) *consultancy support*

Crisis management demands special skills based on practical experience. Any business in the spotlight needs to seek the experience and support
of experts. In advance of the twists and turns of an actual crisis, it is hard to
assess the precise involvement of communications experts or legal advisers.
Nevertheless, it is prudent to define a role for specialist support in preparedness plans.

(v) *long-term costs*

Once the storm has passed, there will be longer-term costs to cover
such areas as operational and security reviews. If consumer injuries or deaths
have occurred, you will face compensation claims, leading to settlements,
either in or out of court.

(vi) *confidence costs*

Public companies face the problem of investor confidence and the risk
of adverse responses from stockholders. At a time of crisis there is always the
risk that stock prices will plummet as media hype and speculation dent
company and product reputation. Surprised by the inexplicably sudden resignation of Barclay's Chief Executive on 27 November 1998, investors knocked
8 per cent off the bank's shares that day, reducing the company's value by
£171 million.[59] Exxon's stock-market capitalization dropped $3 billion in the
two weeks after the *Exxon Valdez* oil spill in Alaska.[60] Following the May 1996
crash of ValuJet Flight 592 in the Florida Everglades, and in spite of a strong
communication plan, stock quickly fell 34 per cent over concern about reduced
bookings, legal expenses from lawsuits, and speculation that the Federal
Aviation Authority investigation would stop all ValuJet flights – which did
eventually happen. Foodmaker's shares fell 11 per cent on Tuesday 19 January,
the day after it was announced that 50 children and adult customers were
being treated for the *e.coli* infection at Jack In The Box.[61]

(vii) *cost containment: the consultant's responsibility*

Business is always at risk from crises. It is the responsibility of management to plan for these situations and minimize potential impact, through the
use of detailed plans and crisis management procedures. In preparing for
high-risk, high-cost scenarios companies need the support of experienced
consultants. Only then can management hope to be truly prepared to face
crisis and manage complex situations with minimal impact on product and
company reputation.

Nike's crisis life-cycle

Sure, you know about the cool shoes and the hip commercials. But what do you really know about Nike?[62]

Nike and its logo, the swoosh, are globally recognized icons. The company, based in Beaverton, Oregon, grew into a multinational concern by making attractive and exciting shoes, and projecting a 'fiery underdog character', that young Americans found especially attractive. Phil Knight and his college track coach each put up $500 in 1964 to start a shoe import business, Blue Ribbon Sports. True to its image of the battling underdog, the company's headquarters was in a laundry room at the home of Knight's mother. In 1972 the first Nike brand running shoe was introduced. By 1990, sales had reached $2 billion a year, and by 1997 the company was the world's biggest sports shoe maker. It is a thoroughly global organization. According to Knight, 'all our experiences had caused us to really believe in the benefits of international trade. The uplifting of impoverished peoples, the better values for consumers.'[63] The company employed half a million people worldwide; 150 factories in Asia alone played a large part in Nike's success. 'Nike shoes make up 5 per cent of the total exports of the whole nation of Vietnam', Knight told journalists in May 1998.[64] Nike was proud of its work in Vietnam but it was there, nevertheless, that the first problems arose.

Stage one: the crisis breaks

In May 1996 several interest groups won attention for campaigns against poor labour practices in the developing world, aiming to raise awareness about the conditions in factories supplying prestigious Western brand-names to western consumers. The groups include Vietnam Labor Watch (VLW), based in New York; Community Aid Abroad (CAA) in Sydney, Australia; Hong Kong Christian Industrial Committee (HKCIC) and Transnational Resource & Action Center (TRAC) in San Francisco. Nike, a globally recognized brand, was an excellent publicity hook, and the first reports claimed that Nike was exploiting workers in Vietnam, Indonesia and China, and employing child labour in Pakistan.

In July, Nike announced a 38 per cent rise in profits. American civil rights leader Jesse Jackson returned from a tour of the Far East and publicly criticized factory conditions. In August President Clinton formed a task force to look into sweatshop labour overseas. Nike rejected a call for independent monitoring of its factories, and in October established a Labour Practices Department of its own.

On 17 October the CBS TV show *48 Hours* reported on Nike in Asia. It disclosed that Nike moved to Indonesia but when working standards there improved, the company expanded to Vietnam. 'New country, same old story. Only longer hours, even lower wages, mainly to women.' Nike managers were reluctant to speak but frightened women employees described abuses in the workplace, including beatings from factory supervisors. A Vietnamese labour official warned: 'If the company intentionally turns away from this, it will have an effect on their reputation.' After the report, the anchorman added: 'Nike now says it plans to hire outside observers to talk to employees and examine working conditions in its Vietnam factories, but the company won't say just when that might happen.'[65]

The CBS coverage, one Nike-watcher says, was 'the report that started it all for us'. Nike was now in a crisis. The mainstream media took up the issue and interest groups enjoyed a publicity bonanza. A factory worker, flown to the USA for the programme, then embarked on a speaking and talk-show tour to air the case for suffering Nike workers in the Asia-Pacific region.

Stage two: the crisis spreads and intensifies

At the end of October, a major protest was staged at the opening of the 'Nike Town' store in New York. In early November a *Washington Post* article broadened the story, alleging that conditions at Nike factories were far worse in China than in Vietnam. The report described women locked in cages guarded by dogs as a punishment for poor sewing.

Nike opened a new football stitching centre in Pakistan, with tight supervision and better pay for the child employees. The company alleged that most European companies controlling the football market did not monitor conditions in their own factories. The media still pursued the Nike story. 'Where does this stuff come from?' asks the *Los Angeles Times*:

Part of what is going on with the sweatshops is that this consumer awareness movement is confronting people with a choice: Exploitation or human rights? They are being asked: Which side do you want to put yourself on?[66]

Many student organizations had already decided. A movement was launched on several campuses to prevent colleges signing contracts with Nike. Students in Los Angeles persuaded their Sports Department to stop buying equipment made by child labour. Nike stores were picketed over Christmas and the New Year.

The media pushed the story hard in 1997: 'The Vietnamese women who work for Nike's manufacturers, exist in conditions barely distinguishable from slavery.'[67] A new 'No Sweat' clothes label is called 'misleading'.[68] 'It's getting to be a tired refrain. First comes an expose of conditions at Nike's manufacturing operations in Vietnam, then a promise from the American athletic-shoe giant that it is addressing the problem.'[69] The findings of the Presidential Task Force were criticized as too weak. 'It's time to flush the swoosh', trumpeted the *Chicago Tribune* in April.[70]

Privately, Nike redeemed its earlier promise to hire outside observers. It had commissioned the independent accounting firm Ernst & Young to investigate conditions in their Vietnamese operations. When the report was completed in January 1997, the inspectors had unearthed problems: workers at the factory near Ho Chi Minh City, which was owned and operated by a Korean subcontractor, were exposed to carcinogens that exceeded local legal standards by 177 times in parts of the plant, and 77 per cent of the employees suffered from respiratory problems. The report also found that employees at the site were forced to work 65 hours a week, far more than Vietnamese law allowed, for $10 a week. Nike kept this information confidential, and in May commissioned Andrew Young, the former US Ambassador to the United Nations, to make a public inspection. Young inspected fifteen Nike factories in two weeks. He found that while there was room for improvement, overall Nike was doing a good job. Nike took out full-page newspaper advertisements announcing Young's findings.

The strategy backfired. Young's credibility was immediately attacked. Media reports detailed incidents of abuse that took place *while* Young was on his tour, and the episode quickly 'developed into a PR embarrassment for the company, which had hoped it would put the ghosts of the sweatshop issue to rest'.[71] The *New Republic* conducted a detailed investigation of its own, and decided that Young's report was 'marred not just by shoddy methodology but by frequent misrepresentations'.[72]

The crisis continued to spread. It was in the media, on the web (sites included 'Boycott Nike', 'Nike Campaign' and 'Praying for Nike's Soul'), on campuses and outside Nike Town stores. It was regularly featured in the Doonesbury cartoon strip, syndicated in 1400 newspapers worldwide. 'A comic strip is not meant to be an accurate depiction of life', Nike's Director of Communications for Asia-Pacific complained to the *South China Morning Post*: 'But I am sure your readers would agree that it should not be a vehicle for spreading hearsay.'[73] Interest groups kept the issue alive. In September, dozens of young people from settlement houses in New York decided to publicly dump their shoes at Nike Town in a protest at a double exploitation of the poor – making shoes for $3 and selling them for $100.

In October, an unhappy Nike employee leaked the confidential and critical Ernst & Young report to Dara O'Rourke, a UN consultant researching labour standards in Vietnam. O'Rourke passed a copy to the interest group TRAC, and TRAC informed the media. O'Rourke had visited the Nike plant near Ho Chi Minh City as part of his duties, and found conditions hardly better than when Ernst & Young reported in January. He told the *New York Times* that women workers were scared to speak, that Ernst & Young's report was not critical enough and that 'wages at the plant were the lowest of any of the fifty factories' he visited in Vietnam.[74] Nike's labour practices manager for Vietnam replied that working hours had been reduced and more fans installed, but acknowledged Nike had not checked to see if chemical levels now met legal limits.

That same month Nike launched a programme to support women entrepreneurs in Vietnam. It was expected that 300 women would receive loans in their first year. The project was to be run by the Vietnam Women's Union, a non-profit interest group based in Colorado. The company also ran a new advertisement campaign aimed at women. In response, US women's organizations attacked Nike's employment record. In November, 53 members of Congress wrote to Phil Knight calling on him to stop exploiting Asian workers, most of whom were women. 'We are deeply embarrassed', wrote the politicians, 'that a company like Nike . . . should be so directly involved in the ruthless exploitation of hundreds of thousands of desperate third world workers.'[75] Nike issued pocket-sized code of conduct cards in eleven languages to ensure workers knew their health, safety and compensation rights and how to exercise them. The media attacked Nike's sponsored stars, including golfer Tiger Woods, football star Ronaldo, tennis players Andre Agassi and Monica Seles and basketballer Michael Jordan. The *Los Angeles Times* called them 'moral jellyfish'.[76] American football star Jerry Rice was cornered by journalists at a Nike store: 'I don't think it's fair for you guys to throw this in my face,' he complained.[77]

Stage three: rebuilding?

Did Nike rebuild its reputation after two years of crisis? Its controversy now merged into other problems: the recession in Asia and job losses among its overseas subcontractors; a trend away from sports shoes to more formal footwear; a sense that the tiresomely ubiquitous swoosh was becoming 'un-cool' with its intended customers. The crisis helped to erode the glamour attached to the product. Large sections of the media now saw nothing glamorous about overpriced bits of rubber glued together in poor countries by underpaid and beaten women. Not just the media: 'Parents are delighted', observed *The Times* when Nike declared its first losses for thirteen years.[78]

Nike's communications, hitherto defensive and piecemeal, began to improve. In May 1998, Phil Knight addressed the American National Press Club in Washington. His failure, he argued to journalists, was to misunderstand the cultural complexities of his Asian operations. When Vietnam opened for business, Taiwanese and Korean managers were brought in to run the operations, without realizing that a 'truly historical hatred' existed between both groups. 'There are too many workers, too many interactions daily, and in Vietnam, too much tension based on nationalities to avoid any incidents.'[79]

'Does anyone think it was an accident that Nike set up shop in human-rights sinkholes?', one syndicated columnist inquired.[80] Nonetheless, a more organized pattern of action and communication began to emerge. Nike's Government Relations Director pledged that abuses by its subcontractors would lead to terminated contracts. Knight himself used his Press Club platform to introduce six anti-sweatshop initiatives:

- To expand current independent monitoring programmes and make public any summaries of inspections.
- To increase the minimum age of footwear factory workers to 18.
- To adopt US occupational safety standards in its overseas factories.
- To expand educational programmes at factories, providing middle- and high-school equivalency courses.
- To increase support of Nike's existing loan programme for Vietnamese women to create small businesses.
- To fund industry research into global manufacturing and responsible business practices.

Some observers noted that pay increases had not been mentioned. 'Vietnam Nike: Yet another promise!' declared the *Saigon Times Daily*, before conceding that workers could indeed 'hope for better working conditions' if the promises were delivered. Mild as the concessions were, opined a US editorial, they at least proved the effectiveness of 'scrutiny, pressure and publicity'.[81] In June 1998, a new book by the Council on Economic Priorities that reviews 250 corporations for the socially responsible investor gave Nike an 'A' but with a question mark for workplace issues (the question mark indicates that the grade is based only on partial information).[82] It is too early to judge whether Nike has at last turned the corner on its Asian problems, but at the time of writing the blanket hostility has to some extent been mitigated.

Nike's long crisis demonstrates several of the principles described earlier:

- *Surprise breeds hesitation.* Nike was focused so strongly on its image among Western consumers, and in the quality of its product, that it lacked the vision to address the problem of labour abuse as a problem in communication. When the crisis emerged, Nike still could not make the adjustment and lost control of the 'script'.
- *Hesitation creates a vacuum.* The scale of the story, covering two continents, Asia and North America, and the brutal simplicity of the subject-matter, with twin themes of cruelty and corporate greed, was bound to prove irresistible to the media. A huge interest was created into which story after story was sucked. Nike twisted in the wind as the media looked to the company's critics to satisfy their hunger for new angles.
- *The company is forced onto the defensive.* By underestimating the strength and influence of its critics, responding to pressure rather than taking a lead, Nike allowed the 'truth' about foreign labour to fall into the hands of others. From then onwards, the company was running to catch up and restore its credibility, a process that consumed time and resources as it battled with other economic problems.
- *Communication is essential, but cannot succeed on its own.* When the 22-year-old golfer and Nike star Tiger Woods returned from a tour of the company's factories in Thailand, he told Philip Knight: 'Your problem isn't with factories; your problem is with public relations.'[83] This is partly correct, but Nike has also had to tackle its crisis by extensive reforms of its overseas operations. The crisis broke because in the public mind Nike failed to demonstrate its commitment to the problem of labour abuses in Asia, by deeds as well as words. Now that the deeds are being done, Nike's communication programme has material to help the company overcome any credibility deficit.

Summary
The crisis life-cycle
- **The breaking crisis**
    1. You are in a fishbowl and the media and other audiences are looking in. Your early messages will carry an impact that is hard for others to forget or for you to amend.

2. Control seems to be slipping out of your hands. Other people shape public perceptions, and communicate in the vacuum left by your company's reluctance to respond.

3. Lack of solid detail about the crisis. Hard-to-provide information demanded by the media, analysts and others. But you will need to say something.

4. Temptation to resort to a short-term focus, to panic and to speculate.

5. For a period of time, everyone loses perspective.

- **Spread and intensification of crisis**

   1. Other stakeholders pulled into the vortex: customers, stockholders, banks, employees, analysts, who may initially draw their information from the media.

   2. Speculation and rumours develop in the absence of hard facts.

   3. Third parties – regulators, politicians, scientists and other experts – add weight to the climate of opinion.

   4. Corporate management comes under intense scrutiny from all these internal and external groups.

- **Rebuilding needs**

   1. To manage reputation. There are opportunities in a crisis to build positive perceptions of your company or product that last beyond the crisis period.

   2. Company communication/culture. The company embarks on a long-term programme to tackle management issues and communication problems that exacerbated the crisis.

Problems and challenges in crisis decision-making

- Surprise and hesitation. The shock of a crisis can create a delay in response that allows your critics and the media to fill the gap with negative comment and speculation.
- Pressure and stress must be channelled by the discipline of a crisis strategy.
- Mistaking information distribution for communication.
- Being open on the terms set by your critics.
- Treating key audiences as 'opponents'.

How can a crisis hurt you?

- **Strategic damage**

   1. To growth plans.

2. To corporate reputation.
3. To personal reputations.

- **Financial damage**
    1. Pulling the product.
    2. Clean-up costs.
    3. Production, marketing and sales costs.
    4. Consultancy costs.
    5. Long-term costs.
    6. Loss of confidence costs.

Notes

1   'What is the truth about these tragic children?' *Daily Mail*, 7 January 1997.
2   Pinsdorf, M. 'Flying different skies: how cultures respond to airline disasters.' *Public Relations Review*, 1991, vol. 17, no. 1, 37–56.
3   'Tilting at elks.' *Time*, 8 December 1997.
4   Hunt, P., Public Affairs Manager, Shell UK. (1997) *Brent Spar: A Drop in the Ocean?* Business in the Community Occasional Paper 5. London: Shell, p. 9.
5   Gilbert, M. *Churchill: A Life*. London: Heinemann, 1991, p. 384.
6   Rudolph, B. 'Coping with catastrophe: crisis management becomes the new corporate discipline.' *Time*, 24 February 1986.
7   Hunt, P. *op. cit.*
8   Howe, Sir Geoffrey. *Conflict of Loyalty*. London: Pan, 1995, p. 668.
9   'A-Class disaster.' *Sunday Times*, 16 November 1997.
10 'Daimler moves fast to save "Baby Benz".' *International Herald Tribune*, 30 October 1997.
11 Kuras, Andrzej. 'Like a bridge over a troubled water.' Interview with Mike Seymour. *Crisis Management*. Undated, p 13.
12 'Trends to watch: Stress, the health hazard of modern life.' *Medical Industry Today*, 25 October 1996.
13 Marino, S. F. 'The stress epidemic: it's costing industry $20 billion annually.' *Industry Week*, 7 April 1997.
14 'Putting stress on the bottom line: defining the thin line separating stress from depression.' *Management Today*, September 1997.
15 Greener, Mark. *The 'Which?' Guide to Managing Stress*. London: Which? Books, 1996.
16 'A brush with anonymity.' *Newsweek*, 29 July 1996.
17 'Trends to watch: Stress, the health hazard of modern life.' *Medical Industry Today*, 25 October 1996.
18 Iacocca, L. (with William Novak). *Iacocca: An Autobiography*. London: Sidgwick & Jackson, 1985, p. 182.

19   Speer, A. *Inside the Third Reich.* London: Sphere, 1971, p. 402.
20   'Is your career killing you?: work related disorders.' *Canadian Business,* 26 September 1997.
21   Marino, S. F. 'The stress epidemic: It's costing industry $20 billion annually.' *Industry Week,* 7 April 1997.
22   *ibid.*
23   Iacocca, L. *op. cit.,* p. 154.
24   'TWA delays family notice: Airline criticized for slow response.' *Pittsburgh Post-Gazette,* 19 July 1996.
25   'Flight 800: Crisis in recovery.' *The Washington Post,* 3 August 1996.
26   'Turbulent Rudy rips TWA on delay of ID process'. *Daily News,* 19 July 1996.
27   Reuters World Service, 18 July 1996.
28   *Pittsburgh Post-Gazette, op. cit.*
29   'The TWA tragedy'. *Newsday,* 19 July 1996.
30   Reuters World Service, 19 July 1996.
31   'Trends to watch: Stress, the health hazard of modern life.' *op. cit.*
32   Sir Geoffrey Howe, *op. cit.,* p. 552.
33   'Putting a jewel in everyone's crown.' *Financial Times,* 28 January 1988.
34   'Success based on "total crap" admits biggest jeweller.' *Press Association,* 23 April 1991.
35   'Ratner's gaffe cuts into sales.' *Marketing,* 23 May 1991.
36   'Golden blunder.' *Sunday Times,* 28 April 1991.
37   *ibid.*
38   'Ratner's cheap gaffe.' *Sunday Times,* 28 April 1991.
39   'Ratnering about rubbish.' *The Economist,* 27 April 1991.
40   'Ratner's stale joke.' *Sunday Telegraph,* 28 April 1991.
41   'Golden blunder.' *Sunday Times,* 28 April 1991.
42   'At last, the dirty little secret is out.' *Maclean's,* 11 January 1999.
43   National Press Club Luncheon address. *Federal News Service,* 12 May 1998.
44   'Two days that sealed fate of redundant rig.' *Independent,* 22 June 1995.
45   Hunt, P. *op. cit.*
46   National Press Club Luncheon address. *Federal News Service,* 12 May 1998.
47   Hunt, P. *op. cit.*
48   'Fast-food phoenix; Jack In The Box rises from the ashes of crisis.' *San Diego Union-Tribune,* 10 August 1997.
49   'Besieged Food Lion says it will roar back.' *Bloomberg Business News* report. *The Ledger* (Lakeland, FL), 8 October 1995.
50   'Odwalla can learn from Jack In The Box.' *Seattle Times,* 1 November 1996.
51   'Embattled Nike still has believers.' *Oregonian,* 21 June 1998.
52   *ibid.*
53   'Shell discovers time and tide wait for no man.' *Financial Times,* 10 March 1998.

54   National Press Club Luncheon address. *op. cit.*
55   'AT&T chief, who cut jobs, defends pay.' *New York Times*, 28 February 1996.
56   *ibid.*
57   'DuPont Releases Third Quarter Earnings.' 23 October 1996. http://www.dupont.com/corp/whats-new/releases/961023.html
58   'Australia: high price of a peanut tasting.' *Australian Financial Review*, 5 July 1996.
59   'Barclays chief quits.' *BBC News*, 27 November 1998. http://news.bbc.co.uk/hi/english/business/the_company_file/newsid_223000/223004.stm
60   'Where to turn when your reputation is at stake.' *Across the Board*, February 1998.
61   'Foodmaker shares dive.' *Chicago Sun-Times*, 20 January 1993.
62   Nike home page, 8 July 1998. www.nikebiz.com
63   'Embattled Nike still has believers.' *Oregonian*, 21 June 1998.
64   National Press Club Luncheon address. *op. cit.*
65   '48 hours.' *CBS News*, 17 October 1996.
66   'Where does this stuff come from?' *Los Angeles Times*, 8 December 1996.
67   *Guardian*, 21 April 1997.
68   'No Sweat label may be misleading.' *Newsday*, 17 April 1997.
69   *Bergen News*, 6 April 1997.
70   *Chicago Tribune*, 4 April 1997.
71   *South China Morning Post*, 6 July 1997.
72   'The young and the feckless'. *New Republic*, 15 September 1997.
73   Letter to the Editor. *South China Morning Post*, 6 June 1997.
74   'Nike shoe plant in Vietnam is called unsafe for worker.' *New York Times*, 8 November 1997.
75   'Nike told: Don't do it.' *Vietnam Investment Review*, 17 November 1997.
76   'Superrich stars in sport; moral jellyfish in life.' *Los Angeles Times*, 17 October 1997.
77   'Who will refuse Nike's blood money?' *The Times Union*, 22 October 1997.
78   'Just do it, says Nike but teenagers say no thanks.' *The Times*, 2 July 1998.
79   National Press Club Luncheon address. *op. cit.*
80   Herbert, R. 'The shoe company has a long way to go in improving worker compensation.' *Pittsburgh Post-Gazette*, 25 May 1998.
81   'A step forward for Nike'. *The Times Union*, 18 May 1998.
82   CEP. *The Corporate Report Card: Rating 250 of America's Corporations for the Socially Responsible Investor.* New York: Dutton, 1998.
83   National Press Club Luncheon address. *op. cit.*

3 **Effective crisis communication**

There is nothing more difficult than the public relations handling of an
operation or activity that involves 'moving from darkness into light'.[1]
Sir Geoffrey Howe, British Foreign Secretary, 1983–9

The character and evolution of a crisis, described in the previous chapters, offer good reasons for a managed approach to crisis. So much of corporate activity is controlled by over-arching systems or specific procedures. Can a similar approach help to bring light to a crisis, the darkest and most anarchic of business situations?

This chapter explores the part played by crisis communication in support of operational and management actions: what it can deliver to troubled companies, what your audiences expect from you, and the hard assumptions that your company has to make about itself in order to weather its crisis. It leads us to Part II of this book, and the specific steps that are required to put your plan into practice.

What crisis communication can do

Why bother?

First, a helpful reality check. Crises happen. They are as inevitable as rainy days. Rain will fall whether you have an umbrella or not. Does that mean you always take an umbrella to work? Companies, like people, cannot spend valuable time worrying about stormy weather every day of the week. Many potential crises just do not arise, or they peter out of their own accord. The media has a short attention span, as does the general public. In a year's time, maybe less, the trouble may be forgotten, and corporate life can get back to normal. Is crisis communication worth the investment? Critics might answer 'no' on the following grounds:

- Crisis communication will never satisfy critics. To them it is PR spin designed to get unrepentant companies over a shortlived controversy.

- Companies do not really need to communicate. A crisis is soon forgotten as media interest switches its focus to another controversy. A crisis is entertainment for a society with congenital Attention Deficit Disorder.

Both arguments have some basis in fact. They should be discussed because no-one should look uncritically at their own field, and because they have something to say about the nature of crises as well as of crisis management. Our examples are drawn from the sports business, a crucible for many crises since – as the aeroplane and Olympic tragedies at Munich mentioned in Chapter 1 demonstrate – famous names and public passions are mutually dependent and occasionally highly combustible.

A company will never satisfy its critics

Interest groups often argue that corporations communicating under pressure cannot be trusted. Few promises are ever kept; no apologies are sincere. The true purpose of their crisis management is to gloss over problems, rather than prove they are being tackled. Nike, as we have seen, has suffered from suspicion that a gap between deeds and words existed on Asian labour. We have also seen how, after two years of firefighting, the company finally closed that gap with a six-point programme that at the time of writing has helped ease public attacks, if not deeper doubts. Whether the reforms were 'window dressing or substantial, we'll have to wait and see', said the executive director of TRAC, an interest group that monitors US factories overseas.[2]

Nike did show that it had at least absorbed the lessons of crisis communication when a new range of shoes created trouble in April 1997. The Islamic Center of Long Island (ICLI), New York, complained that the flaming letters that spelled 'air' on the heels and soles of Air Bakin', Air Melt, Air Grill and Air B-Que on Nike's 'Summer Hoops' line, closely resembled the name for God in Arabic. 'Whether you are Muslim, Jew or Christian', said a spokesman, 'to step on the name of Allah is sacrilege.'[3] A 1000-signature petition was mailed to the company.

At first Nike seemed inclined to defend itself, and a statement revealed that it had already modified the letters in response to an alert from its Middle East distributor. 'The new, changed logo design separates the A from the IR, thus producing a logo that cannot be confused with any other word.' 'We caught it in time', said a Nike spokeswoman confidently. 'We have expressed our sensitivity to the Muslim community by not issuing a design that resembled the word "Allah" in Arabic.' ICLI was not mollified, describing the alteration as a 'small, conciliatory gesture'. 'They didn't even send an apology', grumbled ICLI's communications director.[4]

Five days later, the story expanded. ICLI was joined by the Council on American-Islamic Relations (CAIR) in Washington, which also demanded an apology. Nihad Awad, the Executive Director, held up a pair of shoes at a press conference asking whether 'there are people at the company who want to insult Muslims'.[5] The Houston Rockets star center Hakeem Olajuwon, a Muslim who endorsed another brand of athletic shoe, contacted Nike's president, Tom Clarke: 'The placement of this holy symbol on shoes which will be soiled, walked on and disposed of is very offensive to Muslims', he wrote. 'It is offensive to us when a major corporation such as Nike publicly shows disrespect for Allah's name.'

Nihad Awad, a prominent Arab-American with an international profile, went 'global' with the issue and called on retailers in the Muslim world not to stock the product. Awad was supported by a national youth association in Saudi Arabia, which urged all sports federations in the kingdom to boycott Nike products for 'insulting Muslims'.[6] Saudi consumers purchase half a million sports shoes annually.

The Summer Hoops crisis showed signs of joining the other crises Nike already faced in Asia and the USA. However, the company defused the controversy with a bold and creative stroke. It entered into consultation with CAIR, and in late June a fourteen-point agreement was announced. The product was discontinued, a review board was appointed to oversee all graphic design, Islamic materials were incorporated into Nike's Design Library, and a formal investigation was conducted into the incident. Shipments of the commercial products in question were also diverted from 'sensitive' markets. 'To date, over 30,000 pairs have been diverted from Saudi Arabia, Lebanon, Kuwait, Malaysia, Indonesia and Turkey.' Nike also donated $50,000 to an Islamic Elementary School in the USA. The statement also clarified that 'CAIR is satisfied that no deliberate offense to the Islamic community was intended.'[7]

CAIR described the agreement as a 'victory'. The incident had drawn attention to the waxing strength of the Islamic lobby in America: 'We wanted to reinstate confidence in our community that whenever they see something offensive, there could be something done about it.'[8] The group then recommended that Muslims did *not* boycott Nike products.

Unfortunately, the Nike–CAIR Agreement came under strain after only a year. In July 1998, at a press conference in Saudi Arabia, Nihad Awad attacked Nike for not honouring its pledge to completely remove the logo, criticizing the changes as being too cosmetic. The objectionable logo had been covered with a thin patch and some red paint. Awad told reporters that CAIR's worldwide boycott of Nike was back in business, and announced plans to discuss the issue with Saudi Arabian business groups and youth representatives.

On the face of it, Nike's agreement and the public apology to Muslims demonstrated sensitivity and brilliantly defused a crisis that was on the brink of igniting. It had built an alliance with an influential interest group and given teeth to the message by real changes to company policy and by action over the disputed product. Only a year later, however, one of Nike's new allies in CAIR had resumed his criticism. Were Nike's efforts a waste of time?

Crisis communication is not needed: you'll get away with it in the end

Today's news is tomorrow's fish and chips wrappers. They should keep their heads down for a while.
Newcastle United football fan

Not all companies use managed communication in a crisis, yet somehow they overcome their problems. In early 1998 Freddy Shepherd and Douglas Hall, the Chairman and Vice-Chairman of profitable but competitively struggling Newcastle United Football Club in the UK, flew to a meeting at the Spanish resort of Marbella. The two thought they were going to discuss a lucrative contract with a foreign businessman: in reality their host was a brave tabloid journalist working under deep cover. Over champagne and brandy, a remarkably crass conversation was secretly recorded on tape. Hall (the son of former miner Sir John Hall, one of Britain's richest men and Life President of Newcastle United – the 'Magpies') and Shepherd began to discuss their frequent adulteries and heavy spending on prostitutes. According to the account, Hall boasted they had slept with twelve women at a penthouse party in New York. 'Newcastle girls', he pronounced, 'are all dogs. England is full of them. The girls are ugly and they're dogs.' These were not comments guaranteed to please either Newcastle football fans or Newcastle women. The *tête-à-tête* allegedly touched on other topics: Shepherd divulged his nickname for the club's 'boring' superstar striker Alan Shearer: 'Mary Poppins'. He described how he had sold striker Andy Cole to Manchester United without divulging that Cole faced an operation which could end his career. Hall revealed how the club made £30 million a year selling club shirts for ten times the cost of production. The *News of the World* felt obliged to break the shocking story on Sunday 15 March 1998.

Then followed a classic pattern of mismanaged crisis as the situation escalated. First there was the refusal to comment by Hall, Shepherd and Newcastle United; then the inevitable media rush to other sources for stories and opinion after the club hierarchy had 'gone to ground'. Some of those sources were surprisingly influential. Sports Minister Tony Banks (who, the Newcastle duo had said, should lose his job) demanded to know the truth behind the mark-up on soccer shirts: 'I am looking for a very strong denial from the individuals concerned that the claims are not true.'[9] The Prime Minister Tony Blair pressed for comment as a supporter of Newcastle United Football Club, and the local MP, also a supporter, expressed his 'concern'. The Roman Catholic Cardinal Basil Hume hinted that Hall and Shepherd should go. The club's home city delivered its own uncompromising judgement in an informal poll held by BBC Radio Newcastle, when 90 per cent of the callers wanted the two shamed executives to go. A second poll conducted by the *Newcastle Evening Chronicle* put the figure at 96 per cent.

What might in other circumstances have remained a private scandal quickly enveloped Newcastle United. Like all professional sports clubs, it relies on local support and good relations with the national sports authorities. In addition, Newcastle Football Club was a public company, and its shareholders formed a third audience sensitive to the determined silence that prevailed at the club's St James' Park stadium, and the fact that £9 million of the club's £41 million of sales ($67m, 58m Euros) came from branded products like the now controversial shirts. Consequently, when the stock market opened for business on Monday 16 March, shares in the club slumped and forced the club into action. An emergency meeting was called by the Board of Directors. 'When will the Magpies speak out?', demanded the *Northern Echo*.

Hall and Shepherd, no doubt feeling victims of a sleazy, dishonest 'sting', resisted comment for 72 hours. Then, on the day of the club's next game, a vital contest against Crystal Palace, they issued a statement: 'Both Douglas Hall and Freddy Shepherd sincerely apologize for any offence that has been caused.'[10] They especially apologized to the women of Tyneside. The 'comments attributed to them are totally out of character and do not represent their true views'.[11] Anticipating a hostile demonstration by outraged fans, the two men decided not to attend the Crystal Palace game and asked everyone to get behind the manager, Kenny Dalglish – only Shepherd's second-favourite choice for manager, according to the tabloid exposé. Newcastle United lost the match, and the *News of the World* promised to print more revelations the following weekend, including tales of drug abuse.

The tardiness and brevity of the apology had not gone down well with its intended audiences: 'It's interesting to note that it is an apology, not a denial,' said John Regan, secretary of the Independent Supporters'

Association.[12] 'Their apology, which wasn't even uttered in person, was grudging and petulant. They feel aggrieved, not mortified', noted the *Daily Mail* several days later.[13]

By now £9 million had been wiped off share values, alarming investors and the Board of Directors, who at last told the stock exchange that they were 'deeply disturbed' by the allegations. The crisis had entered its second stage, and spread to new topics: rumours surfaced that the three independent non-executive directors of Newcastle United plc were considering their positions. Hall and Shepherd stuck to their guns, claiming they had drunk too much to remember what was said in Marbella. 'Newcastle in the doghouse', reported the *Sunday Independent*. 'Simon Turnbull describes the mood on Tyneside as the Magpies reel from crisis to crisis; Toon Army becomes the Doom Army as their cherished club's fall from national affection gathers pace.'[14] A representative of the Independent Supporters Association, now used by the national media as a ready source of pungent comment, chipped in: 'Every day that goes on the publicity they receive gets worse and worse. I do not know if they are getting legal or public relations advice, but it is woefully inadequate. It took three days before they apologised and another two days to announce they were not resigning. The pressure for them to go will continue.'[15]

It was pressure the media was more than ready to apply as the story gathered momentum. 'Newcastle United has become a monster of a football club', said the *Sunday Independent*. 'Its complacent management believes it is beyond good and evil.'[16] 'The bawdy Geordies need a public grilling.'[17] The Chief Executive of the Football Association said: 'The anger of supporters is utterly understandable. They have deserved better, much better.'[18] A local MP called the police to ask for action on some of the revelations made in the *News of the World*. Then, on 24 March, ten days after the crisis started: 'At Last! Magpie Bosses Resign'.[19]

The news was broken by the club's public relations company the day after a sixteen-hour board meeting. Sir Terence Harrison, Chairman of the club's public limited company, issued a suitably upbeat and forward-looking statement: 'We hope these changes will enable us to put the difficult circumstances of the past ten days behind us and I call for everyone associated with Newcastle United to work together for its future success.'[20] Sir John Hall himself came out of retirement to restore order to the club. Close to tears, with his wife at his side, he did what his son and Shepherd should have done. He personally apologized, speaking of the pain caused to his own family. His wife contributed a personal interview to *The Times* in which she proudly called herself a 'provincial'.[21]

Newcastle United's shares jumped briefly, adding £8 million to the club's value and incidentally benefiting Hall and Shepherd themselves: 'greedy, seedy, disloyal sexual perverts', according to the *Daily Mail*,[22] but they remained major shareholders. The original focus of the crisis also shifted slightly. Reports about the *News of the World*'s undercover tactics created distaste – if not actual sympathy for Hall and Shepherd – at the way in which they were exposed. On 1 June, Sir John stepped down again as temporary club chairman. The crisis seemed to be over.

At the end of July, two months after Sir John's withdrawal, Douglas Hall and Freddy Shepherd rejoined the Board. They explained the decision in a letter mailed to season ticketholders, at a personal cost of £9000 ($15,000, 13,000 Euros). The apology was repeated, once more in writing rather than in person: 'Yes, we were very stupid in March and we apologise unreservedly for our behaviour . . . Most of the conversation was drunken bragging. We were just stupid.' The club's Chairman and Financial Advisor both resigned.

'I cannot see what has changed', wondered the baffled Chairman of the Independent Supporters Association. The Prime Minister had 'no public comment to make on what has happened'.[23] Had today's crisis become tomorrow's fish and chip wrappers? Other factors appeared to matter more than good crisis communication. There was the fact that Hall and Shepherd owned 66 per cent of the club's shares. 'It was always going to be difficult for people to make decisions with us on the outside', they reminded fans. Newcastle United had also failed to salvage its reputation with investors. Shares had dropped again, and hovered at a penny off their all-time low. Board meetings had been going on all week, and in the end members could not overlook the size of the Shepherd–Hall stake, and the £10 million they guaranteed for buying star players.

From the perspective of crisis communication, Shepherd and Hall had made all the wrong moves: a delayed and halfhearted apology when the crisis broke, a refusal to appear in person or comment publicly as the crisis spread, and absolutely no effort to rebuild their public reputation beyond an impersonal mass mailing. Despite error after error, they had regained their positions only four months after being forced out. When the tide of crisis ebbed, Hall and Shepherd returned to the club and in December 1998 used their majority votes to survive an attempt by smaller shareholders to reject their reinstatement.[24] How could communication, either good or bad, have made any difference to the fiscal realities that underpinned the crisis?

What crisis communication can deliver

Paradoxically, the contributions which crisis communication makes are apparent in the two previous accounts of its shortcomings.

- **Crisis communication responds rapidly to contain 'momentum'.** For all its later, scaled-down, problems, Nike's fast reply on 'Summer Hoops' compares well with the Newcastle directors' reaction to the tabloid tapes. Nike's bold approach to CAIR contained the gathering media momentum, and also allowed the company to show a culturally sensitive side of itself that had been largely ignored in headline coverage of its Asian record. Meanwhile, a flat denial, refusal to comment, or apologies that seem to have been forced out of an unrepentant company or individual lengthen and intensify the crisis, as Newcastle United discovered, along with A. H. Robins over the Dalkon Shield and, for that matter, President Clinton over Monica Lewinsky. An American survey of public attitudes towards corporations in crisis found that 65 per cent of respondents felt 'no comment' implied guilt.[25] A communication strategy provides companies with the internal discipline needed for swift and full response.

- **Crisis communication incorporates perception.** Nike understood, as Hall and Shepherd did not, that as soon as a company's problems enter the public domain, real information and accurate reporting are overtaken by rumour, speculation and accusations. The battle to provide accurate information is becoming an increasing problem for management as technology makes communications easier and faster, and round-the-clock. Facts are largely replaced by perceptions.

    Perception is closely related to reputation. To perceive, the *Oxford English Dictionary* (OED) reminds us, is to 'become aware of by one of the senses; apprehend; understand'. A perception, then, is heavily influenced by emotions and feeling. Corporations do not deal in soft emotions or feeling attitudes. Indeed, they devote much time rationalizing feeling to function more efficiently. Companies fail to understand the level of feeling that can be turned against them in a crisis, and many are frustrated that the first casualties are always facts and the truth, not noting that their reputation is also being damaged by emotionally based perceptions. Effective crisis planning makes reputation and perception management essential elements in the formula for maintaining a competitive edge. Shell has also introduced a procedure termed the 'Spar Test'. 'This is a check on how we FEEL about something as much as what we THINK about it.'[26] An analysis of the emerging field of Reputation Management and its value in Crisis Preparedness Planning appears on page 205.

- **Recovery requires an integrated relationship between operations and communication.** This principle lies at the heart of managing perceptions *and* events. A company must address the physical problem or event that made the crisis. Communication should support operational decisions during the emergency. It should also assist recovery. Sir John Hall recognized this when he came out of retirement to publicly apologize for his son, earning public sympathy that helped guide Newcastle United out of the spotlight during his return to office.

- **Crisis communication disciplines decision-making.** Nike's rapid action to resolve 'Summer Hoops' compared to Newcastle's unplanned, reactive, replies to its tabloid scandal suggests that Nike, at least, realized its decision-making must match the momentum of a crisis. In a crisis a failure to comprehend can stem from personal attitudes, the prevailing corporate culture and the management structure. The result is that the system cannot process decisions quickly enough. Indeed, a crisis places a management structure under severe strain, regardless of its composition. For Shell, the regional autonomy normally employed by the multinational broke down when the Brent Spar controversy hit Germany with extreme violence, and pushed the local headquarters into semi-private opposition to Shell UK. Mitsubishi's problem was precisely the reverse: a monolithic, centralized system failed to comprehend the cultural enormity of sexual harassment as an issue in the USA and allowed an inexperienced team to make a series of fundamental communication errors (see page 23).

  Crisis communication requires a small team of senior executives whose task is to comprehend and contain the crisis by frequent assessment and action, cushioned as far as possible from other responsibilities. The Chief Executive Officer of Johnson & Johnson reportedly said in 1982 when the Tylenol tablets cyanide-tampering crisis broke: 'I am the product manager for Tylenol from now until the end of this crisis'. Details of crisis team management, composition and preparation are offered on page 101 and page 200.

- **Crisis communication puts the media into perspective.** Douglas Hall and Freddy Shepherd failed to overcome their aversion to further contacts with reporters and in consequence failed to supply positive comment via the media to its readers whose support really mattered: the fans and the investors. It is easy to be distracted and even repelled by a short, intense burst of press activity, but media relations should be one part of a synchronized strategy which also involves other skills and disciplines, such as internal communication and rumour management, which are discussed on page 122 and page 135.

Vital audiences

The media may be the most noisy, difficult and demanding group and individuals, but they should not become of greater importance than other audiences. We have said that the media and critics are often a short-term phenomenon. Putting them in perspective begs the question, who else matters in a crisis? A managed response must answer the concerns and questions of your traditional audiences as well as dealing with the allegations and accusations being circulated and escalated by your critics and the media. What responsible company, for instance, wants its investors, customers or employees to obtain information about its activities from web chatrooms, third-party experts or the press? The light you shed must be carefully prepared – messages to one audience will almost certainly reach others who may treat its contents somewhat differently, as Robert Allen at AT&T discovered when he sent his irritated letter to employees defending his pay rise, only to see the contents criticized in the press soon afterwards (see page 54).

Your audiences are diverse, but they are vital to you, the media and critics alike. Their reactions shape the outcome of the crisis, and the scale of the recovery effort. Your audiences must be segmented and their needs tended individually. Without a managed strategy, it will be difficult to address their varied concerns and priorities within the tight deadlines which a crisis imposes.

Since many of these audiences interact and communicate with each other, and with the media, it is essential that you communicate simultaneously with them. This integrated approach requires detailed planning to meet the needs of the following key groups.

Employees

Leaked memoranda from Nike and critical comments to the media from anonymous AT&T managers provide enough evidence to encourage, perhaps, a cynical view of the role which employees play in a crisis. This is, of course, only part of the story. All employees – not only those motivated by conscience or revenge – are part of the crisis, and have a role in its resolution. Their opinions and insights are sought, not only by the media or interest groups, but by family, friends, neighbours and lawyers. Trade unions will also wish to be seen protecting their members' interests. The messages that employees send to these groups contribute to the climate of opinion that surrounds your particular crisis.

Whether or not employees become a hindrance or a help can depend on the decisions made by management in advance of the actual crisis. While it is difficult for any organization to prevent the actions of an individual 'rogue' worker, good crisis preparedness can review the vulnerabilities in a company's 'culture'. Is there a 'mud level', as was noted at Daimler-Benz in Chapter 1, where warnings are screened out and difficult decisions avoided? Or, after the 1987 *Herald of Free Enterprise* disaster, when lawyers for the victims produced evidence 'that officials of P&O Ferries ignored requests from three ship's captains including the master of the *Herald of Free Enterprise* to install warning lights which could have prevented the *Herald* sailing with bow doors open and capsizing'.[27]

Low levels of internal confidence can add momentum to an existing issue and widen the scope for damage. The financial trouble that Body Shop, the ethically sound British cosmetics empire, ran into with its American franchises were exacerbated by internal discontent closer to home. In May 1998 a company memorandum was leaked to the press detailing a host of complaints about poor treatment made by worried British franchisees. 'The Board is not communicating', one shop owner lamented.[28]

A good plan also helps to ensure that during the crisis itself, company employees:

- **do not feel isolated, frustrated or guilty through lack of information.** An anonymous director of Shell Germany told a reporter that the German operation, hard pressed by firebombs and a massive boycott, first learnt of their company's plan to sink the Brent Spar from the television news. 'We knew that this would play disastrously in Germany', he said. 'In London, they didn't seem to understand.'[29]

- **understand the key messages that the company needs to project.** In an international crisis, autonomous regional operations are especially vulnerable as there is a strong temptation to adjust messages from one country to reflect harsh local realities elsewhere. At a press conference in Hamburg, Shell Germany suggested that Shell UK had reversed the decision to sink the Brent Spar rig into the North Sea, which a spokeswoman for Shell UK promptly denied (in fact, the sea disposal was called off three days later).

- **can separate the crisis from their regular activities**, by providing them with a place and a person to refer any inquiries.

- **are less likely, along with their families, to fear for their jobs.** ValuJet identified this problem after the crash of Flight 592, and it approached its employees who – aside from the trauma of the tragedy itself – suffered public attacks on their reputation. The pilots faced reports that they were inexperienced, and rumours that their salaries were only 50–70 per cent of the industry average. First ValuJet voluntarily reduced flights to inspect more aircraft. Then the Federal Aviation Authority (FAA) grounded the airline leaving nearly all 4000 employees temporarily without jobs and uncertain about their future. While the shutdown made layoffs inevitable, management met with employees before the formal announcement to discuss the situation and hear ideas. This inclusive approach encouraged some backing. A majority of ValuJet's flight attendants signed a letter to the US Congress in a show of support for management.[30]

Consumers

Perhaps surprisingly, consumers distrust both companies *and* media in a crisis. In 1993 an opinion survey by the US public relations firm Porter Novelli found 57 per cent of respondents believed companies in crisis withheld damaging information or lied. At the same time, 89 per cent believed that the media blew crises out of proportion.

This suggests that the damage that a crisis can ultimately do is not only caused by the over-hyped *events* of the crisis itself, but the inability of the corporation to protect and enhance its *reputation*: significantly, 95 per cent of the poll's respondents 'said they are more offended by a company's lying about a crisis than they are about the crisis itself'.[31] In 1996, during Australia's biggest food scare, Kraft:

- Recalled all products made with peanuts after a large number of consumers contracted salmonella poisoning.
- Conducted an intensive investigation.
- Identified the problem one week ahead of the health authorities and then took out full-page advertisements assuring consumers that only one batch of roasted peanuts was affected.

Those were the facts behind the crisis, yet they did not bring it to an end. Retail sales of all peanut-related products continued to suffer because the good name of the product itself had been weakened.

Consumers feel motivated to react negatively for several reasons:

- Peer pressure or intimidation. In Germany, for example, motorists brave enough to use Shell petrol during the Brent Spar controversy had to cross picket lines where, if they were lucky, they might find a four-page leaflet explaining the official company position. It would be of little aid: when they left the forecourt a protester might slap 'unpleasant-looking huge, strongly adhesive stickers on their wind-screens', carrying the accusatory message 'Ich kaufe von Shell' (I buy from Shell).[32]
- What are seen as unfair tactics by citizens in one country will be acceptable somewhere else.
- Fears for the safety of themselves or loved ones.
- Initial fears hardening into longer-term distrust because the company took insufficient action to protect its good name or its brand's reputation.

Business community

If your product reaches the consumer through businesses such as agents, distributors, franchisees or retail outlets, they must be built into crisis plans. You are not only aiming to preserve their confidence in the company and the product. The strategy needs to include the business community for other more pressing reasons:

- **A crisis costs them money too.** Business customers may be con-cerned about their own businesses, particularly if services or manufac-turing are suspended, or product is frozen or recalled, or the regulators declare that operations and management are under investigation. Two weeks into Kraft's Australian recall, supermarkets on average were returning around 3000 jars of peanut butter a week. Consumers also avoided peanut products made by other companies, including the supermarkets' own brands. 'It's the cost of the perception of the peanut butter industry, it's the sales cost to the retailers and manufacturer', said a spokesman for one worried retailer, Franklin's Supermarkets.[33]
- **Legal bother.** It is possible that your suppliers or retailers have been plunged into a crisis of their own because you either purchased or supplied flawed goods. Foodmaker clearly believed itself wronged when it sued its wholesale suppliers for providing *e.coli*-infected meat to its Jack In The Box restaurants. The suppliers promptly counter-sued, alleging that damaging statements by the burger chain's parent com-pany were undermining its own business.

- **Suppliers are at risk.** The effect of the salmonella scare in Kraft's peanuts inevitably rebounded onto Australia's A$150 million (US $95m, 80.5m Euros) peanut-growing industry. The biggest producer wrote to its customers that 'contrary to media reports, it has not been established that the contamination resulted from Peanut Company of Australia [PCA] peanuts'. Nevertheless, it also began regular salmonella testing of its products for the first time. After a circumstantial link with a run of PCA nuts was finally made by Kraft and the health authorities, one prominent grower, who also happened to be a former State premier, likened the effect of the crisis on peanut producers to that of mad cow disease on British beef farmers.

Investment community

Analysts, institutional and individual investors, the banks and financial media: the investment community is one that every public company in trouble tries hard to address. In crisis, you may experience two developments:

- **An intrusive hunt for the 'truth'.** Nervous elements of the investment community, particularly analysts, stockholders and the financial media, will embark on a massive and persistent hunt for information if your crisis is big enough. Their task is to assemble a mosaic of information from differing sources in order to assess how the company will be affected.
- **A dramatic collapse in share values.** The investment community and financial markets depend on confidence when plying their trade. Crises serve to undermine any sense of confidence and trust in a company and its management. The frantic search for facts may be paralleled by violent dips as dissatisfied or information-starved investors dump shares. The last good quarter may not count for much. A crisis, nebulous and shifting, is hard to measure. The absence of anything to measure breeds uncertainty, which leads in turn to extreme acts of precaution. Shares can drop because of non-quantifiable fears that a reputation has been seriously harmed, which was the case with Ratners and Newcastle United plc.

Local community

Every company will have a local community with whom it must communicate. It is the city where a troubled facility is located; the town or prefecture that has been hurt by your tanker, aircraft, lorry or bacteria; the district where you plan to dump waste. Most of Australia's peanut production takes place in the state of Queensland, which made Kraft's crisis a regional economic problem with strong political overtones. In such cases a neighbourhood – whatever its size – is an area that feels one or more of the following about your crisis:

- Concern about its possible impact on employment and supporting services in the area.
- Anger at any environmental or personal harm.
- Strong and publicly aired differences of opinion over your activities.
- A readiness to be mobilized by external interest groups wishing to promote a national or global issue – the 'think local, act global' approach in action.

Politicians, local and national authorities

If the crisis is large enough, politicians and regulatory authorities are certain to be involved.

- Regulatory authorities must be told about rules that were broken or failed to meet the demands of the situation.
- Health and safety officials/inspectors must be kept up-to-date about the situation.
- Ministers may expect to be asked questions, especially if they have responsibility for the industry or business sector. Naturally, they would prefer to be fully prepared.
- Politicians will be asked for opinions – especially local ones.[34] A 'local' perspective is highly persuasive. A 1998 American survey found that local television news (which of course relies on local opinion leaders) remains the most influential and popular information source.[35]

Frequent communication and cooperation with these groups is essential for a company to demonstrate publicly that it is acting responsibly, and to protect its position with these key audiences. If ministers or politicians are convinced that a company's activities do not serve the public interest, or their own popularity, or both, they are quite capable of dropping previously held positions. In some crises, the result can be decisive. In spite of its careful, sophisticated and longstanding government relations network, at the climax of the Brent Spar crisis Shell found itself: 'With the exceptions of the UK and Norwegian Governments . . . without any governmental support in the legal process we were following.'[36] Soon, Shell changed its decision and left the last two political allies fuming on the sidelines.

Independent experts

One feature of contemporary crises, whether corporate, personal or political, is the large number of experts now accessible to the media for opinion and analysis. Every field has a number of independent experts, such as scientists, analysts or academics, who are ready to comment on the unfolding crisis in the popular and trade press or on air. Experts play several conflicting but nonetheless influential roles:

- **As informed outsiders.** The third-party, objective nature of expert commentary lends authority to their views, since they appear to stand outside the crisis.
- **As indirect participants.** Expert views, taken up and repeated elsewhere, form the body of opinion encapsulated in such weighty phrases as 'industry sources say', or 'experts believe'.

You may already know the identity of the media's favourite 'experts' on your industry, or on sensitive issues related to it. They, and others, will be adding their weight to the commentary that surrounds your crisis. The Porter Novelli survey found that independent experts enjoyed an 89 per cent positive rating with the public, making them the second most believable source after actual witnesses (at 92 per cent). Effective crisis communication should include them in your direct communication effort. Alliance-building with third parties is best accomplished in advance of the crisis, as part of preparedness planning and preparation to anticipate and handle crises. This topic is discussed in Chapter 6, on Issues Management (pages 167 and 184) and Chapter 7, on Preparedness (page 196).

Reality checks

When the crisis strikes, effective communication rests upon a thorough understanding of what a crisis is, how it unfolds, and what a strategic approach can bring to the process of resolution. These have been the subjects of Part 1 of this book. Response and preparedness, the subjects of Part II, build on that foundation of understanding. Knowing what can happen in a crisis underpins the reality checks that should form the basis of a crisis strategy. Those reality checks, or considerations, require a frank appraisal of the company for which you work and the activities in which it is engaged:

- Does your business carry a negative legacy which breeds suspicion and carries a lack of trust? You may well accept this already, and can point to a host of initiatives along the lines of 'sustainable growth' or 'responsible care'. This consideration should also be included in your crisis communication planning; negative attitudes need constant correction and management.
- Is your industry hard to understand? Are your operations complicated, your motives suspect and your operations exposed to misunderstanding and emotional responses from ill-informed groups and individuals? Be ready to explain yourself in simple terms which take account of the fears and prejudices held by the outside world.
- Accept that more and more in the future your licenses to operate will lie within the gift of unqualified groups and individuals. Realize that their views and decisions will place high emphasis on emotional arguments. The consequence of this unpalatable fact is that you will need to devote more time to explaining your plans and actions in consultation with a wide range of local and national groups and individuals. This process will take increased time but it is likely to reap long-term benefits.
- Realize that communication skills will increasingly take on as much importance in the portfolio of management skills as you now attach to technical excellence, financial acumen and operational experience. You need to identify, promote, recruit and retain the best communicators as well as the best engineers, marketers and managers.
- Remember your industry operates on a playing field where you are surrounded by a series of diverse groups that will scrutinize and demand ever-higher ethical standards in all your operational activities. Accept that the media and interest groups, with their potential to influence and shape opinions, is here to stay and grow in the next century. As an industry you need to learn how to work with interest groups and through the media, not only for promoting products, but for the unique opportunity to communicate fast to the wide range of groups and individuals that have a stake, or an interest, in your industry and your company.

Summary

Properly used, effective crisis communication will:

- Put the media into proper perspective.
- Enable a rapid response to changing events.
- Align deeds with words.
- Work with perceptions as well as the facts to rebuild your reputation.
- Create an integrated relationship between operations and communication.
- Radically re-shape managerial structures to cope with crisis conditions.
- Establish direct communications with your permanent, and most important audiences:

    Employees
    Consumers
    Business community
    Investment community
    Local community
    Politicians, local and national authorities
    Independent experts.

The factors that drive a crisis

A crisis is something drastically out of the ordinary, and as we have discussed, the factors that drive it forward may be unfamiliar. The crisis will generate emotional by-products: the initial shock and the pressures of being placed under the public microscope, the fear that everything is about to collapse, and hostility towards the media and your critics. Understanding these factors will help us to deal with the crisis in an effective manner.

A crisis forces you to overcome some formidable hurdles:

- You will need to recognize that you are facing a crisis.
- You will need to make communications a priority.
- You will need to establish yourself as a credible source of information.
- You will need to be honest and open.
- You will need to be sensitive to the human side of the story.
- You will need to take cultural differences seriously.
- You will need to explain yourself in uncomplicated, non-technical language.
- You will need to see the situation as your audiences see it.

- You will need to understand the motivations of all your audiences, including critics, and not ignore them.
- You will need to reorganize your operations to deal with the crisis.
- You must use and recognize the importance of feelings and emotion.
- You will need to identify good opportunities to deliver your messages.
- You must rebuild your reputation for the future.

The task of crisis response will be explored in Part II.

Notes

1 Howe, Sir Geoffrey. *Conflict of Loyalty*. London: Pan, 1995, p. 552.
2 'Nike hones its image on rights in Asia'. *International Herald Tribune*, 26 June 1998.
3 'Nike sneaker logo offends Muslims'. *Newsday*, 5 April 1997.
4 *ibid.*
5 'Muslims ask apology'. *Chattanooga Free Press*, 10 April 1997.
6 'Boycott Nike for insulting Islam'. *Moneyclips*, 25 May 1997.
7 'Nike reaches accord with Islamic group'. *PR Newswire*, 24 June 1997.
8 *The Patriot Ledger* (Quincy, MA), 24 June 1997.
9 *Press Association Newsfile*, 16 March 1998.
10 *Evening Standard*, 18 March 1998.
11 *Daily Telegraph*, 19 March 1998.
12 *Evening Herald* (Plymouth), 18 March 1998.
13 *Daily Mail*, 25 March 1998.
14 *Sunday Independent* (London), 22 March 1998. Non-British (and indeed some British) readers may be interested to know that 'Toon' is 'town' in the local 'Geordie' accent.
15 *Evening News* (Edinburgh), 20 March 1998.
16 *Sunday Independent*, 22 March 1998.
17 *Daily Mail*, 23 March 1998.
18 *Northern Echo*, 24 March 1998.
19 *ibid.*
20 *ibid.*
21 'Family before football for this Geordie', *The Times*, 28 March 1998.
22 *Daily Mail*, 25 March 1998.
23 *The Scotsman*, 25 July 1998.
24 'Newcastle directors defy small shareholders. Unrest boils over at St James' Park.' *BBC News*, 21 December 1998. http://news.bbc.co.uk/hi/english/business/the_company_file/newsid_239000/239584.stm
25 Porter Novelli survey, August 1993. 'U.S. corporations lack credibility'. *Toronto Star*, 14 August 1993.

26 Hunt, P., Public Affairs Manager, Shell UK. (1997) *Brent Spar: A Drop in the Ocean?* Business in the Community Occasional Paper 5. London: Shell, p. 9.

27 'P & O "ignored requests" for warning light on Herald of Free Enterprise'. *Guardian*, 15 September 1990.

28 'Body Shop franchise rift widens'. *Mail on Sunday*, 17 May 1998.

29 'Is Shell going up in smoke?'. *Independent*, 20 June 1995.

30 *PR Newswire* 23 July 1996.

31 'Few trust company officials in crisis, survey says'. *Reuter European Business Report*, 13 August 1993.

32 Hunt, P., *op. cit.*, p. 8.

33 'High price of a peanut tasting'. *Australian Financial Review*, 5 July 1996.

34 Seymour, M. 'Product safety under public scrutiny'. In Hodges, C., Tyler, M. and Abbott, H. *Product Safety*. London: Sweet & Maxwell, 1991, p. 315.

35 'Local TV news is top info source, survey says', *Dallas Business Journal*, 29 December 1998.

36 Hunt, P., *op. cit.*, p. 9.

Part II

Principles and techniques of effective crisis communication

A wise company does not approach its crisis communication in a confrontational frame of mind, as if it was one side in a heated courtroom battle. Nor should it behave as though engaged in a peculiarly intense form of product marketing. A good strategy employs many techniques, all of which aim to manage the events of the crisis, the public perception of the company's actions, and also its reputation as management emerges from the crisis and rebuilds the company's good name.

These techniques and their guiding principles are the subjects of Part II, which moves from an account of the general steps needed to regain control in an unexpected crisis, to a review of special techniques, and the situations presented by extortion, product recall, sexual harassment and law courts. The last two chapters discuss methods for containing risks and issues with the power to spark major crises, and the creation of a sound Preparedness Plan well in advance of the crisis itself.

Case study: Bluepage

Jennifer Stone hurried into the office at 9.45 a.m. The security guard glared at her as the phones rang. 'They're in Boardroom A. It's been like this all morning', he added, and jerked the receiver towards his ear in an angry motion. As she stepped into the lift, she heard him speak abruptly into the mouthpiece.

Four other people were there: Michael Bates, Frank Asser the lawyer, dressed for a day at the golf course, and (she realized nervously) George Turnbull, the Chief Financial Officer. Christine Baker from Customer Services was also there, subdued, and fidgeting with a large notepad. The table was covered with newspapers open to the inside pages. Jennifer picked one up: 'Faulty Alarm Kills 87-year-old.' Another newspaper was open at page three. She read the article to the final sentence: 'Bluepage, which only yesterday promised that its systems were fully operational and ready for the year 2000, could not be reached for comment.' It was not a long story: but it was enough.

'That's one of the better ones', said Frank Asser grimly. 'I've told Reception not to say anything until we've spoken. I don't want the hole to get any deeper.'

'OK,' said Turnbull. 'Let me tell you what the problem is.' As the senior company officer in the room, it was right that he should start the meeting. 'I have analysts and institutional investors backing up to talk to me. I've got to get back to them. We're planning an expansion to America and I don't want this ridiculous episode to affect it. We need to tell them that the situation is under control. Of course the alarms aren't broken.'

'Of course.' Michael nodded his head, thinking about the customers.

'What are we doing?', Jennifer asked.

There was a significant pause. 'Where's Bob Wallace?', she asked Turnbull, a large and occasionally overbearing figure. If anyone would know where the CEO was, it should be him.

'Not sure. He was going away this weekend with the family. I don't have a clue', Turnbull blustered. He appeared oddly defensive over this turn of events.

Now we're in trouble, Jennifer realized. We can't take any big decisions without Bob. It's the silly season: parliament is out of session, and the media is looking for stories to plug the political gap.

'What do we know?', Michael asked.

The answer, it appeared, was very little. They talked at length, ranging over the volume of calls, the reputation of the company, the identity of the people who were attacking them, until finally Asser said in irritation, 'We can't do anything without the contractors. They got us into this mess.'

'You're right.' Turnbull rose. 'I'm going to call Synex. I know their President – she's on a pager', he added ironically. The group adjourned for half an hour to check their messages.

In Turnbull's office the phone was ringing. Reluctantly, Turnbull picked it up. It was a BBC journalist, a breed at once unfamiliar and rather distasteful to him. But there was no escape.

'We don't really have any comment to make until we know the full situation.'

'Don't you trust your own product?'

'Naturally, but—'. Turnbull paused and mopped his brow. The 'but' had been almost beyond his control, an attempt to protect himself and the company. What would investors think about the 'but'? He remembered the confidence and certainty that exuded from Bluepage's last quarterly statement, and felt suddenly nervous.

'But?'

'But . . . we're talking to the company who made the alarms to make sure they were properly assembled.'

'Oh? Contractor? What's their name?'

'Synex.' Turnbull boomed. He gave their switchboard number reluctantly, but with a feeling of relief that pressure might at least be lifting from Bluepage. Then he quickly dialled the pager for the CEO of Synex.

Jennifer listened to her messages in horror. She had never experienced anything like this. Appalling questions from journalists, some of them her friends; a couple of anxious shareholders; two from Age Watch, a radical group fighting for the rights of the elderly; one from a lawyer; several from anxious employees; and three from actual customers, tearful and scared. Apparently the security guard began directing calls almost at random as the pressure grew.

We've got to get the receptionist to come in, she realized. The calls had to be routed and controlled. At the moment Bluepage was looking incompetent: a particularly ironic position to be in for a company whose business was in providing absolutely reliable communication.

Against her instincts, but half fascinated, Jennifer entered the chatroom and discovered a new link to a site called 'Bluepage Blues'. It was filled with complaints, allegations and rumours.

When the group assembled again, it was clear that the others had suffered similar experiences.

'There's a rumour going around that our operators are badly paid and don't respond fast enough. I had a call from the agency asking what to do about the new ads.' Michael scratched the back of his hands, a sure sign he was nervous. 'They're coming out on Sunday in all the main newspapers – Telegraph, Times, Mail and Express.'

'It's worse than that', said Christine Baker in a halting voice. She was feeling her junior position in the group. 'The operators are being swamped by frightened people testing the system. The lines are jamming and they can't sort out any genuine emergencies.'

'We never needed those ads more,' Turnbull bellowed. He was thinking of his investors. 'They need to be reassured that we're still in charge. We've got to show them that it's business as usual.'

Jennifer listened to the discussion. She felt helpless, as if the group was adrift, just talking for the sake of talking. The table was piled with paper: notes, e-mails, call back slips, newspapers. No, they weren't floating, they were drowning. This wasn't business as usual. A memory of her consultancy job came to her. A training session she had once attended.

'Excuse me', she said, so quietly that they all stopped and looked at her.

'I don't think we can run the ads', she began. 'for—'

'What the hell do you mean?', Turnbull shot back. His anger surprised her.

'We'll look stupid. When the media see them, it'll just add fuel to the fire.'

'I disagree. I disagree entirely', replied Turnbull. His voice rose steadily. 'I repeat: we have to show everyone we're in charge. Mike?'

Michael Bates looked from one to the other of them; his watery blue eyes seemed even more indefinite than usual. He was scared. Scared about the company, about the cost of withdrawing the ads, about his job, and most of all scared of Turnbull, a Board Director and next in line to the Corporate Throne. Slowly, he nodded. 'I agree.'

'Well I damn well don't,' Asser said unexpectedly. 'Jennifer is right. If we run those things we're exposing ourselves to even more legal trouble than we're already in. I'd hate to see that stuff produced in court.'

'And it also looks as though we don't care,' Jennifer interjected. She was remembering more about that training session. Maybe she even had some notes somewhere.

'But perhaps we can use the space to put in another ad,' she continued. 'Not an advert, an announcement.'

'Announcement?', Turnbull asked warily. 'What sort of announcement?'

Jennifer swallowed. 'That we're recalling the product.'

There was a long silence in the room. The thought that had been in everyone's mind had been spoken.

'Do you realize,' said Turnbull, 'the cost of doing that? Do you realize the cost to, to . . .'. He threw up his hands. 'Everything. To our growth plans. To . . . everything! We have thousands of customers all over the UK.'

'Yes.' Her voice fell lower. 'Not just the UK. Holland. We'll have to recall from there, as well.'

Phones continued ringing in empty offices. It was a beautiful day all over England.

Somewhere in Gloucestershire, the CEO of Bluepage was relaxing, unaware that his company had entered the early stages of disaster.

Age Watch had never seen anything like it. Nothing they had done in the past had made such an impact. We've frightened people into action, Max Jackson reflected as he wrote up a statement for the press conference scheduled later that morning. Instead of making them feel guilty, we've made them feel scared. I should have known that would work better. Superb publicity! Age Watch seemed everywhere this weekend.

The interest group had been busy all day. Its staff of volunteers, people of all ages, had been manning the phone lines, answering questions, distributing information kits, directing callers to websites or, if they were important enough, to Jackson himself. Eventually, snowed under by enquiries, he had scheduled a news conference.

Jackson worked hard at his statement, periodically taking calls and providing the sort of vivid, urgent quotations that the media wanted. 'Thousands of people are living under a cloud.' 'It's not an alarm, it's a time bomb', and so on, each message sprinkled with others about the problems suffered by older people. Recent surveys . . . over a third of elderly people in America say their children haven't helped them in a time of need during the past five years . . .

A knock on the door. 'Coming', he called, and went down to the small, overheated meeting room now crammed to bursting point with people, lights and cameras.

Judith Graves, the CEO of Synex, had been keeping abreast of the crisis from home and trying vainly to get through to Bluepage's offices. She had moved fast, and engineers were re-testing the product. She turned the problem over in her mind for the hundredth time. Was it the product? Or the Bluepage operators? Or customers not using them properly?

Restless, she turned on the radio and caught the end of a news report. 'The situation is still unclear, but a source at Bluepage speculates that a flaw in the equipment may be the problem. The alarms are made by another company, Synex, based in Reading.'

A few moments later, her own telephone started to ring as if it would never stop.

'Is that true what they're saying?'

The off-duty Bluepage operator shrugged. 'How would I know? I'm just an operator. It's not my responsibility.'

'Well,' her neighbour persisted. 'Don't they train you?'

'Oh yes, yes. They do a bit of training. We need to find out how serious the injury is, and how to keep the person talking until help arrives. It's a very clever system.'

'Well, why isn't it working now? All those people out there who could be in trouble. It's not nice.'

The operator shrugged. She was embarrassed and felt almost worthless.

'All I can say is we've – they've – never had a problem in the past with any of this.'

The neighbour did not seem at all reassured. Her father was a Bluepage customer.

After two hours of heated discussion, the group at Bluepage had got precisely nowhere. Jennifer was in favour of recalling the product. Christine Baker was in favour but her opinion was not influential. Frank Asser was in favour of recall but against a recall announcement that had not been carefully reviewed by his office – a process which he made a particular fuss about, and that sounded as if it could waste vital hours. Turnbull was strongly against withdrawal. The prospect of shattered expansion plans and investor confidence held him obstinately to his position. Michael Bates wavered, but in any case his prevarication did not really matter since Turnbull, as the senior person, would have the final say.

Other people had dribbled in and were manning telephones and relaying information to the group. On her own initiative, Jennifer had penned a short note to be read out to enquirers. It said: 'Bluepage regrets the concern but remains confident that the problem will be resolved soon, in collaboration with Synex. Meanwhile, we urge our customers not to call our emergency operators until our next announcement. The situation is under control.' She hated the statement. It was impersonal, and plainly the situation was not under control.

'We're not seeing the wood for the trees', she said, aware that Turnbull was becoming increasingly angry with her. Half of her thought: why should I care? It's his company. But the other, stronger, half made her say: 'My old consultancy has a crisis unit. We've got to get outside experts in here.'

'Crap.' Turnbull was sinking into denial. 'I've heard enough.' He shook his head like a bull ready to charge a wall. 'We're going to put out the ads, and when this problem with Synex is sorted out we'll announce it. There isn't going to be a recall!' He glowered around the table. 'Any objections?' Christine Baker and Michael dropped their gaze. Asser seemed to be struggling with the decision, but said nothing. Jennifer shrugged her shoulders. Mentally, she was trying to distance herself from the problem, and the odour of approaching calamity. She tried one last time: 'We need a plan.'

'One minute.'

They turned around. Bob Wallace stood in the doorway. He had heard every word of the conversation. 'I heard the news in the car before lunch and came back immediately. They let me in the back to avoid the press.' The CEO turned to Jennifer. 'Tell me again what you just said.'

4 The unexpected crisis: retrieving control

A review of the framework

You must do the thing you think you cannot do.
Eleanor Roosevelt[1]

At the moment a crisis hits, normal business organizations, structures and procedures must be rapidly replaced by crisis teams and management. Day-to-day processes for assembling and handling information and decision-making must switch to three distinct functions capable of operating simultaneously:

- Operationally solving the problem – be it real or merely perceived.
- Managing and coordinating all communications in order to wrest back and maintain control of the situation.
- Running the rest of the business – which in itself helps to restore a sense of normality to concerned and frightened managers, employees, customers and suppliers.

This chapter considers the methods used to improve communications in the maelstrom of a crisis.

While every crisis situation will be different, we should briefly remind ourselves of common factors which will influence the key role of communications:

- Any serious incident, issue or emergency will be played out in the public domain, with all the accompanying implications for transparent management.
- The first victim of any crisis is truth and accurate information. Facts are replaced by perceptions, as speculation, allegations and accusations swirl around and within the company.
- Unless rapid and tight control is exerted, misinformation and rumour will rapidly escalate the crisis out of control.

Understandably, managers can find many reasons for not communicating, if only because there will be other pressing operational matters to be tackled. Faced with a lack of real information and a wall of noise, there will be reservations over the legal risks of admitting liability or of causing unnecessary panic by careless talk. Above all, managers will be faced with a torrent of queries, concerns and accusations about a situation which they are struggling to understand and do not yet know how to resolve.

Communication in a crisis is not merely a set of defensive tools, but a necessary pro-active means of influencing and shaping opinions, rumours and damaging speculation or accusations to positive advantage. As we have seen, a communications vacuum will be filled by groups and individuals who welcome the opportunity to advance their own agendas by discussing your company, your problems and ultimately your crisis. At the same time research suggests that a 'no comment' from a harassed executive, or a blank refusal to respond to media demands for an interview or statement, will be interpreted as an attempt to hide or an admission of guilt by roughly two-thirds of any audience.[2]

We have also seen that in any crisis the media play a central role in driving communication forwards with all the consequent effects in terms of pressure upon management and the decision-making processes. Many corporate managers can relate anecdotes about when a journalist 'printed the wrong story' or 'distorted the situation' in a report or apparently 'failed to listen' to what a company actually said. Some can even cite incidents where the media misunderstood or 'totally mis-reported' important facts or information. Often, such problems stem from a failure of management to understand the motives that drive a journalist or shape the needs of a news editor (see page 45). The agenda of the media in a crisis can be summarized as:

- Looking for a good story, which will engage the interest of their readers, listeners and viewers.
- Seeking the 'cause' of your crisis.
- Seeking to attribute blame – they must find their heroes and the villains.

This process of researching and delivering a story must be undertaken against a background of demanding deadlines, driven by the need to get the news out before the competition. With instant communications and 24-hour news, deadlines are dead; the story of your crisis must be rapidly researched, prepared and packaged in time for the next newscast or print edition.

In a crisis, corporate reputation is on the line under trying circumstances. Every effort must be made to ensure that messages are clear, accurate and effective. The following rules are useful checks against integrated crisis communications:

- The five 'Cs' rule suggests that internal and external communications – written, verbal or visual – need to meet the following criteria: Care, Commitment, Consistency and Coherence, Clarity.

    Care. The tone should indicate that the company cares about the problem and empathizes with those who have been affected.

    Commitment. Corporate management must declare and act to demonstrate the will to solve the problem, find the cause and minimize the chances of a recurrence.

    Consistency and Coherence. Unless all spokespeople and all written communications are saying the same thing, a suspicion will develop that someone is lying or obfuscating the truth.

    Clarity. In an increasingly complex and technical world and given the range of audiences discussed above, it is becoming more difficult to explain crisis problems in terms which can be understood by all, free from jargon and scientific language.

- The three 'Ts' rule simply demands that corporate management *Tell The Truth* to the best of their ability. If a company lies, the truth will come out eventually, and the long-term effects are likely to be worse than if the truth was told in the first place. This honest approach should extend to taking control of the truth; and admitting when we do not know and why – something that senior executives on occasion find difficult to do.

Since communications occupies a central role beside operational action in a crisis, it is important to have contingency plans in place. While detailed procedures and systems will vary between companies, the following key elements should be in place and will be discussed over the next two chapters:

- Systems for centralizing the flow of information coming into and going out of the company. This control measure ensures that decision-makers receive the best and most current information. At the same time the company will be speaking with a single voice.
- Crisis speed demands communication systems that can react and respond at the same pace to answer the needs of internal and external audiences.

- Rumours – ever present in a crisis – need to be monitored to ensure that corporate management can anticipate and counter information before it takes hold and drags the situation out of control.
- Since surprise and lack of time will press in on managers, communications information and materials need to be at hand and pre-prepared wherever possible.
- Acting as a spokesperson, particularly with the media, requires aptitude, skills and up-to-date information. A company in a crisis should have trained and briefed spokespeople working to a co-ordinated plan, and it should be understood that the media will also expect field managers from the affected location to provide comment.

The final step in preparing to communicate in a crisis involves preparedness planning to ensure that key management can anticipate and handle serious issues, incidents and emergencies while in the spotlight. This process, which should develop in parallel to operational crisis planning, should cover:

- Procedures and systems which integrate operations and communications under one crisis management team.
- The creation of a programme of communication activities within the framework of operational plans and backed up by key messages.
- Identifying and training a portfolio of spokespeople with the experience and knowledge to cover the corporate, operational, marketing, financial, technical and scientific/medical aspects of any potential crisis.
- Exposing crisis teams, plans, systems and procedures to a series of realistic and demanding scenarios to test and validate them.
- In conjunction with regular risk and threat reviews, a programme for updating and reviewing plans, procedures and systems.

A company whose corporate managers have undertaken this preparedness planning process will be ready to face serious problems heated by crisis. To do less, or to resort to the well known mantra of 'it can't happen to us' – is not just negligent, it is irresponsible. The task of preparedness is examined in Chapter 7.

What, though, should be done if you are caught unprepared? This chapter will explore in more detail the components needed for an effective response to an unexpected crisis.

Operations

If you say something before you really know the facts, you are speculating.
If it is subsequently wrong, you are a liar. If you don't say anything, you
are a stonewaller.
Warren Anderson, former Chief Executive Officer, Union Carbide.[3]

Whatever the crisis, it is undoubtedly happening right now. Let us assume that no-one in your company is prepared for it. What has to be done, and in what order? Finding an order in which to do things may seem impossible: everything might be happening at once – the incident that sparked the crisis, the search for information, the rush of inquiries from your loyal audiences, intense media pressure and even public criticism. Larry Kamer, a crisis consultant based in San Francisco, argues that three numbers should act as 'milestones' in a crisis: 60, 3 and 1. Within 60 minutes of the event, a communication should be distributed indicating what is known about the incident and the steps being taken to deal with it. Within 3 hours a crisis organization to handle communication should be in place, at least in skeletal form. By the close of the first day, a 'short-term communication plan needs to be in place'.[4]

Assemble a crisis team

The Second World War presented the Churchill government with the joint problems of fighting a global war and running the regular business of the country. Clearly, the traditional form of Cabinet government, consisting of around twenty Ministers, was too large and unwieldy for the fast, concentrated and voluminous decision-making required to achieve victory. Churchill's solution after coming to power in 1940 was to appoint a smaller Defence Committee of the War Cabinet to function alongside the regular Cabinet machine and to concentrate on producing the equipment and the strategy needed to beat the Axis Powers. Churchill's official biographer has recorded: 'The Defence Committee quickly became the arbiter of all war operations. The War Cabinet was the arbiter of all decisions outside the sphere of operations.'[5]

The Defence Committee consisted of just six Ministers. It is a model replicated by sensible corporations in a business crisis, and reinforced by Churchill's explanation of the Committee's purpose: 'to help me in giving a vigorous and positive direction in the conduct of the war, and in overcoming the dead weight of inertia and delay which has so far led us to being forestalled on every occasion by the enemy'.[6]

Business, like Cabinet government, cannot respond to an invasive crisis without a Core Crisis Management Team (CCMT) to decide strategy. The usual procedures of committees, consultation, minute research; the balancing of interests and priorities with resources; these sensible components of decision-making are too slow and unwieldy in a crisis. They must therefore be reserved for regular operations; and in spite of the crisis, regular operations do continue: goods and services continue to be made, bought or sold; customers sought; research and development undertaken. The CCMT should be small – no more than ten – and liberated from regular management duties, at least as fully as the crisis requires.

Once the CCMT has been convened, one of the first decisions should be to establish a schedule for meetings (typically every two to three hours depending on the situation). Neither the CCMT or any other crisis manager should enter into an uninterrupted and more-or-less continuous meeting. Such an approach leads to a talking shop which deteriorates into a rumour exchange with no time for putting into action any decisions that might be made. When one of the authors of this book worked on a product recall for a multinational drinks company involving 17 million bottles in 152 markets, he adhered strictly to a daytime programme of two-hour cycles with CCMT meetings lasting no longer than 25 minutes. At the same time he advised, and had it accepted, that the CCMT would never schedule or conduct conference calls during these meetings. Indeed it was agreed that these time-consuming calls should always have a separate pre-set agenda and never last longer than 20 minutes.

The team's agenda should strictly adhere to a cycle of activities:

1. Reports on action taken in previous period.
2. Situation review and analysis.
3. Definition of decisions required in long and short term.
4. Allocation of operational and communication tasks and actions required before next meeting.
5. Allocation of briefing and updating tasks to internal management – particularly senior/corporate management.
6. Briefing and directing other support teams for such functions as product recall and recovery, communications, quality assurance and customer briefings.

See page 200 for further details on developing a CCMT and the support teams that may be required as part of a Crisis Preparedness Plan.

Your messages

A company's messages to its audiences must demonstrate:

- You can be relied on to keep your audiences up-to-date with the situation, even if the situation remains unchanged.
- You are prepared.
- You are taking action.
- You are being open and fair-minded.
- You care about what happened – you have feelings, too.
- You are working alongside any regulatory authorities that may also be involved.

Frequent criticism, the threat of legal action and psychological pressures present obstacles to this approach. At the same time, much is hanging on the message: the long-term damage to product and reputation; the short-term heat generated during the crisis; the degree of cohesion within the company.

The success of a message is the joint legacy of its content and form. In a crisis, the first embodiments of that message are early control of the communication flow, the opening Initial Holding Statement, the effectiveness with which you handle hard questions, the quality, accuracy and currency of the information you provide or make available to the media and other key audiences and the credibility of your spokesperson. We will now explore these factors in more detail.

Harness the communication flow

The noise generated by a crisis exerts a sizeable influence on the quality of decision-making.

- It can seriously impede information-gathering. For unprepared companies, the tidal wave of incoming inquiries, requests, questions, demands or complaints via phone, fax, internet or in person can physically obstruct management attempts to gather essential information.
- It encourages reaction rather than initiative. Executives find themselves struggling to respond instead of developing a strategy that leads their company out of trouble.

- It threatens the development of a coordinated message. Nobody connected with the affected company is immune from personal contact with the public: from employees to the landlord of the nearby pub, from analysts to the family of senior managers. The more dramatic or significant the crisis, the wider the net cast by those seeking information and comment.

One of the first challenges that a crisis team faces is to bring order to the flood of communication. This must be achieved by creating a channel to attract as much of the overflow as possible, and systematically monitoring the content. This operational decision is an urgent priority. After recalling its line of Pepperami sausages, Mattesson Walls received over 1300 calls in 24 hours. Hoover's disastrous free-flight promotion in the UK, which produced massive numbers of claimants, generated 2000–3000 daily calls and up to 4000 letters a week at the height of the crisis.[7] After the Oklahoma bombing, an attempt by one evacuated business to install a toll-free number for inquiries failed because local lines were jammed and the telephone company's people were all involved in rescue operations. A second attempt was made through a company in Atlanta, Georgia, but the extent of the emergency was not fully appreciated by that distant outfit and many delays were suffered. Finally, someone remembered a room in a branch office in Oklahoma City itself which had fifteen telephone lines.[8] Separate crisis lines unblock the daily operations of the company. They also channel the crisis to representatives who are entitled to talk in detail on the company's behalf. The regular switchboard, reception desk or other employees should not answer questions about the crisis unless they are working under the direction of the crisis team.

Several options are available:

- The company keeps dormant telephone line(s), which can be activated at the time of crisis. These are in addition to (and probably totally different from) normal numbers. While this is a quick technological option, there is always the problem of who should staff them – accepting that any published number will be inundated with calls from concerned, worried or frightened consumers and the general public, not to mention journalists in pursuit of new angles. Logistical challenges include the location of this bank of operators and the means of keeping them trained and up-to-date.
- The second and more frequently used option is to expand existing information/consumer/complaint lines. This carries the same problems as for the dormant line option (plus the possible risk that the capacity

will not be available to handle the overload of call traffic). The other problem is that crisis calls can overcome all normal usage of the service, leading to an impression that the company is in deepening crisis.

- The third option, if internal facilities and staff cannot immediately be made available, is to make a formal arrangement with an agency or telephone bank service. In addition to the cost of retaining this standby service it is necessary to:

  1. brief the agency in full detail and ensure they have all the necessary information to speak and act on behalf of the company, using the correct tone and approach to customers and consumers. A comprehensive Question and Answer (Q&A) document will be required, prepared specifically to answer the needs of the operators. Thereafter as the crisis develops, the agency will need constant updates of the brief and their Q&A and information documents. A company representative should work alongside management at the telephone agency to troubleshoot and keep operators up-to-date on what will be rapidly changing situations.

  2. insist on a rapid feedback system so that the agency keeps the CCMT fully up-to-date on the levels of traffic, as well as the lines of questions, concerns and comments being raised by callers.

What should be done with calls?

- **They should be logged.** Every caller's name, affiliation and question should be recorded on electronic or paper forms to establish patterns of inquiry. Which people and which organizations call frequently or urgently? These are the interested audiences whose opinions will help shape your crisis. What common questions are being asked? If your telephone responders do not know the answer, the forms can be forwarded to the relevant expert who can jot down the replies for use in return calls.

- **They should be evaluated.** In a crisis, hotlines and information services become a rich source of information on the attitudes and perceptions of customers, consumers and the general public in relation to the problem or issue. Particularly influential callers require more than switchboard service. The crisis team will need to evaluate inquiries from customers, journalists, politicians, analysts, community leaders, interest groups and regulatory authorities in order to develop a more personal approach. A system for recording details of calls and callers should be introduced with data being analysed and fed to a central point in the crisis management team. When linked with media monitoring and press handling information, senior management can use data from hotlines to pick up early warning signals of new rumours or press speculation, thus permitting anticipatory planning.

- **They should be answered.** Your story needs to be told as quickly and as fully as possible. Questions must be responded to, even if it is simply to say that you are not yet able to give an answer until more is known about the situation. If an answer is required, it should be given or announced when it becomes available.

- **They should be directed to objective sources of information.** The credibility of a corporate response is affected by the clarity with which complex issues are explained and a readiness to refer audiences to respected independent sources of information. Independent experts are among the most believed sources of opinion in a crisis, and an effective crisis response must take account of that fact when dealing with the media and other important audiences. 'This is an important lesson', one media relations manager has said when recollecting his own experience of the New York World Trade Center bombing. 'You must quickly supply the media with engineers and executives – the experts with credibility.'[9] Working with Edelman Public Relations, Odwalla used the Web in the crucial hours after its *e.coli* crisis in October 1996 to establish a site with links to expert sites that provided callers with information, not just about the crisis, but about the dangers and treatments for *e.coli*. *Forbes* magazine later observed that the 'quick timing was critical' to the effectiveness of the site and to building credibility for Odwalla's response:

> Within the first 48 hours, it received more than 20,000 hits; a number of those visitors took advantage of hypertext links to the Centers for Disease Control, the U.S. Food and Drug Administration, and even a Japanese site that gave treatment information.

Odwalla's President recognized that: 'For getting complex information out about which we were not authorities, the Web was ideal.'[10]

Hotlines and information services

It will be apparent from the above paragraphs that technology now permits companies in crisis to set up and run information services and hotlines at short notice, permitting them to handle large numbers of calls. If well used this facility can demonstrate care and concern while answering the many and diverse questions that will be raised by the general public. At the same time this public demonstration of a willingness to communicate can be detrimental to the reputation of management and the company.

If products or promotional materials carry a customer service number, it will be used as a way to reach the company. If a new or special number is published, through the media or retail outlets, then that number will be rung by thousands of consumers. It is essential to plan in advance so that the hotline is seen as a credible route into the company:

- Ensure sufficient telephone lines and switch gear is available to handle anticipated traffic – which will always outstrip expectations.
- Make available fully briefed and specially trained operators to handle the flood of calls. This is not the work for an unprepared secretary or receptionist because callers will be aggravated, frightened and even aggressive. Operators will receive the brunt of blame and abuse for the problem, which has escalated into the public domain.

Crisis situations attract general interest accompanied by illogical and unbalanced behaviour. Hence a freephone or toll-free number will attract many 'crazies', as they are known in Germany and The Netherlands. Special arrangements are needed to transfer 'loony calls' away from the main traffic so that valuable operator time and line space is not taken up.

Monitor media coverage

Companies need to see how their messages are interpreted, and to track and react to emerging areas of concern. This requires constant awareness of what is being said or written about the crisis. Debra Traverso, a US crisis consultant, has warned that:

> Reading a transcript of a television news report may not prompt the same reaction or impression that seeing the report would provide. Transcripts cannot relay inflection in voice, sarcasm in tone, laughter or background graphics. An employee watching a television or listening to a radio in your offices can provide this information.[11]

Corporate management should never be presented with a pile of audio/ video recording, print clips or broadcast transcripts which have not been analysed. If senior managers are allowed to wade through what can be frightening piles of criticism and worse, they start to believe the headlines. They need a summary of media activity, preferably over each 24-hour period, which covers:

- The main themes or stories that the media are running.
- Assessment of the success of the company's communication efforts – particularly whether key messages are being picked up and delivered by the media.
- Forecasts of possible ways media coverage will move next.
- Recommendations on media strategy for the next period.

If time permits, market research should also be undertaken and be presented to the CCMT, in order to offset or balance out what the media are saying against the perceptions of such key audiences as consumers and customers.

Choose a spokesperson, a deputy and a back-up

As Heraclitus put it, 'dogs bark at a person whom they do not know'.[12] It is the task of a company under attack to ensure that it is known. For that, a good spokesperson is needed.

A crisis needs a face. Bad (and for that matter good) news boils down to human interest. The media and their reading public like to associate a face or personality with the organization. A company without a face is a 'faceless company': defensive, secretive, scared, arrogant, uncaring. In the trial of public controversy, a spokesperson is as important to a company as its lawyers.

It is not an easy position: the spokesperson must deal with hard, very public criticism. The pressures can be immense, and the scope for confrontation enormous. In 1997, the Polish government's chief spokeswoman removed the spokesman for the crisis committee grappling with floods that swamped 440 towns and villages. He had sent a statement to television representatives accusing them of 'biased and untrue' coverage and of a 'reluctance' to show the committee's work.[13] An ill-prepared and untrained spokesperson can have a lasting impact. Britain's Ministry of Defence is still enduring the legacy left by its lacklustre civil service spokesman during the 1982 Falklands crisis. Handicapped by a reluctance to give information and a tendency to sound like a 'dalek', he became 'a figure of fun'.[14] The performance of American military spokespersons during the Gulf War was more effective, though still subject to media complaints that the information supply was too restricted, and that the top commanders made too few appearances. On the other hand, technology, events, messages and setting were wrapped thematically together by public relations personnel and presented with greater frequency and professionalism than had been the case during the Falklands campaign.

Is the best spokesperson in a crisis the top commander – the Chief Executive Officer (CEO)? While Steven Fink discovered in *Crisis Management* that 97 per cent of Fortune 500 CEOs felt they could respond well in a crisis (which 89 per cent believed were inevitable)[15], it is not clear over a decade later that CEOs fully understand the intense communication demands that will be made of them. Jeffrey Erickson, TWA's Chief Executive, described as a 'gruff, low-key engineer',[16] had hurried back to New York from London after the crash of Flight 800 on 17 July 1996, and made a brief appearance at the press conference at noon the next day. He spoke a few words and let the TWA spokesperson handle questions. *Newsday*, the New York newspaper, called Erickson's performance 'One Big Shrug'.

He probably shouldn't have bothered.

'This is a personal tragedy for all of us', the CEO said in a smarmy, melodramatic tone.

And that was pretty much that.

Thirty seconds later, the man was marching off.

'He would not take responsibility for anything.' *Newsday* concluded. TWA's next choice of spokesperson did little better: 'After Erickson skunked away from the hangar, he left behind his hapless PR man. Mark Abels, this fellow is named. And he made matters only worse.'[17] Reuters compared Erikson's appearance unfavourably with the response of Valujet's CEO, Lewis Jordan, who 'conducted press briefings and interviews immediately' after the Everglades crash. Jordan was indeed quickly visible, extending his 'heartfelt sympathy and genuine concern for the family, friends and loved ones of all customers and crew members'. He even used the media as a forum to respond to the mounting criticism and speculation. On ABC's *This Week with David Brinkley*, Jordan pleaded: 'We need a little help in stopping this rushing to judgement and convicting us without a fair trial.'

Nonetheless, a CEO does not have to convert himself or herself into the company's sole public representative. The spokesperson has many vital and time-consuming tasks to perform:

- to meet regularly with the media
- to build a personal relationship of trust with the media
- to protect and enhance corporate credibility
- to provide prompt and accurate comment on developments
- to avoid speculation, and build the message only around the available facts
- to be accessible at all times
- to be open, professional, and 'human'
- to be an integral part of the crisis management team. Communications must not be excluded from decision-making.
- to become the central point for all public announcements by the company to minimize the dangers of conflicting sources of information.

Ideally, the media want to hear all the time from the people in charge of the company; but the responsibilities of a spokesperson can be too large for one person alone, still less for a CEO who must address operational as well as communication needs. The crisis may be too large for senior executives to commit themselves to regular media appearances.

While a CEO needs to be present and take responsibility for key announcements in a high-profile crisis, the regular task of updating and informing should be reserved for someone especially trained for the task, and whose time must be fully dedicated to it. More details about preparing spokespeople for crisis are provided on page 197.

Initial Holding Statement

The first message must be almost as instantaneous as the crisis itself. It is the most crucial message of all, since it will deeply influence the tone for the rest of the crisis. The effects of a bad opening statement are harder to shake off at a later stage. It would be counter-productive to raise the expectation of the media only to be disappointed by (in their terms) a thin catalogue of facts that they probably know already from other sources. At the same time the company must point out why it cannot say more and indicate when it anticipates being able to update the media and other audiences. If a crisis is truly running, it is also necessary to use an Initial Holding Statement to alert management; the company will not want them to hear first from the media.

Within an hour of the incident that sparked the crisis, the Initial Holding Statement should be developed. It should:

- **Explain what happened.** Provide as full, detailed and non-technical an account as possible. When important details are initially unavailable, do not be afraid to say so, and undertake to provide those details as soon as they become known. Do not attempt to blame other people or organizations, or the media: it will be read as a defensive attempt to dodge responsibility.
- **Describe what you are doing.** Even in the chaos of a breaking crisis, a company is always taking action. It may be assessing the extent of a disaster at one of its facilities or a risk to its product; it may have dispatched a team to the scene of the incident. There is always something to explain: what will the team be doing when it arrives? Will it be working closely with any other organizations? What is already known about the nature of this threat to health or safety?
- **Show how your company feels.** This is the most difficult and important portion of the Initial Holding Statement. Your audience will not want you to confine yourself to practical explanations. The public affairs manager for Bowater South admitted, after a 99-vehicle crash in Tennessee in which the company was implicated and which killed twelve people: 'There were times when we were so busy that we forgot to say sorry for the families who lost loved ones.'[18] The Initial Holding Statement (and subsequent communications) should show, without appearing mawkish, defensive, trite or insincere, that you care as much as anybody about what happened, realize that a tragedy has occurred and are sorry for the people who are affected. This does not necessarily mean that you are accepting liability or offering to pay medical bills: although an early apology from a company that is liable may ease the situation. Alan Rogers, a bereaved survivor of the *Herald of Free Enterprise* tragedy, has said: 'You know, the worst thing is that to this day, no one from P&O has even written us a letter saying sorry. That would have gone a long way, wouldn't it?'[19]

Offer an apology when it is required

Saying sorry is not the same as admitting that you are at fault and legally liable. It is the natural, expected, human reaction to tragedy. Expressing sorrow for an incident can be critical and therefore repays close examination. Organizations apologize all the time, and for some there is plenty to apologize for. In Japan, 1997 has even been called the 'Year of Apologies' by the press in reference to the number of corporate officers, celebrities and politicians lining up to say sorry for a variety of misdeeds including adultery, appointing convicted bribetakers to the Cabinet, paying money to Japanese mobsters, and lying about Japan's worst nuclear accident. Apologies are usually made for the sake of form, or the sake of fashion, or for honest and dishonest mistakes.

Yet even the relative readiness to apologize in Japan can fail the expectations of its particular culture. It becomes devalued by overuse, and the Japanese public in 1997 and 1998 witnessed too many senior civil servants, politicians and businessmen calling press conferences in order to apologize. A Japanese academic has stated: 'People seem to think apologies become a way of avoiding the real problem.' Shohei Nozawa, President of Yamaichi Securities, even coupled his apology for Japan's largest postwar business failure with tears and sobs. Bowing deeply, he said: 'We don't know how to ask the forgiveness of our customers, shareholders and other associates.' One woman told a reporter: 'It looked like a performance – totally false. He ought to be ashamed of himself.'[20]

When are apologies expected? There are occasions when the need is blindingly obvious. Service Corporation International (SCI), a funeral homes multinational operating in Britain, was surprised by a television documentary. The programme, *Undercover Britain: Last Rights*, featured backroom scenes secretly filmed at an SCI funeral parlour. Attendants used coffins containing corpses to deposit litter, handled bodies roughly and in one scene used a dead woman's arm as a mock beer pump. Not surprisingly, SCI announced that it was 'shocked and saddened . . . we apologize to anyone who found the scenes disturbing'.[21] Sony promoted a computer games Playstation in the UK by sending bogus medical test results to householders in October 1998. The fake X-ray results carried a fake doctor's signature under a card: 'I am writing as a matter of urgency with your scan results – they reveal early stages of a progressive condition for which I am prescribing immediate treatment.' Householders who were actually awaiting real test results were somewhat upset, including one woman who had gone for a scan a few days earlier. Sony apologized 'unreservedly' and stopped the promotion, although not before the woman's Member of Parliament intervened and the Advertising Standards Authority ordered an investigation.[22]

But apologies might also be expected even when nothing has happened. A fault in a compressor safety system at a petrochemical plant in Fife, Scotland, sent gas flares higher than usual into the clear night sky over the region. Many people imagined that a disaster had occurred and called the fire brigade, which was forced to deal with over one hundred false alarms. Nobody was ever in danger, but a spokeswoman for the plant sensibly empathized: 'We apologize for any inconvenience or concern caused by the flaring.'[23]

The information highway is a rich source of crises and one not restricted to hi-tech companies. Boots the Chemist, a multinational based in Nottingham, England, e-mailed a market research questionnaire to its website visitors, but an error led to people receiving multiple copies. Boots apologized for the telephone lines that jammed as websurfers from Ireland to Australia grappled with questionnaires that streamed in over 24 hours. In another incident, one of the 6000 subscribers to Richard Branson's Virgin Net used the service to promote 'Dunblane Massacre', a computer game based on the school mass murder of the same name. 'Players' took shots at smiling children, and anyone using under one hundred bullets could print a badge carrying the legend 'the fastest gun in Dunblane'. Virgin Net's Technical Director reacted quickly and withdrew access to the site as soon as it was discovered: 'We certainly apologize for any hurt and distress that the part we play may have caused.'

Apologies are demanded for historical wounds as well as contemporary scandals or misjudgements. 20th Century Fox experienced both with the inhabitants of Dalbeattie, Scotland, who were incensed that one of the town's sons, the First Officer on the *Titanic*, was incorrectly portrayed as a coward in the 1998 hit movie. Nokia, the Finnish mobile telephone company, made errors in historical judgement on two continents at almost the same time. In June 1998 Nokia's instruction manuals for China made the mistake of describing Hong Kong, Macao and Taiwan as separate countries. Less than a month earlier, the company ran an advertisement in a German newspaper that used the phrase 'Arbeit macht frei' (work makes you free), a legend that once adorned the front gate of Buchenwald concentration camp.

An apology might have to be offered when the problem is not necessarily yours, as in the case of Virgin Net. An international brewer once conducted a recall because their French bottle makers had cooled eight batches too quickly leading to brittleness, with consequent cracking at the neck and under the crown caps. Nevertheless, the brewer still apologized to drinkers.

How should apologies be made?
- **They should be clear, expressive and ungrudging.** TWA's CEO and the directors of Newcastle United Football Club (see page 74) are among those who have learnt that a badly expressed, reluctant or tardy expression of regret only fuels the flames.

- **They should be immediate.** The emotions surrounding a crisis do not permit hesitation. Nokia understood this and apologized quickly for its inflammatory instruction manual. In a letter published in *Wenhui*, a Shanghai newspaper, the company wrote: 'We accept the criticism of your newspaper, and wish to convey our most sincere apologies to the newspaper, your readers, and our large number of customers.' A larger and politically sensitive crisis was averted. A Nokia spokeswoman commented, 'This has not spread to a national level, partly because we acted so quickly.'[24]

- **They should be public.** The media and general public need to see that you have expressed your contrition to the people damaged by your actions. The number of affected people may be small and localized, but the national or international media may wish to relay their story to a larger audience. This was no doubt one reason why corporate giant 20th Century Fox dispatched an executive to Dalbeattie in the wake of *Titanic*, to offer what one newspaper called a 'humble apology' for the film's depiction of First Officer William Murdoch:

> The film was made as entertainment and was not meant to be a factual record and if we have upset Murdoch's family and the people of Dalbeattie, I apologize for that.[25]

The belatedness of the *Titanic* apology by 20th Century Fox undermined its effectiveness, but the First Officer's nephew was still able to say: 'I cannot completely forgive them. But what they have done today makes it a little easier.' This is the response that all corporate apologies should aim to achieve. 'If the public perceives you are truly sorry and that you genuinely want to do the right thing,' said one CEO after bringing his company's crisis to a safe conclusion, 'they will usually forgive you rather quickly.'[26]

The advance planning of an Initial Holding Statement is examined on page 197.

International crisis coordination

Since more and more companies are multinational, or work through multimarket organizations, crisis management will be demanded simultaneously in more than one country or jurisdiction. Such circumstances pose unique problems for which special plans and procedures are required. While it is not possible to offer a single solution to every circumstance, two scenarios in particular need thought:

- Corporate headquarters and functions in one market are separate from the country where the serious incident or issue is being played out.
- The major incident, issue or emergency envelops more than one market.

Many factors need to be taken into account, but the main considerations for senior decision-makers are:

- From where should the main corporate crisis management effort be driven?
- What level of devolved authority is required to ensure timely and effective operational and communication responses?
- How can information be gathered and assessed in a multimarket situation?
- What roles and responsibilities are required for spokespeople and media handlers?
- From where is coordination and communications direction and implementation driven and executed?

Although solutions will vary, the following principles should be applied when planning and executing multinational and multimarket crisis management:

- The lead time zone should always be where the key strategic decisions are being made – usually where the CCMT is located. If the company is stock-quoted it is likely that the CCMT will conform to the regulations and time constraints of the most important stock markets.
- Every effort must be made to ensure that managers in all markets are informed internally before any news is broken in the public domain, particularly by the media.
- Situation monitoring, information gathering, collation and analysis must be coordinated to ensure that strategic decisions are made only on timely and best available data. This may require a round-the-clock receipt and analysis capability at corporate headquarters.
- At the height of any crisis, the CCMT and other key decision-makers should be available to management in affiliates or subsidiaries on a 24-hour basis.
- Media handling and coordination of activity by spokespeople should be organized for round-the-clock responses and communication activity.
- Procedures for response, clearance and authorization for communi-

cation activities are reduced to the minimum while ensuring that communication actions deliver coordinated and consistent responses across the company and time zones.

- A cycle of updates and briefings is implemented to keep key internal and external groups and individuals up to speed and involved in their own markets and time zones.

Success is only possible in multinational and multimarket crisis situations if the key decision-makers (usually the CCMT) keep fully up-to-date on operational activities, attitudes, perceptions and future plans in all the effected markets. This requirement will demand well coordinated procedures and responses from the corporate team. At no time must key management and external groups perceive that they are on the periphery or out of the picture.

Audiences

While in a crisis the media will be the most vocal and demanding group, executives must remember all those to whom they must communicate. The challenge is not just to turn back the tide of rumour and speculation but to answer concerns, queries and fears, since many audiences can assist by accurately describing the situation when they are in turn approached for comment. What general approaches must be taken with audiences if an unanticipated crisis strikes? One corporate communications manager observed after a crisis:

> Simply having well-defined corporate principles and a social conscience is no more effective in managing a crisis than referring to a PR textbook. It is the prompt translation of that corporate culture that is critical.[27]

Once a crisis reaches the public domain, management must conduct a programme of integrated communications to make their corporation's principles and concern clear to a wide range of audiences. In an emergency, these audiences can be split into manageable groups:

- The media.
- The family of the Company:
    1. Employees and their families, because they will be approached.
    2. Supervisors and middle managers, because they have to be able to answer employee queries and fears.

3. Product management.
4. National/regional managers.
5. Corporate headquarters.
6. The salesforce, because they are facing customers every day.
7. Unions and works councils.
8. Security, switchboard and reception staff, because they will receive the first visitors and calls.

- The Business Community:
  1. End users/consumers.
  2. Business partners/customers.
  3. Investors.
  4. Suppliers.
  5. Distributors and agents, because their business could be affected.
  6. All the experts or commentators who could be asked, for example industry associations, commentators and financial analysts in your sector.
- The Influencing Circle:
  1. Regulatory authorities and officials.
  2. Local authorities.
  3. Residents and community leaders.
  4. Politicians at local, regional and national level.
  5. Regional and national governments.
  6. Ministers, their officials and special advisers, because they may be held responsible.
  7. Technical experts and specialists who will be asked for their opinion.
- Lawyers

The media

The opening moments in a major crisis are driven by the media. Corporate reputation and morale is directly affected by the activities of reporters hunting for their stories. An organized company response is advisable for, as one former journalist pointed out: 'If no one was willing to tell me what was happening, I would either conjure up the worst possible image in my own mind or talk to people who would give me what purported to be information, although it might be very inaccurate.'[28] When the crisis strikes, the crisis team must ensure that their messages are clear, prompt, honest and consistent; and that the technical facilities are on hand to help the media to do its job.

Questions and responses

It is imperative to prepare for an unrelenting flood of questions. The temptation to say something just to relieve the pressure can be overwhelming. 'I've said some things I'll probably always regret', said journalist Joe Klein of his own 'mind-boggling' time in the media spotlight after being uncovered as the author of *Primary Colors*.[29] Even Sir Bernard Ingham, Margaret Thatcher's seasoned Press Officer, reported 'feeling extremely exposed', at the time of the 1982 Falklands crisis and concluded simply: 'It was nerve-wracking and I never wish to experience it again'.[30]

A crisis does not have to involve military conflict to test the nerve. An incorrect, hasty or testy reply to a difficult query, a supposed 'off-the-record' remark, or showing favour to some reporters over others could carry serious personal or legal consequences. At the other extreme, a bald 'no comment' is liable to be viewed as a sign of guilt. Lack of preparation in particular leads organizations into deep waters. In 1990 NASA actually managed to create a crisis at its pre-flight press conference for the Hubble space telescope; which represented an exciting step out of the Challenger tragedy quagmire. An analysis later concluded: 'The agency oversold the telescope and provided inaccurate information about its capabilities.' This approach fell apart at the press conference. The NASA officials were unready and unable to give the subject of the first photographs, when they would be available and whether the media would be allowed to cover the first images. In consequence, 'NASA's poor handling of these questions caused anger and skepticism among the media.' Eventually, the media attacked NASA when it finally conceded that the cameras were not working. Two days after that concession, NASA announced that the space shuttle fleet would be grounded because of fuel leaks. Congressional representatives called hearings to find out the source of the problems with Hubble and the shuttles, and NASA's credibility crisis, escalated by a mishandled press conference, had spread to influential political audiences.[31]

In an emerging crisis a 'Questions and Responses' (Q&R) list should be speedily prepared, to anticipate and reply consistently and clearly to the most likely, difficult, explosive and hostile media inquiries.

In order to equip spokespeople and media handlers the Q&R list needs to comprise:

1. Key messages to which we should seek to return on all occasions.
2. Questions and the structure of responses to keep in line with key messages.

While the questions are inevitably tailored to the specifics of the crisis, they fall into these broad categories:

- What happened?
- Who or what is responsible?
- How dangerous is it?
- What are you doing about it?

Replies should conform to the Initial Holding Statement. One PR director of an international hotel chain has commented *apropos* her company's crisis plan: 'don't go outside of the box of that statement until you're ready to make a new statement'.[32] If you do not know the answer to a particular question, do not be afraid to say so, and promise to provide the answer as soon as it becomes known. Do not try to place blame, however strong the temptation. The desire to relieve pressure by implicating other people or organizations generally backfires. Remember that Daimler-Benz at first (though not for very long) blamed the 'Baby Benz' Elk Test fiasco on the new car's tyre manufacturer; NASA tried to shift responsibility for the Hubble failure to its contractor. In both cases this reaction only led the media, and in the case of NASA the regulatory authorities as well, to criticize the supervisory and quality control standards set by NASA and Daimler-Benz.

A sample Q&R list is included on pages 198 to 200.

The facilities

At scenes of human tragedy, particularly airports or large construction companies, there is a natural desire to herd, corral or barricade the press away from the sight of an accident or disaster, for very good practical reasons. The police in the UK talk about 'sealing off the accident area' from the press. This is unrealistic in light of the all-consuming need for pictures or footage. Any journalist or picture crew worth their salt will do whatever is necessary to get pictures of the seat of the explosion, the crash debris and the twisted bodies of victims, along with a poignant shot of the single abandoned shoe or child's toy. Communications should be managed as close as possible to the crisis scene. When onsite briefings are required, an operations room with telephones, faxes, television, radio and internet links would be ideal for both media and the crisis team. Media reporting involves waiting: waiting for a person to appear, or for a new development to be announced.

It is helpful to deal with that vacuum yourself rather than leave it to be filled by others. Provide a constant supply of information, news conferences, updates and refreshment; if there has been no change in the situation, announce it. People who are waiting need to be reassured that they have not been forgotten.

Quick provision of facilities is a step forward in gaining understanding for the challenges you face, and can be accomplished even in the most difficult circumstances. After the World Trade Center (WTC) bomb blast in New York City in 1993, the Port Authority of New York and New Jersey, which owned the building, decided 'to hold daily news briefings and provide early access to the blast site'.

> An emergency communication center was set up in a visible spot on the concourse level of the World Trade Center, using makeshift trestle tables and blackboards. Twelve to 14 PR professionals staffed this chaotic office to ensure the steady flow of information every day from 7 am to midnight or later.[33]

The Port Authority's Executive Director, Chief Engineer and the Director of the WTC gave 30–40 per cent of their time to media relations. Site access itself was granted within 48 hours of the explosion, and TV cameras were brought into the command centre of the engineers rebuilding the Center. The engineers themselves were uncomfortable with this decision, but 'it was something we had to do to turn this story around', recalled a Port Authority media relations supervisor, Peter Yerkes. It worked: once reporters saw the five-storey-high bomb crater for themselves, they stopped asking why the Port Authority's emergency systems failed to work. According to Yerkes:

> It wasn't sensationalism or voyeurism. It had to do with helping reporters understand what we were up against.[34]

At the same time it ought to also be stressed that there are legitimate causes for media exclusion zones:

- When there is serious danger or a safety consideration.
- When the preservation of forensic or police evidence is paramount.

Under such circumstances rigid constraints are reasonable provided they are publicly explained, and the media will accept them (albeit grudgingly).

Maintain intensive communications for as long as the media needs

After the World Trade Center bombing, the Port Authority held 7.30 a.m. planning sessions and mid-morning press conferences 'every day, seven days a week, for six weeks, beginning the morning after the blast'.[35] Frequent updates, briefings, interviews and news releases should continue as long as necessary, and changes in the status of the crisis should be promptly announced. In time, reporters look elsewhere for lead stories once they are satisfied that your organization has nothing controversial to offer, and is being honest and timely in its media relations. Toward the end of 1990, Hubble started producing pictures which NASA immediately made available at news conferences and scientific symposia. 'The efforts paid off; the media began to focus on what the telescope could do instead of what it could not.'[36]

Similarly, the rapid media communication effort that went into the WTC bombing on 26 February saw the Port Authority successfully through the early, intense phases of the crisis life-cycle:

> as coverage became routine, the focus was directed away from the disaster to repairs, tenant concerns, safety precautions, security improvements and the reopening of the Towers. Finally, on March 18, New York Governor Mario Cuomo became the first tenant to move back into his office in Two World Trade.[37]

Show that you are taking action

Journalists must see that you are taking the necessary operational steps to resolve your crisis. Different crises require different operational solutions: a product recall does not, for instance, generate the same activities as a plant explosion or a courtroom battle. Regardless of the crisis, however, the message of constructive activity needs to be understood by the press. Organizations must be prepared to publicly demonstrate what they are doing to improve the situation. The intimacy of the bond between media perception and corporate activity is especially apparent during a product recall, since the former depends on a high-profile communication of the latter. Johnson & Johnson (J&J) lit the path in 1982 during their famous crisis over cyanide-sabotaged Tylenol tablets. The incident has been heavily studied and in many ways represents the beginning of crisis communication as a discipline in its own right. J&J's key audience was the American consumer, which meant that its recall operations had to be extensively and publicly communicated. The product was taken off shelves across the country, a toll-free hotline established, full-page advertisements placed in newspapers and videotapes produced to explain the story in detail. The company sent over 450,000 electronic messages to the medical community, and executives devoted much time and energy to media interviews.[38]

The family of the company

In a crisis it can be forgotten that employees will have views, concerns and fears about their company, their jobs and their future. The attitudes and perceptions are exacerbated and exaggerated in the opening hours of a crisis, particularly when the media swarms over the company in a hunt for stories and answers. Work slows as anxious staff wait nervously for information and speculate among themselves and to their union representatives. 'We will be looking for assurances from the bank that the positive relationship we have been building over the last year will continue and the welfare of staff remains a high priority for the bank,' warned a representative for the banking union BIFU after the unexpected resignation of Barclays Chief Executive, Martin Taylor.[39] An employee motivated by guilt, nervousness or insecurity may come under massive pressure to speak into a microphone or make a damaging 'off-the-record' remark. Even a well-prepared crisis team which has moved to harness and centralize the communication flow cannot prevent every approach. 'It's very difficult to police every employee you have', one lawyer has warned. 'A lot of those contacts take place outside of the formal interview.'[40]

Trades union involvement may complicate the situation. Union leaders reacted to the Everglades crash of Flight 592 with public criticism of ValuJet, which until then had discouraged unionization in an effort to maintain its low costs. The Association of Flight Attendants submitted testimony to the authorities, going as far as to suggest that Chairman Robert Priddy and President Lewis Jordan were unfit to manage the airline.[41]

When the crisis strikes, therefore, immediate communication with all employees becomes essential to building internal confidence and shaping a unified message to external audiences. The crisis team must inform employees ahead of the media, providing details of the incident, an assessment of the immediate effects on employees, and the action the company is taking. As with the media, delays in acquiring information should be explained to employees, and updates provided periodically, even when, as with the media, there has been no significant change in the situation.

The methods used to reach employees in a fast, personal and sincere manner vary from company to company. Letters, meetings, e-mail, company websites and inhouse journals all have a role to play, especially to ensure employees are kept up-to-date ahead of media announcements. Bowater South contacted employees 'quickly and completely' by letter after the massive vehicle crash blamed on poor visibility created by emissions from a Bowater facility, although that simple statement belies the effort that went into the process. Five separate letters went to each employee, and thirteen separate lawyers edited each letter. This initiative, nevertheless, was felt to be worthwhile. The letters 'did serve their purpose to inform and reassure the employees, gaining their trust and maintaining their ambassadorship'.[42] However, the company, a branch of Bowater Incorporated, did not communicate with other company mills or corporate headquarters, who in consequence 'were receiving inquiries about a crisis that they knew nothing about'.[43] The October 1989 San Francisco earthquake damaged the historic Fairmont Hotel, which had also suffered in the infamous earthquake of 1906. The director of public relations, aware of how the ensuing media coverage might affect room bookings, ensured that the staff were included in the communications loop by holding regular meetings and involving them in the community clean-up effort.

Salespeople can play a vital part in getting messages to customers quickly. They are also a valuable way of combating rumour, particularly when competitors come forward with their own interpretation and suggest consequences of the crisis with which you are struggling. The sales network should also be seen as an important source of feedback direct from the marketplace. Careful planning and coordination are needed to put in place the necessary briefing, updating and feedback systems and procedures; and some thought is necessary in advance on how salespeople can be contacted and briefed when they are on the road and with clients. The available tools include pagers, mobile phones, e-mail messages directly into any computerized order systems, even messages left at home.

The business community

Companies in crisis must not only win the war, but the peace that follows. You must show the business community that you are restoring your operations, and rebuilding your reputation and your stock. Given the importance that investors give to non-measurable assets such as public perception and reputation, it is of course essential to provide a steady stream of statements, interpretation and news independent of whatever is offered in the press.

Some corporations may have to invest heavily in restoring the trust of the business community after mistakes have been exposed, while others, disrupted by events beyond their control, can focus on showing that normal operations have been resumed. The latter task is essentially one of promotion, exemplified by the Fairmont Hotel's attempts to show that it was open despite the earthquake:

> A task force was formed with the convention-and-visitors bureau to get the word out that hotel business in San Francisco – specifically at the Fairmont – could continue. Sales representatives contacted travel agents and meeting planners to inform them that the hotel was fully operational.[44]

If the audience is too large for person-to-person contact in the heat of crisis, conference calls and correspondence must play a part. Norman Augustine, a prominent crisis manager and company president, has described how at Lockheed Martin: 'we maintain at a central location all the supplies we need to communicate in writing with every member of each key constituency group. A letter can arrive at the home of each of 170,000 employees or 45,000 shareholders within two or three days.'[45]

The influencing circle

The members of the 'influencing circle' are interdependent and feed off one another for information and opinion, either directly or through the media. In serious crises, communication is needed to ensure that these groups hold their nerve and do not cave into ill-informed but noisy discussions in the media and public domain; companies find it surprising that they might have to steady nerves of ministers or senior regulatory figures through their respective key advisers. A crisis-hit company must reach these audiences with its own messages to help shape perceptions of the crisis and its own reputation among opinion-formers and, ultimately, the media and public at large. The task involves demonstrating:

- **Concern.** In the event of a threatening incident, the 'influencing circle' must see that you place people above profit. Exxon, for instance, reacted to a massive refinery explosion at Baton Rouge in Louisiana in August 1993 by publicly stating that 'Exxon's primary concern will continue to be for the safety of those who work in the plant and for those who live in the surrounding community.'[46] A hotline for the community was also installed to allow for dialogue and quick responses to emerging concerns.

- **Leadership.** It must be made clear that your organization is on top of its crisis. In the case of the refinery explosion, Exxon announced that it had immediately begun monitoring the neighbourhood for hazards and provided information about the clean-up effort.
- **Cooperation with the authorities.** This is, of course, a necessity, but a clarification of your willingness to cooperate with the effort demonstrates that the response is a joint effort, rather than an investigation of your shortcomings or a publicly funded mop-up of the mess that you have made. Burroughs Wellcome tackled two cyanide deaths linked to their Sudafed 12-hour capsules in March 1991, by ensuring that their communication 'flowed from the principle that the company was trying to protect consumers and support law enforcement officials'.[47]
- **Dialogue.** Relationships are strengthened by community participation rather than simple distribution of information. As the crisis progresses, public meetings, neighbourhood panels, seminars and tours help to minimize the scope for misunderstandings, rumour and confrontation.

Lawyers

According to one commentator, NASA lawyers faced with the Challenger Shuttle disaster:

basically knew that the engine turbine blades didn't cause the explosion. However, they were so concerned with not making a mistake that they refused to let NASA comment on the issue, thus fuelling further media speculation and mistrust of the agency.[48]

In the litigious world in which all companies conduct business, corporate management are reminded frequently by legal counsel of the risks of admitting liability or making a statement which comes back to haunt the defence in subsequent litigation cases. It has been argued in these pages that no Chief Executive can fairly be penalized for genuinely expressing sorrow when injuries have occurred, or safety or health appear to have been threatened, but careful legal and communication coordination is needed to ensure that the company speaks with a single voice to prevent suspicious observers from finding differences that imply insincerity, cover-ups or attempts to lie. In these circumstances, a good working relationship between legal counsel and crisis communicators is critical. Successful and legally safe communications can only be achieved by the joint management of legal and communication experts acting under the ultimate authority of corporate decision-making.

Tensions can develop between communications and legal opinion. This is unsurprising, given the difference between intervening in an immediate and free-flowing public controversy and in a long-term regulated and constrained legal environment. This difference can lead to serious dispute when management of an affiliate or subsidiary are dealing with a series of local crises. Corporate legal counsel – from the litigious USA, for instance – may not always understand the priorities and pressures that prevail in such jurisdictions as China, or post-communist Central Europe.

In 1995 a group of US academics assessed the relative dominance of public relations or legal strategies in crisis situations by looking at organizations facing public charges of sexual harassment. Legal strategies were defined as denial of guilt, saying little, or not commenting. Public relations strategies were equated with announcing an investigation, expressing how the company feels in human terms, stating policy, admitting that a problem exists, and announcing corrective measures. It was found that legal strategies dominated in almost two-thirds of the 39 cases studied. The authors argued persuasively from the evidence that companies in crisis should:

1.   reconcile the legal and communications counsel
2.   take a more collaborative approach to crisis communication.[49]

These recommendations have been implemented in the past, notably by Johnson & Johnson. Their famous 'Credo' was first published in 1943 and revised over the years to become and remain a living document. The English-language version currently begins: 'We believe our first responsibility is to the doctors, nurses and patients, to mothers and fathers and all others who use our products and services.'[50] This clear allocation of priority has enabled J&J's legal and communication functions to work together through several crises, beginning of course with the Tylenol crisis. 'We set as the number one priority the safety of the consumer', J&J general counsel George Frazza told an American Bar Association meeting in August 1983. 'We took immediate steps to find out as quickly as possible what caused the tragedy, then to do all within our power to contain it, regardless of whether the product was found to be blameless or at fault.'[51] Willard D. Nielsen, a Director of Corporate Communications for J&J, has even recounted a crisis where at one moment he found himself discussing legal information while a company lawyer dealt with communications.[52]

In disputes between long-term legal considerations and shorter-term needs to change attitudes or influence opinions through communications, the CCMT must be the final arbitrator, since it is responsible for key strategic decisions.

Recovery

Recovery will be achieved when management is perceived to have fixed the problem or have demonstrated the commitment to do all that is possible to solve it *and* to have successfully communicated to all key internal and external audiences. A crisis presents an opportunity for the company to coordinate the story of its recovery, which is likely to involve one or more of these areas:

Operations

Enacting and announcing operational change is an obvious priority if the crisis has threatened or taken lives. Following the deaths of four children and the illness suffered by 700 customers who ate *e.coli*-tainted Jack In The Box burgers in 1993, Foodmaker, the parent company, began the process of winning back consumer confidence by publicly reforming its operations. A new system for food handling was launched: 'Hazard Analysis Critical Control Point' (HACCP), developed from NASA's system to ensure food safety for its astronauts in the 1960s. The analysis follows food on its journey from the supplier into the mouths of consumers by using checklists and reports written out by employees working six-hour shifts. The system monitors temperatures on delivery lorries, down to 33 critical points in the restaurant, including the scrubbing of equipment and handling of food. Temperatures of cooking surfaces are tested twice daily, and timers are used to determine how long food is cooked on each side. Chefs must pierce the burger to confirm it is cooked through. Company auditors visit the 1300 restaurants once a month and monitor the process.

Foodmaker has also used HACCP to set an example of responsible leadership by:

1. working with interest groups like Safe Tables Our Priority (STOP), formed by parents of *e.coli* O157:H7 victims;
2. sharing the results of the programme at scientific gatherings and industry meetings;
3. according to a Foodmaker executive: 'actively supporting legislation that makes food safety systems like ours mandatory throughout the food industry'.

The new system, 'comparable to those used by health inspectors', has received valuable and public third-party endorsement from two government agencies: the US Department of Agriculture and the Food and Drug Administration.[53] HACCP has been described as providing Jack In The Box's customers with the assurance they need and 'most important to its recent sales figures' when Foodmaker returned to profitability three years after the tragedy.[54]

Culture

The aftermath of a severe or badly handled crisis should lead to a reappraisal of a company's culture: a review – sometimes painful – of the decision-making process, the potential for blockages and denial, and the ability of the company under pressure to speak the same language and act as effectively as its external audiences. 'Of course', commented Daimler-Benz's Chairman after the Elk Test, 'we will have to go back to our organizational structure to make sure bad news travels as readily as good news.'[55] This need not degenerate into turf wars and defensive managerial manoeuvring provided the audit is a participative, open procedure. Nike has publicly linked its culture to a specific ideal of responsible citizenship since the attacks on its Asian labour record. Chief Executive Phil Knight announced: 'We'll fund industry research – we'll fund university research – and open forums to explore issues related to global manufacturing and responsible business practices, such as independent monitoring and health issues.'[56] On a more comprehensive plane, Shell's humiliation by the environmental lobby over Brent Spar, and attacks on its human rights record in Nigeria, piled on top of a series of financial results described as 'ordinary' by one senior company officer. Managers realized that the prevailing corporate culture could not bear the strain that modern crises placed upon it, or produce the enterprise needed to realize the enormous potential of the biggest company in Europe: 'There was', one observer declared, 'a bias towards technical competence at the expense of commercial savviness.' The head of Shell's worldwide chemical unit conceded as much: 'We were a company with very few businessmen.'[57] The public attacks on the company by environmentalists and human rights groups had hurt internal morale, and exposed flaws in Shell's centralized structure. The *Financial Times* concluded that Brent Spar:

> shook Shell's management structure to its foundations . . . managers had never thought that a decision by a Shell operating company in one country could trigger violent attacks against a Shell company in another.[58]

A new executive recruited by Shell to manage the internal change reported: 'I see a lot of lack of confidence in management levels three or four rungs down from the top.' One outcome of the process has been a drastic reform of the complex corporate chain of command, traditionally arranged geographically by country or region. The new system obliges local companies to report direct to five business organizations responsible for Shell's main activities, including exploration, production, refining and marketing. The organizations will be led by business committees with no chief executive as leader and a mandate to act 'collegially' over 'wider issues where a collective approach is required'.[59]

The change in Shell's capacity to anticipate global crises extends to a more comprehensive approach to communication as prevention. 'Out goes the "decide, announce, defend" philosophy that held scientists and technologists as gods', reported an industry publication, 'in comes "engagement" of various "stakeholders".'[60] John Wybrew, the company's director of public affairs and planning, acknowledged that 'in order to protect [Shell's] image it had to win the hearts and minds of the public'.[61] The 'Spar Test' that assesses feelings as well as technical challenges surrounding projects, recounted on page 75, was an early signal of Shell's new approach to problem-solving; an attempt to resolve 'the conflict between internal feelings and rational, scientific solutions'.[62]

Relaunch

A product damaged, delayed or recalled by a crisis must be successfully returned to market to overcome the memory of the damage it created and the caution of a less trusting public. Daimler-Benz had such a task on its hands after the 1997 Elk Test. The company did not face complete ruin when its A-Class car was publicly vanquished by the Swedish elk: analysts remained confident that the eventual launch would survive the incident, although some revised their earnings expectations. Meanwhile, Daimler-Benz suspended delivery for three months and suffered 2000 cancelled orders in the three weeks following the crash (which was balanced by an equal number of incoming orders).

In spite of some initial defensiveness, the unfavourable attention and a rash of jokes on late-night German television, Daimler-Benz was redeemed by an internal culture that took pride in its tradition of quality and reacted well to the technical challenge. The 100,000 customers were assured by the company chairman that the problem would be solved. Tyres were changed on some models, shocks and stabilizers were redesigned, the rear axle width increased and a traction control system was introduced. The launch was handled with great care, particularly in Germany, where an advertising campaign featured tennis star Boris Becker suffering falls and setbacks before winning a championship. The car itself was proclaimed Germany's Car of the Year in 1998 by the country's most popular newspaper. The international media response was also positive, from Malaysia ('No more flips')[63] to Britain ('provided the British buying public can get over last year's hysteria, the Benz's star is going to shine very brightly').[64] Daimler-Benz declared the crisis over in its results for the first quarter of 1998: 'We not only managed to secure new customer groups with the successful relaunch of the technically-modified A-class and the M-class, the CLK Roadster and the SLK roadster, we also recorded substantially higher incoming orders.'[65]

Relaunch of a product following a crisis needs careful preparation and planning, especially if it had been necessary to recall or change the original formulation and/or packaging. The following points have been found useful when considering a product relaunch following a crisis:

1. Market research should have been initiated as soon as the brand or product reputation came under threat of suspicion (and recall was considered). Once the crisis is over, market research including focus groups should be used to establish:
   - what consumers/end-users and the general public remember or understand of the crisis;
   - what changes are necessary to the product or the packaging to restore any lost confidence and ensure that the new product is recognized as different (and thus safer and better);
   - if there are any real barriers to proposed pricing of the relaunched product.
2. Production and distribution plans are needed to decide whether a local (test) relaunch is necessary, or whether a regional or national operation is feasible.
3. A relaunch programme is created to provide an overall theme and coordinated plans for advertising and media support.
4. Communication plans are drawn up to cover:
   - production and sales management and employee briefings
   - salesforce briefings
   - customer briefings
   - management briefings
   - any necessary regulatory briefings
   - if a quoted company, briefings for shareholder and financial analysts

- one-to-one briefings with journalists, especially from the trade press.
5. A press conference or briefing may be necessary on the relaunch day to coincide with the start of any advertising campaign.
6. Market research should continue after the relaunch to ensure that customer and consumer confidence is holding up and growing.

Summary

Responding to an unexpected crisis requires:

- Coordination of all communications, both internally and externally.
- Key managers assigned to run the rest of the business, away from those involved in crisis management.

The steps that must be taken:

- Assemble a crisis team.
- Distribute an Initial Holding Statement.
- Harness the communication flow.
- Choose spokespeople.
- Build media relations by:
    1. preparation of Questions and Responses;
    2. providing facilities to help the media do their job;
    3. providing a flow of interviews, statements and clear evidence of the scale of the problem;
    4. maintaining intensive communications for as long as the media needs;
    5. showing that you are taking action.
- Reach non-media audiences:
    1. the family of the company (employees and their families, management, salesforce, security, reception and switchboard);
    2. the business community (consumers, customers, distributors or agents, industry associations, sector analysts and commentators);
    3. the influencing circle (local authorities and community leaders, politicians, regulators and officials, technical and scientific experts).
    4. lawyers.
- Develop recovery plans. A company must prepare to communicate the story of its recovery, which may involve:

1. operational changes;
2. changes to company culture;
3. product relaunch.

Notes

1   Ward, G.C. *A First-Class Temperament*. New York: Harper Perennial, 1989, p. 448.
2   'Few trust company officials in crisis, survey says.' *Reuter European Business Report*, 13 August 1993.
3   Kaufmann, J., Kesner, I. F., and Hazen, T. L. 'The myth of full disclosure: a look at organizational communications during crises'. *Business Horizons*, vol. 37, no. 4, p. 29, July 1994.
4   Kamer, Larry. 'Crisis planning's most important implement: the drill.' *Communication World*, December 1997.
5   Gilbert, Martin. *Churchill: A Life*. London: Heinemann, 1991, p. 673.
6   *ibid.*
7   Seymour, Michael. 'Product safety under public scrutiny'. In Hodges, C., Tyler, M. and Abbott, H. *Product Safety*. London: Sweet & Maxwell, 1991, pp. 318–19.
8   Dozier, Dow. 'Employee communications at Kerr-McGee in the aftermath of the Oklahoma City bombing'. *Public Relations Quarterly*, 22 June 1998.
9   'Terror in the towers: A media relations pro tells his story'. *Public Relations Journal*, December 1993.
10   'PR finds a cool new tool. When the fates gave corporations a beating, savvy spin doctors got a web smart'. *Forbes*, 6 October 1997.
11   Traverso, Debra K. 'Opening a credible dialogue with your community'. *Public Relations Journal*, August 1992.
12   Wheelwright, P. *Heraclitus*. New York: Atheneum, 1964, p. 83.
13   'Spokesman for government crisis team recalled'. Polish Press Agency, *PAP Newswire*, 4 August 1997.
14   Ingham, Bernard. *Kill the Messenger*. London: Fontana, 1991, p. 289.
15   Fink, Steven. *Crisis Management: Planning for the Inevitable*. New York: American Management Association, 1986, p. 67.
16   'How TWA faced the nightmare'. *Business Week*, 5 August 1996.
17   'The explosion on flight 800/On facts, TWA pulls evasive maneuvers'. *Newsday*, 19 July 1996.
18   Maggart, Lisa. 'Bowater Incorporated – a lesson in crisis communications.' *Public Relations Quarterly*, 22 September 1994.
19   *Independent*, 5 May 1994.
20   'Japanese directors bow out in sorry style'. *Guardian*, 1 December 1997.

21 'Funeral company apologises after documentary'. *Press Association Newsfile*, 13 May 1998.

22 'Anger over Sony's "cancer" mailshot'. *BBC News*, 24 October 1998. http://news.bbc.co.uk/hi/english/health/newsid_200000/200628.stm

23 'Lothian's burning!' *Evening News* (Edinburgh), 16 April 1998.

24 'Nokia apologizes for errors in Chinese mobile telephone manuals'. *Agence France Presse*, 1 July 1998.

25 'An epic apology'. *Daily Mail*, 16 April 1998.

26 Kaufmann, J. *et al.*, *op. cit.*

27 'Avoiding speculation during PR crisis plan for product recall'. *O'Dwyer's PR Services Report*, October 1992.

28 'Terror in the towers: A media relations pro tells his story'. *Public Relations Journal*, December 1993.

29 'A brush with anonymity'. *Newsweek*, 29 July 1996.

30 Ingham, Bernard, *op. cit.*, p. 291.

31 Kauffman, James. 'NASA in crisis: The space agency's public relations efforts regarding the Hubble space telescope'. *Public Relations Review*, no. 1, vol. 23, p. 1. 22 March 1997.

32 'Crisis to calm: Hotel crisis management'. *Hotel & Motel Management*, 11 August 1997.

33 'Terror in the towers: A media relations pro tells his story'. *Public Relations Journal*, December 1993.

34 *ibid.*

35 *ibid.*

36 Kauffman, James. 'NASA in crisis'. *op. cit.*

37 'Terror in the towers'. *op. cit.*

38 These details are extracted from a thought-provoking critique of the role played by disclosure in crises. Kaufmann, J. *et al.* 'The myth of full disclosure'. *op. cit.*

39 'Barclays chief quits'. *BBC News*, 27 November 1998. http://news.bbc.co.uk/hi/english/business/the_company_file/newsid_223000/223004.stm

40 'Crisis to calm: Hotel crisis management'. *op. cit.*

41 'ValuJet attendants hit top execs.' *Chicago Sun-Times*, 23 July 1996.

42 Maggart, Lisa. 'Bowater Incorporated – a lesson in crisis communications'. *Public Relations Quarterly*, 22 September 1994.

43 *ibid.*

44 'Crisis to calm: Hotel crisis management'. *op. cit.*

45 Augustine, Norman. 'Managing the crisis you tried to prevent'. *Harvard Business Review*, November 1995.

46 Duhe, Sonya Forte and Zoch, Lynn M. 'A case study – framing the media's agenda during a crisis; Exxon Corp's public relations management'. *Public Relations Quarterly*, 22 December 1994.

47   'Avoiding speculation during PR crisis plan for product recall'. *O'Dwyer's PR Services Report*, October 1992.

48   Coulter, Patrick. 'A merger is nothing but a "planned" crisis'. *Communication World*, December 1996.

49   Fitzpatrick, Kathy R. and Rubon, Maureen Shubow. 'Public relations vs. legal strategies in organizational crisis decisions'. *Public Relations Review*, 22 March 1995, vol. 21, no. 1, 21.

50   Johnson & Johnson, 'Our Credo', 12 April 1999. http://www.jnj.com/who_is_jnj/cr_usa.html

51   'When is a "recall" not a recall?' *FDA Consumer*, October 1995.

52   'Effective crisis planning'. *Public Relations Society of America*, VHS Videotape, 1990.

53   'On the hamburger trail'. *Los Angeles Times*. 22 September 1994; 'Fast-food phoenix: Jack In The Box rises from the ashes of crisis'. *San Diego Union-Tribune*, 10 August 1997; 'Setting the food safety standard', 14 April 1999. http://jackinthebox.com/main.html

54   'Foodmaker back to making money: Food-handling program one key to the comeback'. *San Diego Union-Tribune*, 28 April 1998.

55   'Tilting at elks'. *Time*, 8 December 1997.

56   National Press Club Luncheon address. *Federal News Service*, 12 May 1998.

57   'Shell discovers time and tide wait for no man'. *Financial Times*, 10 March 1998.

58   *ibid*.

59   'Barons swept out of fiefdoms: Shell's far-reaching shake-up is dramatic but necessary'. *Financial Times*, 30 March 1995.

60   'In pursuit of repute.' *Utility Week*, 15 August 1997.

61   'Shell puts more emphasis on PR'. *PR Week*, 22 September 1995.

62   *ibid*.

63   'No more flips'. *New Straits Times*, 9 August 1998.

64   'It's not a class war, it's a revolution'. *Evening Herald*, 7 August 1998.

65   'Company earnings: Daimler-Benz (Q1 car sales growth due to new models)'. *AFX News*, 8 April 1998.

5 Special techniques

WHILE EVERY INCIDENT PRESENTS unique challenges within the framework described in the last chapter, some do share broadly similar patterns and occur frequently enough for special techniques to have developed to tackle them. These techniques supplement crisis response in significant ways and it is helpful to discuss them in some detail.

Rumour management

The first of three introductory comments is to remind ourselves that rumour will always fill *any* communications vacuum; 'the vacuum' is a major rationale for crisis communications.

The second important aspect of rumour is that it always appears to be more interesting and more attractive than the plain truth, and invites the inventive process of developing speculation and allegations.

The third comment involves what might be termed 'The Chinese Whispering Game Factor'. As with this children's game of passing a message down a long line of participants, so also company information suffers distortion and misinterpretation at each communications interface – every listener slightly mishears and then each speaker adds their own 'five pennyworth'.

The business world, used to concrete targets and accurate measurement, has trouble addressing irrational and persistent rumours. Companies, especially large companies, are not inherently transparent. They do not readily expose their inner operations to public scrutiny, often for sound commercial reasons. At the same time, they deeply influence the daily lives of individual citizens. This gap between knowledge and impact is filled on occasion by rumours and suspicions. As one American commentator has said: 'There's an implicit belief that for anyone to become really economically powerful, there must be some implicit deal with the forces of evil.'[1]

Rumours are a playful or downright malicious by-product of conspiracy theorizing. Americans are particularly fluent in the language of conspiracy, from John F. Kennedy to alien abductions. 'The trick of higher paranoid scholarship', observed the historian Richard Hofstadter, 'is to start with defensible assumptions, gather certain "facts," and let it all amount to "evidence" in careful preparation for "the big leap from the undeniable to the unbelievable".'[2] Conspiracy thinking, noted the British *New Statesman*, is 'bound to flourish' in a country:

> where political propaganda, commercial advertising and the entertain-ment industry create everyday deception or, as anthropologist Jules Henry called it, 'a tissue of contradictions and lies'. America's Christian, 'good versus evil' mindset adds to the mix, for it calls for an active search for evil. And there is always the American often-cited love for simple explanations, and the discomfort with causes that aren't at least as powerful as their effects.[3]

It is true that corporate rumour is especially prevalent in the USA, but many of the necessary pre-conditions are commercial rather than national, and not unique to one country. Globalization has led many foreign companies into the American marketplace, where awareness of local attitudes and customs is as important as in any other country. American companies have also expanded overseas, and regional operations are not likely to escape the consequences of a rumour arising in another location.

The process is encouraged by information technology, electronic media and even voicemail, all of which offer rumourmongers the prospect of rapid dissemination plus universal and instant impact. Many rumours have their own web page. Visitors to www.UrbanLegends.com can trawl 800 rumours about people or companies. The web has also reduced the time for a company to decide whether or not to respond. According to the creator of one website devoted to rumours: 'The time it takes for a story to spread has gone from days, weeks, months to hours, minutes, seconds.'[4] Television news and gossip shows add credibility by packaging rumours in an informational format via trusted and popular presenters. News stories are produced, then repeated, recast in different forms, edited, expanded, reshaped and relayed to fit the space and time needs of the medium. In these ways communication technol-ogies instill rumours with energy and variety, instead of only acting as transmitters. Companies can face serious (and totally unwarranted or untrue) rumours being discussed and escalated in online chatrooms, devoted to discussing a company or industry. The situation is made worse since the chatrooms operate under the title of – or refer directly to – the company name, thus attracting more attention. Furthermore, the legal position is far from clear when it comes to combating remarks made on the internet, especially since authors may hide their identities. Deciding how to counter such rumours raises the question of whether or not to enter the debate or stand aloof and trust that common sense, disbelief or boredom will prevail.

Rumours abound about corporate actions or products, and are harder for companies to deal with than facts. From the perspective of crisis management, rumours are always untrue, since if they were based on truths they would enter the realm of fact and the techniques described earlier could be applied: data collection, firm and credible confirmation or denial. These actions, difficult enough by themselves, are not always enough if the rumour itself is the whole problem. The nebulous nature of a rumour, shifting its shape and accruing real or unsubstantiated events to back it up, is something people often enjoy believing in, regardless of the reality.

Rumours and external audiences

In March 1991 Procter & Gamble (P&G)'s president appeared on the popular *Phil Donahue Show* and divulged to viewers that a portion of the company's profits were donated to the Church of Satan. It was time, he said, for 'coming out of the closet' on this issue. 'There are not enough Christians in the US to make a difference.' Almost immediately, a list of 49 P&G products to boycott began circulating in the southern states of the USA.[5]

It does not take an expert to realize that in those circumstances any company would have a massive crisis on its hands. P&G did not, of course, because the story was a ridiculous fabrication, a lie, a rumour put out to discredit the Cincinnati, Ohio manufacturers whose products include Crest toothpaste, Tide laundry detergent, Ivory soap and Pampers nappies. The boycott, however, gathered momentum. It reinforced an earlier rumour, circulating since 1980, about P&G's familiar logo, the profile of a Man in the Moon, with curly beard and surrounded by stars. There were curls in the man's beard, it was said, that resembled the satanic number '666', and the thirteen stars were yet another mark of P&G's fiendish tendencies.

External rumours possess several interesting characteristics:

- **Rumours can hibernate.** The *Donahue* incident revived a rumour that had been lying dormant until a story came forward to give it new momentum. In another instance an article was circulated in charismatic churches accusing P&G of regularly offering 'employee seminars that contain some degree of New Age practices such as mind control, visualization, self-hypnosis, channeling, biofeedback, Eastern mysticism or psychic activity'.[6] Calls and letters to P&G about Satanism pursued a fitful pattern, peaking with the generation of new rumours in 1982, 1985, 1990 and again in 1995. Between 1980 and 1995, P&G answered more than 200,000 inquiries on the subject.[7]

- **Rumours generate problems regardless of a company's previous good name.** In 1991 Snapple Beverages launched a fruit juice, Tropical Fantasy, but word circulated that the new product was created by the Ku Klux Klan to cause sterility in African Americans. This story was embroidered by allegations that the 'k' on Snapple labels stood for the Klan (it actually stood for 'kosher'), and the picture of a ship that also appears on the label was a slave ship (in reality an old print of the Boston Tea Party). Snapple's record of support for continuing education and scholarships made no difference to the situation. A boycott began in the southern states and California, where the rumour was thought to originate.
- **Rumours need not reach the entire public to have an impact:** they need only reach a company's key audiences. A respected New York firm, Swanke Hayden Connell Architects, was 'hurt' in 1990 by industry rumours that it was in financial trouble and 'going out of business' in the then-current recession.[8]

The first and most important action is to establish as much detail as is available on:

- the rumour that is circulating;
- where it might have originated;
- who might have started it and who is now driving it onward.
- How our audiences are viewing the rumour. Often a company will discover that customers or regulators are either unaware of the rumour or have already dismissed it.

Intel has closely monitored the internet for rumours ever since a 'rogue' website, N-Tel Secrets, helped foment a major crisis over a flawed Pentium Chip in 1994. Monitoring comment has allowed Intel to head off rumours and controversies at an early stage, including a second announcement from N-Tel Secrets of a supposed error in the Pentium II Chip.[9]

Companies should be monitoring a rumour from the outset and should do so until they are sure it has disappeared. Leaving this 'overwatch' process until a late stage exposes a company to the risk of eventually fighting stories that have moved on or even changed course.

Armed with detail, the company can decide how to approach the problem. A three-tiered approach should be considered.

- **Ignore it.** Rumours can vanish as swiftly as they arise. Hoping a particular rumour goes away is an instinctive first step, since any response will draw attention to whatever is being said. Online chatrooms rely on a steady stream of speculation: to stay still would serve no purpose. Many companies simply do not monitor chatrooms. Others produce a short memo summarizing the daily comment. In either case, the effort is understandably minimal: it would take too much time to chase after vast quantities of idle speculation. It is better first to assess whether a rumour could diminish and fade and *then* decide if being seen to ignore the story is the correct corporate position. That said, corporate management must be ready to explain why they have decided to take this line in case a key individual or group becomes exercised by the story being circulated, and starts asking difficult questions.
- **Isolate it.** If the rumour does *not* go away, and actually becomes an annoyance, the first step must be to contain the problem, either geographically or by addressing the limited audiences involved. Snapple launched an advertising campaign in the San Francisco Bay area where the Ku Klux Klan rumour had originated, and obtained public support from the local president of the National Association for the Advancement of Colored Persons (NAACP).

  An American importer of Corona beer, after trying to ignore tales (maliciously spread by competitors) that the product had been adulterated with urine and fearing eventual media attention, eventually reacted by sending an information packet to wholesalers which documented the beer's purity without actually mentioning the rumours.[10]

  Swanke Hayden Connell's (SHC) audiences were smaller still, and local enough to be managed even more directly. On the principle that people are most inclined to believe the evidence of their own eyes, the firm threw two large parties, one for clients and prospective clients, the other for consultants, designers and dealers, 'to let them know we're alive and well'. Both parties were held at SHC's new midtown offices, which boasted a large terrace overlooking Central Park. SHC's director of corporate communications noted: 'the events dramatically put the lie to inaccurate stories circulating about our imminent demise'.[11]

- **Fight it.** The final, reluctant step is a comprehensive public assault on the rumour with all the means at a company's disposal. These include:

    An information campaign. P&G sent letters to churches and news outlets, and developed an information kit to explain the prosaic origins of their trademark, which was registered in 1882 and evolved from a popular mark wharf-hands put on boxes of Star Brand candles in the 1850s. The thirteen stars stood for the thirteen colonies. An answering system was also installed to deal with inquiries: it was certainly unfortunate that in order to access it callers were invited to press the number '6'. A website is also in place: 'The Facts About Procter & Gamble's Trademark'.[12]

    Third-party endorsement. The kit and website included an endorsement from Phil Donahue, confirming that no-one from P&G had ever appeared on his programme. 'Anyone who claims to have seen such a broadcast is either mistaken or lying. It never happened!' P&G's site features other letters of support from figures and organizations most likely to be trusted by likely 'boycotters': the Archbishop of Cincinnati, Jerry Falwell, the Southern Baptist Convention, the Episcopal Diocese of Southern Ohio and Billy Graham's Evangelistic Association.

    Removing the excuse for the rumour. In 1985, P&G took what to many seemed the ultimate step: the famous Man in the Moon was dropped from products, but preserved for corporate stationery and internal use. In 1995 he reappeared, with the curls flattened.

    Lawsuits. Careful consideration is needed before taking this elaborate (and costly) route. The other pro-active options should *definitely* be examined first. There are two problems connected with litigation:

    1. It is fighting an immediate problem with a long-term solution. Rumour is a problem facing the company now, whereas a legal case will take months if not years to resolve.

    2. Taking the heavyhanded legal route may pump oxygen to the rumourmongers and their stories. The 'McLibel' case, originally centred around a leaflet attacking the environmental record of the McDonald's fast-food chain, is a classic example where two individuals with a 'no hope' case tied up a major multinational for seven years in the courts. The case generated many media stories which were mainly supportive of the 'innocent' small people facing up to the US giant. The outcome, when the judgement was eventually given, had ceased to be material.[13]

Procter & Gamble adopted a policy of filing suit whenever the origina-
tor of a rumour can be traced. 'These ridiculous lies have cost the company a
lot of time and energy over the past ten years', P&G's vice-president of public
affairs complained after one successful legal battle.[14] In August 1995, Procter
& Gamble launched its fifteenth lawsuit over Satanism. The defendant was a
leading member of rival Amway's independent Distributors Association
Council, who allegedly spread the rumour to other independent distributors
using Amway's voicemail system. According to P&G, the Utah distributor's
voicemail message went out in April or May, 'around the time consumer calls
to P&G regarding the rumor rose to 200 a day from the usual average of 22'.
Some of the distributors exploited the message to provoke a boycott of
P&G.[15] 'We know', a P&G spokesperson revealed, 'consumers around the
world have been diverted from buying our products.'[16] Amway itself has said
it is cooperating with P&G to combat the story, and 'does not condone the
spreading of false and malicious rumors against Procter & Gamble or any
other company'.[17]

Rumours within the company

In any situation, where the business, professional or business reputations of the company, its management or products are potentially being
exposed to risk, internal rumour or speculation is bound to arise. The
following principles apply:

- Monitor the rumour to keep abreast of its twists and turns.
- Examine the situation in light of the latest rumour(s), or the latest
  version of existing rumours.
- Be ready to communicate to counter rumour or correct inaccuracies or
  speculation. Kaiser Permanente, a large California Health Maintenance
  Organization, established an online service called 'Rumor Check' for
  its 30,000 employees spread over 32 medical facilities in Northern
  California. The forum attracts over 100 postings a day on all subjects
  'from potential labor disputes to requests by stumped employees for
  help on continuing education projects', and is monitored by a retired
  public affairs officer working from home. Rumor Check is designed for
  employees 'to gripe, pose questions, and interact as an electronic
  community'.[18]
- Make every effort to tell management and employees *before* they hear
  news from other sources, particularly the media.
- Consider the constraints on communicating internally (and externally).

- The Core Crisis Management Team (CCMT) must then identify the first opportunity and the fastest means possible to brief managers, followed by employees, if security constraints permit.
- Accept that rumours always generate interest and are often more attractive than the facts or truth.
- Silence – or a vacuum caused by lack of communication – will always be filled by rumour and speculation.
- Any organization of ten or more people will always have a series of rumours circulating. Thus monitoring and pick-up systems are required, especially when a company is facing or handling a crisis situation. Under these circumstances rumour can contribute to and exacerbate already serious problems.
- Never put managers in a position whereby their people ask them about something they have not been told about themselves.
- As soon as management initiates communications, a commitment is being implied. Once the company starts the process it will have to continue, or virulent rumours will start circulating once more.
- Be frank with your employees whenever possible:
  1. Explain exactly why you cannot tell them more; they will usually accept it.
  2. *Ask* them not to talk to the media, rather than issuing a gagging order – they are more likely to comply.
  3. Accept that your company is big enough and important enough for people outside to ask your people about what is happening, and that your employees will find it very hard to respond with 'no comment'.
  4. Realize that anything you write down and distribute to individuals or notice boards could be printed, forwarded, photocopied and faxed at any time. Ensure that you could live with seeing your words today in tomorrow's news.
  5. Accept that in any organization of 100 employees there will be two or three people with direct access to the media. They could include:

     Husbands wives, partners, siblings or just good friends of journalists.

     'Stringers' who will be paid a weekly or monthly retainer to report any unusual or interesting incident or activity at their company.

     Someone who enjoys the self-importance of reporting company events as an 'informer'.

This rough statistic takes no account of embittered ex-employees and whistleblowers, who may emerge to harry the company for a variety of reasons.

A key group in the management of rumour (internal or external) is the salesforce. They are critical because:

- They are at the interface with your customers (and represent the company and its values/ethos for them).
- Salespeople are natural communicators and usually find it impossible not to respond if asked about a rumour.
- Salespeople cannot be seen not to know. They may feel pressured to make up information they lack.

When it is decided to counter rumour, the salesforce must be a high priority for the task of correcting information.

Product recall

As soon as safety problems are catapulted onto the public agenda, corporate management must consider the ultimate solution of product recall. Eventually, if customer and consumer trust appears to be severely undermined, then recall may be the only option.[19] Most recalls are voluntary, undertaken not only to protect the public and the reputation of the company, brand or product, but also because it is more responsible and less damaging than seizures or court injunctions by the regulatory authorities. They are common, growing in frequency by 300 per cent in the UK between 1995 and 1997. Infoplan International found recalls in Britain ran at an average of over sixteen a month over eighteen months to November 1997.[20] The affected products can be many and varied. In October 1998, recalled British products included two toy masks with flammable hair; a toothbrush mug and soap dish with knobs that could come off and therefore be swallowed, and a toy elephant with a dangerous cot strap popper.[21] The following month, companies or federal agencies in the USA recalled 10 million playpens, some nearly 40 years old, because children could strangle themselves on protruding parts; 600,000 pounds of beefburgers to check whether they were contaminated by *e.coli*; 71,000 fitness treadmills because of dangerous electrical problems; 37,000 wooden bunk beds because of a strangulation threat presented by limited space on the top level; 458 cases of cheddar cheese-filled pretzels which might contain peanut butter not marked on the label; 80,000 barbecue grills with a potentially dangerous propane gas hose; 1.5 million pounds of hot dogs, and also luncheon meat, possibly infected by listeria.

This catalogue of activity demonstrates that health and safety issues are common reasons for recall. The recall itself can take different forms. In a consumer product manufacturing company, a crisis could result in any one of the following actions:

- Product freeze, hold or destruction within manufacturer's production or warehouse facilities.
- Freeze, hold and withdrawal from distributor warehouses or distribution chain.
- Hold and pick-up from wholesale or retail central warehouse facilities.
- Local, regional, national or even international recall from retail stores, including clearance of shelves.
- Fully public operational and communications campaign to recall affected products from consumers or end-users.

The American Food and Drug Administration (FDA) takes a highly structured approach to recall. Its standards have been followed in other markets and are instructive to review. FDA officials assess the effectiveness of a recall in three key areas:

- Depth, or how far down the distribution chain the recall must reach, from company through wholesaler, retailer and consumer.
- The extent of public warnings made by the company and the FDA, which becomes particularly important if the product is a health or safety hazard.
- Effectiveness check levels. Firms are graded from 'A' to 'E' on conducting 'effectiveness checks' to verify that audiences at the chosen depth of recall have received the message and acted on it.

Most US firms embarking on a recall notify the FDA for guidance and support, though there is no legal obligation to do so. Once the process has started, the FDA's district office will investigate the company and on the basis of its documented findings about the product, covering such areas as its health and safety record, complaints received and quality controls, sends a Recall Recommendation (RR) to the relevant FDA centre (for foods and cosmetics, drugs, devices, biologics and veterinary medicine).

The FDA centres employ a three-level health hazard evaluation, which helps to decide the scope of the recall and provides some companies with a useful model to integrate into their operations.

- Class I recalls cover 'a strong likelihood that a product will cause serious adverse health consequences or death'.
- Class II recalls are those 'in which use of the product may cause temporary or medically reversible adverse health consequences'. Although evaluations are always conducted on a case-by-case basis, past recalls under this category have included food products contaminated with pieces of glass too small to make injury likely.
- Class III 'involves a product not likely to cause adverse health consequences'. Cases in this category have included mislabelling a food product as another, without a risk to health.[22]

Recalls are practised by some industries more than others. In Britain in 1993 food and drink led the way, followed by electrical goods, baby and children's products, health products and clothing.[23] The exact order can mirror changing national preoccupations: in the USA, cars are repeatedly recalled, either by the federal authorities or the manufacturers themselves. One study found that the agency for highway traffic safety recalled 10.1 million vehicles in 1992 and 11 million in 1993, described by one firm as a 17-year high.[24]

The logistics of recall are not always handled effectively, whether conducted by the company or a regulatory authority. In America the Consumer Product Safety Commission (CPSC) found in 1990 that 'consumer response to CPSC recalls ranges typically from 2 per cent to 15 per cent'. Television, with its capacity to demonstrate vividly the dangers in some products, appears to be the most effective medium for informing consumers, although the results can vary. One dramatic recall in the USA, using television, radio and press and a news conference held by the CPSC chairman, only achieved an 18 per cent return rate.[25]

If blanket publicity does not always achieve the hoped-for result, the problems faced during recalls indicate that reforming the communication process could bring improvements. US research suggests that the main problems include:

- Media perception that the recall is not 'newsworthy'.
- Consumer belief that the news is not relevant to them.
- 'Recall saturation'. The public receives so many recall warnings that critical messages are lost or forgotten.

- The nature of the publicity achieved. Television visuals, and mail with telephone follow-up to endangered consumers, appear to be most effective.[26]

For a company, these issues also form an obstacle, not only to achieving a high return rate, but also to perceptions that it is behaving responsibly and honestly when one of its products places consumers at risk. There are a number of factors which point to the success of a coordinated communication plan:

- **Clarity and promptness of action**[27]

A prompt recall decision by companies is easier to make when there is agreement that its product poses a threat, and is itself compromised. Lifescan Canada, for instance, voluntarily launched a recall of its Surestep Glucose Meters in July 1998, because a particular batch (sold through pharmacies and hospitals) issued an error message instead of a high blood-glucose reading for high levels of blood sugar. The misreading endangered diabetics who might conceivably avoid getting medical attention. Lifescan:

1. Notified the Health Protection Branch (HPB) of Health Canada, the responsible federal agency.
2. Identified the affected batch.
3. Attempted to reach all registered users of the affected model.
4. Informed doctors, pharmacists and diabetes educators who might be in contact with users.[28]
5. Described how to bypass the mistake and check against the real result.
6. Undertook to replace the defective meters and provided a telephone number to arrange for replacement.

In the UK, a fault on product line filters caused bone slivers to pass into a bone marrow baby feed. As soon as consumer complaints were received, Heinz, the manufacturers, made a wide assessment of the potential impact on this popular product, and ordered an immediate and complete withdrawal.[29] It is important to note that the recall decision was taken even though the bone slivers were smaller than a grain of rice and medical advice confirmed that these tiny contaminant pieces could not have caused a child to choke when swallowing. The real concern lay in the habit of infants to snuffle or ingest solids up into the nasal passages, which can lead to choking. Nevertheless, executives understood the urgent need to protect their overall portfolio of baby foods and bolster their trust with mothers, at the expense of losing one successful product within the range.

The FDA holds firms responsible for conducting the actual recall, and monitors their efforts to contact purchasers promptly with information including:

1. The product being recalled.
2. Identifying information such as lot numbers and serial numbers.
3. The reason for the recall and any hazard involved.
4. Instructions to stop distributing the product and what to do with it.

*   **Balancing the cost of recall against the cost to reputation**

When corporate management accepts the need to recall a product, the Chief Financial Officer will see shares decline, withdrawal costs mount, compensation given to consumers and spending on replacement stock.[30] At the same time the hidden costs can never be accurately calculated for such items as management time and operational disruption. These costs must be set against the threat to the integrity of the brand. Life Brand Olive Oil was recalled by its Canadian distributors in August 1998 because of fears that it was mislabelled and contained castor oil, a health hazard to pregnant women, senior citizens and cardiac patients. Canada's leading drugstore group, Shoppers Drug Mart/Pharmaprix, acted voluntarily to protect consumers and public trust in its exclusively sold 'Life' brand products.[31] In many countries, the alternative to voluntary recall is unattractive, and in the USA has been explained by an FDA official: 'If we request a recall, we are prepared to seize the product and go to the press.'[32] Companies need to accept that regulatory authorites around the world look to the US FDA as a benchmark when defining regulations and or assessing health and safety hazards.

*   **Defining the risks and scope of the recall problem**

The logistical and operational challenges of any product recall will be daunting. A confusing thicket of authorities may also be involved, which should be anticipated and identified by preparedness planning. In Australia, a survey on product recall reported by the Federal Bureau of Consumer Affairs (FBCA) in February 1997, has recommended simplifying the system. It found the recall process bedevilled by a surfeit of government agencies, leading to 'uncertainty, duplication of work and higher costs'.

For example [the FBCA reported] in its response to the survey on behalf of its members, the Federal Chamber of Automotive Industries provided a list of 17 government contacts for notification of motor vehicle recalls. This figure included both legislative and non-legislative requirements.[33]

In parenthesis, it is interesting to note that the report's recommendations for overcoming bureaucratic duplication involved taking advantage of information technology:

1.   An internet site be established to provide sufficient information to consumers to enable them to be informed of the risk a product may pose so that they can take appropriate action.
2.   The internet site be able to be used by government agencies to share information about recalls.
3.   If notification of a recall is entered on the internet site by a regulator, that notification will discharge any obligation which the business has to advise other regulators about the recall.[34]

Aside from working with the correct authorities, limited product freezes or distribution 'holds' or national product 'lifts' raise complex tracing and recovery problems.

The authors of a *Harvard Business Review* study of recalls recommend that 'logistics and information systems should . . . incorporate recall planning into management information systems, including databases, thereby maintaining product traceability records attached to customer files'.[35] Nevertheless, recalls at multinational levels can present difficulties inside international distribution networks, where assessing risks to consumers may be hard to define in detail. A long distribution chain through different shippers, agents and hauliers makes it more difficult to track the depth and spread of a troubled product. It has been rightly pointed out in *Harvard Business Review* that:

logistics and information systems should be able to trace any product that has been handled. That is, the systems should be able to isolate a product defect by batch, plant, process or shift through the use of identifiers such as serial numbers.[36]

Unfortunately, batch coding might not always be used in the product lifecycle (from production to sale), especially in emerging markets such as Central and Eastern Europe or parts of the Pacific Rim. Finally, the likely volume of the problem must be taken into account in advance planning.

When conducting a multinational recall of 17 million bottles in 152 markets, one drinks company found that the large volumes made it challenging to determine whether any problem bottles had reached retail outlets to put consumers at risk, although rigorous tracking systems were in place.[37]

- **Placing communications within a recall plan**

Operations and communication must share the same close relationship in recalls as in other types of crisis-threatening popular products and brands. Failure to do so can jeopardize the success of the recall and public trust in the company itself. Perrier managers discovered this when an FDA laboratory in North Carolina found benzene traces in their bottled water, sold in the USA as 'chic, sophisticated and pure'.[38] The amount varied from only 4 to 19 parts per billion, but benzene is a carcinogenic chemical. Source Perrier in France initially minimized the problem and left subsidiaries to manage their own responses. In Paris, a company spokesman speculated that the benzene was caused by a 'greasy rag'.[39] Rumours began to circulate that the problem was the Perrier spring itself, and the resulting confusion caused by conflicting messages undermined the confidence of the public. At one press conference Perrier 'evaded questions on the extent of the recall until frustrated reporters began to chant "the facts! The facts!" '.[40] When the company finally decided on a worldwide recall, the Paris news conference was flooded with the international press, as hundreds of journalists fought to get in.

Eventually, Perrier regained control of the crisis by a $30 million (25m Euros) recall of 160 million bottles worth around $70 million (60m Euros), tighter control of communication, and a carefully planned relaunch. A study conducted by the international 'Perception Management/Crisis Management' consultants Burson-Marsteller found 90 per cent of consumers believed the company acted responsibly.[41] Even under those favourable auspices there were problems. In the UK, for example, there were questions on why the new 75cl international-standard bottles were sold at only slightly less than the older one-litre bottles, and the supermarket chain J. Sainsbury refused to stock the product because it was labelled 'naturally carbonated'.[42] Ultimately share prices did not fully recover, and Perrier was taken over by Nestlé. The original problem was eventually discovered to be a faulty filter at the bottling plant.

Management must be ready to reply to queries and explain the situation in a coherent, consistent and prompt manner. Advertisements, letters, telephone briefing scripts, press releases and briefings to employees and salesforce were created by Quaker Oats in the UK for use in sixteen markets for the recall of 'Honey Monster' and 'Sugar Puffs' breakfast cereals.[43] Fisher-Price prepared a website to support its recall of 10 million 'Power Wheels' children's vehicles in October 1998. The site offered:

1.   Updates on the progress of the recall.
2.   Press releases.
3.   The identification of local service centres.
4.   Lists of unaffected models.
5.   Words and pictures explaining where the problem lay.
6.   A search engine for customers to determine whether their models were affected.
7.   Contacts for further questions.[44]

Once consumer concerns begin to ease, an assessment can be made of future options beyond recall, including relaunch. See page 129 for a fuller review of the relaunch option.

Litigation crises

Litigation raises unique challenges in crisis communication. A legal system usually reflects the history, outlook and preoccupations of a particular country, and it is difficult to establish an approach to legal crises that works across all countries or cultures. In Japan, where public confrontation is discouraged, it is routine for damage claims to take over a decade. Two thousand victims of mercury poisoning at the Japanese port of Minimata in 1955 took 40 years to reach a settlement. In America 'Litigation PR' is a distinct and highly controversial discipline, employing high-profile methods outside the courtroom to influence events inside. A particular approach taken by a company on trial in one country may not work in another, although it could still suffer consequences in both.

Another complication is the relationship between crisis deadlines and litigation timescales. Legal strategy and consequent tactics – especially when facing liability claims – can be planned in terms of years, against a series of fallback positions and strategies. Meanwhile, crises can be measured in deadlines of hours, and often minutes when the electronic media have been engaged by the situation.

Litigation in the wake of death and injuries can confront multinationals in any country and any region. It consumes valuable corporate time and energy. Victims may decide to go to law regardless of the company's initial response, giving fresh life to media coverage, putting new strain on the corporation's public reputation, and heightening the tension between the need to respond and comment or stick to a self-imposed silence. American airline companies, unlike some of their Asian and European competitors, have traditionally been more reluctant to offer financial help to victims' families because of fear that it will be seen as admitting liability. A. H. Robins dragged its feet over the Dalkon Shield IUD, and reacted so aggressively to lawsuits filed by injured women that in the end one angry federal judge ordered investigators into the company, who discovered substantial evidence that management knew the Shield's dangers years before they conceded as much to the public.[45] Seven years after the Bhopal tragedy, with many cases unresolved, the Indian government issued an arrest warrant for the former chief executive of Union Carbide, Warren Anderson, which drew heavy media coverage. 'It is likely', predicted one academic article on public disclosure, 'that Union Carbide will continue to experience much negative publicity associated with each stage of the settlement process.'[46] Foodmaker, the parent of *e.coli*-tainted Jack In The Box burgers, reacted to the breaking crisis by soliciting victims, some of whom were in hospital, to sign releases which in return for a few hundred dollars would prevent legal action.[47]

Sexual harassment is another common cause of litigation in the USA. The damaging consequences of Mitsubishi's first ill-judged and arrogant reaction to the lawsuits filed by victims of sexual harassment in Normal, Illinois have already been discussed in this book.[48] In a 1991 survey, over 90 per cent of Fortune 500 companies ran programmes to educate employees on the subject of unwelcome verbal or physical sexual attention. For many corporations, isolated incidents may not be an incentive to tackle the problem but the threat of mass actions by several employees can be very unwelcome. Astra USA, with 1500 employees located in a Boston suburb, is an arm of a Swedish pharmaceutical company that makes asthma medications and a popular anaesthetic, Xylocaine. In 1996, six former employees filed a federal lawsuit alleging that Astra's US executives created 'an organised pattern of sexual harassment in order to satisfy their personal desires'. Lars Bildman, head of Astra USA, was accused of replacing older and married women with 'extremely attractive' younger women and of pressuring female employees to have sex.[49] The three targeted executives and Bildman denied the allegations, but Astra AB, the parent company in Sweden, suspended and later fired Bildman and his officers, recognized that it was at fault by ignoring earlier complaints and instituted staff training about harassment and discrimination.

Astra, in short, effectively applied the principles of crisis communication despite the legal dimensions of its crisis:

- **Public contrition.** Silence does not reduce the likelihood of lawsuits. Albright & Wilson refused to acknowledge letters or calls from

Greenpeace over their emissions into the Irish Sea until they were taken to court for breaking pollution laws. Lawyers feel compelled to avoid disclosure to lessen the danger of litigation, but many crisis managers argue that a positive approach to communication will silence or quell indignation. James Lukaszwieski, an experienced crisis consultant, has described the components of 'trust-busting' behaviour: avoidance of comment, placing communication solely in the hands of lawyers and only talking to fend off litigation.[50] Astra AB's spokesman made no effort to evade the issue: 'I will not defend this in any way . . . It is an awful mess and it is very important that we clear it up.'[51]

- **Taking responsibility.** Hakan Mogren, Astra AB's chief executive, did not hide behind legal obfuscation and, apparently satisfied by the evidence, told reporters that some of the allegations were probably true, a statement repeated by Astra's spokesman in the USA.[52]

- **Isolating the problem by rapid and positive action.** Astra AB quickly separated itself from its Astra USA subsidiary, fielding awkward media speculation that executives at the parent company must have known about Bildman's activities during his 15-year tenure as chief executive in America before *Business Week* faxed them its exposé in April 1996 – especially given numerous visits made by Swedish executives to the American facility, and the fact that, as a respected author and business commentator in Sweden observed to an American reporter, 'Office parties can be kind of feisty here.'[53] Feistiness notwithstanding, Astra's new US team launched an internal investigation, suspended several senior US executives within days, created a vice-president for Human Resources and installed a hotline for Astra employees to talk anonymously with company investigators. An interim chief executive, dispatched from Sweden, undertook to take calls from employees for one hour a week. These measures won praise from the local director of '9 to 5', the National Association of Working Women: 'I'm used to hearing about companies that dismiss sexual harassment, don't take it very seriously, avoid it, don't want to think about it. I really have to praise Astra for taking it very seriously.'[54]

- **Timely communication with employees.** On 12 May, a day before *Business Week* published the article that broke the scandal, the acting head of Astra USA sent a memo to staff pointing out: 'Your family, friends, and neighbors will undoubtedly have many comments and questions about this article', and asking – not ordering – them to 'please keep in mind Astra AB acted promptly upon learning of the serious allegations that it raises'.[55] As the incoming team began to take apart Bildman's system, some employees began publicly to endorse the reforms. 'Now, men and women who have been harassed know they have the law on their side', one worker reported after a training session on harassment. 'Previously, you were alone.'[56]

• **Rebuilding.** As Astra's messages fell into place, the media began to concentrate on the record of Lars Bildman and his wayward associates, rather than the company. The new team at Astra USA turned the crisis into an opportunity to show its commitment to what Lynn Tetrault, the new head of Human Resources, described as 'major cultural change'. A work–family taskforce was launched to help employees balance their work and personal lives; potted plants and family photos were permitted on walls; and lunch no longer had to be taken at set times. 'We have shifted to a new CEO with a vastly different style, one that is more inclusive and team oriented', Tetrault explained to a reporter from the local *Boston Globe*, while also recognizing that much remained to be done.[57] A follow-up story in *Business Week* observed that: 'To some degree, demonizing Bildman may serve to deflect blame from Astra itself', but backed the internal 'housecleaning' effort by concluding that Astra USA 'already has done more than most companies in similar circumstances'.[58]

• **Quick settlements.** Speedy and just settlement in litigation crises bring a degree of closure for many victims and for a company's external and internal audiences. By September 1996, Astra USA had reached out-of-court settlements with twelve former employees who complained of sexual harassment, leaving at least seven more cases to be agreed. In April 1997, a federal judge ruled that the parent company was not responsible for the actions of its US managers. Foodmaker came to realize the value of this approach after its earlier assertiveness to *e.coli* victims. A $44.5 million class-action suit brought by franchisees was settled a few months after the tragedy, a shareholder class-action for over $8 million three years later, and agreements were reached with 500 victims for amounts between several thousand and $15 million.[59] Foodmaker's chairman and president often attended mediation hearings in person.

The official responsible for family affairs at the US Transportation Safety Board has observed at first hand the value of an open, concerned and prompt corporate response:

> Many family members I've talked to in the past have said they didn't really want to file suits, but they just felt like the airline

didn't care, and the airline and the underwriters gave them such a hard time that they were going to sort of punish them.[60]

Endnote: crime

Crime has been ranked among the most likely causes of crisis by senior executives in the UK,[61] perhaps because this subversive threat seems the least controllable and most unpredictable. Crime is a species of crisis that should be noted here but not, regrettably, in detail since the tactical or strategic principles involved must be discussed with corporate management in terms of client confidentiality. In general, however:

- Companies face criminal threats in markets around the world, including:
  1. Criminal threat and extortion.
  2. Consumer terrorism, a term used to cover on-shelf tampering and malicious product tampering.
  3. Blackmail.
  4. Kidnapping.
- The handling of these complex and difficult situations varies from market to market and depends on the law enforcement agencies and laws of the countries involved.
- Companies need to recognize these as areas of risk where they can become targeted by criminal elements (and sometimes discontented or malicious employees). In planning for these eventualities they should seek the advice of law enforcement agencies and the support of consultants and agencies who specialize in crisis management and security matters.
- Special communication restraints will apply under these circumstances when security and sensitivity concerns may impose limits on how, what and when information can be communicated to internal and external audiences.

Summary

Certain types of crisis require special techniques.

Rumour management

- Rumours among external audiences:
  1. Can hibernate.

2. Can generate problems regardless of a company's previous good name.
3. Do not have to be media events. They need only reach key audiences to be effective.

A three-tiered approach to a rumour should be considered:

Ignore it. Rumours can vanish as swiftly as they arise.
Isolate it. Contain the problem, either geographically or by addressing the key audiences involved.
Fight it. The last step is a comprehensive public assault on the rumour, including:
   1. Monitoring.
   2. Lawsuits.
   3. Information campaigns.
   4. Third-party endorsement.
   5. Removing the excuse for the rumour.
- Rumours within the company:
   1. Accept that rumours always generate interest.
   2. Accept that silence invites speculation.
   3. Find ways of establishing details of rumours.
   4. Be ready to communicate to counter rumour or correct inaccuracies or speculation.
   5. Dispel rumour by informing management and employees *before* they hear news from other sources.
   6. Never put managers in a position whereby their people ask them about something they have not been told.
   7. Accept that once you have started communicating, you will have to continue. The tap cannot be turned off.
   8. Be frank with your employees whenever possible.

Product recall

Effective recalls face several obstacles:

- media perception that the recall is not 'newsworthy';
- consumer belief that the news is not relevant to them;
- 'recall saturation'. The public receives so many recall warnings that critical messages may be lost or forgotten.

A number of factors govern recall success:

- clarity and promptness of action;
- balancing the cost of reputation;
- defining the risks and scope of the recall problem;
- coordinated communications within the recall plan.

Litigation crises

Despite the unique sensitivities of litigation, the principles of crisis communication can often be applied in close consultation with legal counsel:

- Public contrition.
- Isolating the problem by rapid and positive action. Take immediate steps to show that you are sensitive to the issues raised by the litigation.
- Timely communication with employees.
- Rebuilding. Show that you have learned and changed from the experience.
- Quick settlement. Speedy and just settlement in litigation crises helps bring a degree of closure for many victims and for a company's external and internal audiences.

Notes

1   *Business Week*, 11 September 1995.
2   'They're all in it together: Americans and conspiracies'. *New Statesman & Society*, 29 September 1995.
3   *ibid.*
4   Rosenberger, Rob. *The Fresno Bee*, 15 December 1996.
5   'Procter & Gamble's devil of a problem: Anti-satanism watchdogs turn up the heat'. *Washington Post*, 15 July 1991.
6   'Procter & Gamble: Fighting the enduring persistence of a popular urban legend'. www.atheists.org/flash.line/p&g.htm
7   'P&G obtains $75,000 judgment in Satanism suit'. *PR Newswire*, 19 March 1991; 'P&G bedeviled once again by satanism rumors'. *Detroit News*, 5 September 1995.
8   Mintz, Gilda. 'Making professional services grow'. *Public Relations Journal*, May 1992.
9   'Pentium flap gives birth to rogue Intel site'. *Forbes*, 6 October 1997.
10   'Loose lips can sink sales: rumormongers damage company images'. *Los Angeles Times*, 16 August 1987.
11   Mintz, Gilda. *op. cit.*
12   'The facts about Procter & Gamble's trademark'. 15 January 1999. http://www.pg.com/rumor/index.html

13   Vidal, John. *McLibel*. London: Pan, 1997.

14   'P&G obtains $75,000 judgment in Satanism suit'. *PR Newswire*, 19 March 1991.

15   'P&G sues over rumor'. *Advertising Age*, 11 September 1995.

16   'Procter & Gamble: Fighting the enduring persistence of a popular urban legend'. *op. cit.*

17   'P&G bedeviled once again by satanism rumors'. *Detroit News*, 5 September 1995.

18   'Kaiser Intranet lets employees rant'. *Forbes*, 6 October 1997.

19   Seymour, M. Product safety under public scrutiny'. In Hodges, C., Tyler, M. and Abbott, H. *Product Safety*. London: Sweet & Maxwell, 1991, pp. 310–11.

20   *1997 Review of Crisis and Risk Management*. London: Infoplan International.

21   'UK product recalls', 4 June 1999. http://www.xodesign.co.uk/tsnet/pages/recall.htm.

22   'Recalls: FDA, industry cooperate to protect consumers'. *FDA Consumer*. October 1995. More information on the FDA's recall and other activities can be obtained at their website: http://www.fda.gov/ or contacting: FDA (HFE-88), 5600 Fishers Lane, Rockville, MD 20857, USA.

23   'Training to be calm in a crisis'. *PR Week*, 17 February 1995.

24   Gibson, Dirk C. 'Public relations considerations of consumer product recalls'. *Public Relations Review*, no. 3, vol. 21, 22 September 1995, p. 225.

25   Selzer, H. 'Summary memo of working group on product recalls, Office of Special Adviser to the President for Consumer Affairs'. 23 May 1990, p. 3.

26   Gibson, Dirk C. *op. cit.*

27   These factors are adopted and adapted from Seymour, M. In *Product Safety*. *op. cit.*

28   'Certain Lifescan Surestep Glucose Meters recalled'. *Health Canada Warning*, 31 July 1998.

29   Seymour, M. In *Product Safety*, *op. cit.*, p. 311.

30   *ibid.*

31   'Life brand olive oil recalled'. *Health Canada Warning*, 14 August 1998.

32   'Recalls: FDA, industry cooperate to protect consumers'. *FDA Consumer*. October 1995.

33   'Regulation of product recalls'. Discussion Paper. *Federal Bureau of Consumer Affairs*. Canberra, Australia. February 1997.

34   'Product safety recalls website project', *c.* January 1999. http://recalls.consumer.gov.au/info.html

35   Smith, Craig, and Thomas, Robert and Quelch, John. 'A strategic approach to managing product recalls'. *Harvard Business Review*, September 1996, p. 102.

36   *ibid.*

37   Seymour, M. In *Product Safety, op. cit.*, p. 315.

38   'Perrier's crisis management strategy was put severely to the test when disaster struck earlier this year'. *Management Today*, August 1990.

39   *ibid.*

40   Crumley, B. 'Fizzz went the crisis'. *International Management*, p. 45. Cited in Gibson, Dirk C. *op. cit.*, p. 225.

41   'Perrier launches comeback'. *Boston Globe*, 2 May 1990.

42   'Perrier claims recapture of market lead after sales freeze'. *Financial Times*, 21 April 1990.

43   Seymour, M. In *Product Safety, op. cit.*, p 315.

44   'Power wheels safety notification and replacement plan', 29 November 1999. Fisher-Price. http://www.powerwheels.com/special/affected.html

45   Kaufmann, J., Kesner, I. F., and Hazen, T. L. 'The myth of full disclosure: a look at organizational communications during crises'. *Business Horizons*, vol. 37, no. 4, p. 29, July 1994.

46   *ibid.*

47   'Jack In The Box agrees to quit asking for releases from e.coli victims'. *Seattle Times*, 6 March 1993.

48   See page 24.

49   'The astonishing tale of sexual harassment at Astra USA'. *Business Week*, 13 May 1996.

50   Lukaszwieski, James. 'Establishing individual and corporate crisis communication standards'. *Public Relations Quarterly*, no. 3, vol. 42, 22 September 1997, p. 7.

51   'Astra looks to enforce harassment policy'. *Boston Globe*, 7 May 1996.

52   'New Astra CEO makes changes. In Sweden, sex harassment dominates Annual Meeting'. *Boston Globe*, 14 May 1996.

53   'In Sweden, Astra tries to dance around scandal spotlight'. *Boston Globe*, 24 June 1996.

54   'Astra looks to enforce harassment policy'. *Boston Globe*, 7 May 1996.

55   *ibid.*

56   ' "Going a new way." Still under cloud of lawsuits, Westborough firm working to redefine corporate culture'. *Boston Globe*, 4 December 1996.

57   *ibid.*

58   'Day of reckoning at Astra'. *Business Week*, 8 July 1996.

59   'Jack In The Box rises from the ashes of crisis'. *San Diego Union-Tribune*, 10 August 1997.

60   'Moments that build or destroy reputations'. *Financial Times*, 29 September 1998.

61   *1997 Review of Crisis and Risk Management. op. cit.*

6 Issues management and risk communication

Two linked disciplines

Risks comprise real or perceived threats (to health, safety, financial or general well-being), which trigger concerns, and then fears. Few products or services today do not have a risk attached to them:

- risks in production
- risks in use
- risks in disposal
- risks inherent in inappropriate management behaviour
- risks caused by inappropriate handling, use or consumption.

If there are no risks attached to a product or service (which would be unusual in the commercial world), an issue may hang over the company itself. An issue is created by discussion, debate, or outright conflict of opinions – usually with a scientific, technical or medical content or other input which raises complex problems and communication challenges. Such issues may be driven by any one or combination of factors:

- environmental
- ethical or moral
- related to health or safety
- related to an aspect of social justice such as employment equity, discrimination, inappropriate language or sexual harassment
- related to international issues such as cheap labour or political oppression
- cultural differences: at its most extreme but perhaps most vivid, one perennial problem facing US or European multinational executives is: 'do we give "favours", or do we lose valuable business because we do not follow local custom to oil the wheels of regulation and permissions?'

Some companies deal with both issues and risks in their various operations. From the perspective of communication, the specific problem is less significant than its potential to rouse public concerns or fears, attract attention and comments of 'experts' and interest groups, which in the process attracts media attention and results in widespread discussion and analysis of every aspect of the issue. This effectively inflames the worries and fears of all parties. It is usually wisest for a company to communicate about its issue *before* the crisis, and before the task of explanation is made much more difficult under the giant pall cast by dramatic events.

Issues and risk management is often, as noted in Chapter 1, a slow-moving business that lifts, or is lifted, in and out of the public domain. The contributing factors may take months or even years to move onto converging paths – let alone combust together – and become a matter of public and media interest. The slow movements and accumulation of factors, and the fluctuating nature of issues, are the aspects that challenge companies. They must anticipate the point at which an issue or crisis is *approaching* the public domain or has crossed the line between issues management and crisis management.

Companies that have identified an approaching issue or risk before it has exploded into crisis must give careful thought to the nature of their communication: it involves education, dialogue and persuasion rather than promotion, debate or dictation. On occasion, it must even be continuous, a point made by Shell UK in *Brent Spar: A Drop in the Ocean?* In the 1970s the international oil companies in the North Sea

> were seen as the nation's saviours . . . We rode high in public esteem. We communicated a lot of what we were doing . . . and then we reached the stage where we said that 'everyone knows this stuff, it costs us a lot of money to do all this communicating, let's not bother any more'.

'We have failed', wrote Hunt, 'to continue to communicate to people the benefits that they get in the UK from having an offshore oil and gas industry.'[1] Given the dramatic reaction to the Brent Spar crisis in Germany described in the preceding chapters, it is plain that Shell's failure to communicate fully on the issue of North Sea oil also affected other parts of Europe.

The longer a sensitive problem is ignored, the greater is the potential for physical and corporate damage. This principle is exemplified by the mass poisoning at Minimata Bay in Japan, caused when Chisso Corporation dumped organic mercury compounds into the sea. The tragedy took 40 years to resolve, became a symbol for the environmental damage created by Japan's postwar boom, and in the words of the Japanese Prime Minister who announced the final settlement: 'has often been referred to as the first disease caused by pollution'.[2] For Chisso, the hundreds of deaths and thousands of injuries also represented a financial burden, aside from the fact that it would be linked with Minimata. The 'association factor' lingers over other companies: Union Carbide and Bhopal; Exxon, the *Exxon Valdez* and oil spills; the *Herald of Free Enterprise*, ferry safety, and P&O.

Although the tactics for tackling issues and risks are often interchangeable, there are important differences between the two fields which occur at an earlier stage. It is helpful to review those differences before discussing programme development.

Issues are social concerns

Issues management is the attempt to form and shape public opinion on subjects which both the communicator and audience deem of wider concern to society. It is often used on behalf of worthy causes and helpful products; in 1991, for example, the Wellcome Foundation launched a successful media campaign in the UK to raise awareness of cold sores and their treatment; but issues management can also be a valuable component of crisis management. We have already seen that issues management is the *raison d'être* of interest groups, and often of politicians. Many of the issues they pursue have an impact on business. In turn, some companies track issues that may affect their operations, and create programmes which enable them to present their own point of view, preferably while public opinion is still largely undecided and open to persuasion.

To fail to prepare fully is dangerous because every company carries the potential for issues to hit them at any time. Corporate crises are prolonged and complicated when a neglected issue seasons the initial event with outrage. Many crises are eminently preventable, or can at least be contained, if companies tackle those pre-existing problems. In some cases, several of which are discussed in this chapter, companies courageously bring issues to the attention of the public on their own initiative, turning issues management into a form of crisis prevention.

Risks are personal fears

When an influential audience feels personally threatened by an organization, that organization is presented with a problem of risk communication. A risk is more volatile than an issue. Instincts are age-old and not always rational: the rituals that surround nomadic cultures, or the paleolithic hunters and their quarry who stalk across the cave walls of western Europe, illustrate that humanity has sought to face and cope with its worst fears from the very earliest times. Modern worries over health, safety and the environment indicate that people today remain as fearful as at any other period in history. Illness, accidents, random acts of violence, authority, even eating safely or healthily are all subjects that have long preoccupied humanity.

The constant need to face and cope with fear is of course a tacit admission that fear is not likely to be totally defeated. If one illness is conquered, another rises to take its place in public discussion; if a company handling toxic materials has an accident-free record, another company may be less fortunate; if we avoid beef to avert mad cow disease, should we also worry about the risk from scrapie in sheep? If we refuse all meat products, do we need to be concerned about our exposure to pesticides and fungicides used on fruit and vegetables?

If there are differences between the fear of yesterday and today, they are – from the point of view of crisis communicators – that new technology always plays an enlarged role, creating new things to fear and new ways to transmit and enlarge that fear; and, less immediately obvious, that groups and governments in our increasingly complex society can intervene in more detail to shape individual attitudes to risks or danger. Risk communication has evolved because organizations have found it necessary to explain their activities to these audiences. Neglecting a risk, or failing to explain adequately can ensure that crises and issues are occasionally triggered by a stimulating infusion of public fear. At the turn of the twentieth century, Upton Sinclair, one of the original crusading journalists dedicated to exposing business greed and cruelty, attempted to expose the atrocious conditions suffered by workers in the slaughterhouses of Chicago. He wrote *The Jungle*, a book which shocked the American public and helped bring radical changes to standards in America's stockyards and canneries. The reason for its success was quite unexpected: Americans did not like the idea of eating contaminated food. As Sinclair himself put it: 'I aimed at the public's heart but by accident I hit it in the stomach.'[3] The US Congress was bombarded with complaints from angry and scared voters. A series of reforms of the food industry passed quickly into law and pushed out smaller, badly run meat packers to the benefit of big business. Inadvertently, Sinclair had triggered the fear needed to bring social change.

Risks are less rational than issues

The environment for a risk is often more chaotic than for an issue. Issues generate general concern and discussion which may accumulate in the form of gradual public pressure. Risks usually generate personal fear, which contains an emotional element. Attitudes to risks then become driven by perceptual values, which creates unfamiliarity and distorts judgement of personal risks from competing risk factors. These irrational elements, in their turn, contribute to perceptions of company reputation and corporate responsibility. Corporate management does not always appreciate the role played by fear and emotion, and resorts to 'corporate speak' and cold responses. A good risk communications strategy recognizes the following assumptions:

- Fear is based on emotional responses.
- Fear cannot be dismissed; it will not go away.
- The risk does not have to be real; it has only to be perceived.
- Fear has a massive influence on public attitudes and actions.
- Fear feeds crisis.
- Personal fear is a more powerful force than concern for others.
- Fear is countered by empathy, attentiveness and education.

The unreality of some risks is perhaps hardest for a business to understand or appreciate unless, like Shell, you have been at the centre of a crisis which has apparently been triggered and escalated by threats based on misconceptions and distortion, exaggeration and scare tactics by other parties.

Modern reactions to risk are also heavily influenced by the actions of statutory authorities which can, if not educated about the scare, damage companies by precipitate action. When there are several governments involved, each with its own domestic agenda to pursue, the capacity of risk communications to tackle the problem is severely tested. In 1994 and 1995, for instance, official over-reaction to a non-existent risk created an international crisis of confidence in Australia's A\$3 billion a year beef industry (US \$1.9bn, 1.6bn Euros), sparked the agricultural industry's biggest ever lawsuit, and in the opinion of the Cattlemen's Union president, created an industrial relations débâcle for the industry's image and market share.

A drought in Queensland and New South Wales in 1994 had led beef farmers to feed their herds on 'cotton trash,' high-protein pellets of cotton leaf made from the local crop. The beef was destined for export to Asia and the USA, until random abbatoir samplings discovered traces of a ton-toxic pesticide, Chlorfluazuron (CFZ). The culprit was swiftly unmasked as Helix, an ICI spray used on cotton plants to destroy caterpillars.

Researchers also discovered that the detected levels of CFZ were minimal and that the beef was safe. 'You would have to eat about 30 tonnes of meat with high levels of contamination at one sitting for it to have any detrimental effect on human health', an industry official pointed out.[4] Indeed, the news made no impact on Australian consumers. Overseas, the story was dramatically different, and the logic harder to swallow. Some official agencies, including the USA, had never heard of CFZ before, but the dread word 'pesticide' was all that was needed to provoke a response. Government agencies in six countries held up Australian beef imports, trapping A$250 million (US $159m, 137m Euros) worth of product in the export pipeline. The issue became front-page news. Schools and shops from Japan to the USA voluntarily withdrew Australian beef. Cattle producers were outraged. It was absurd, fumed the Executive Director of Australia's Meat Council, that a pesticide harmless to humans could create such turmoil and sully Australia's reputation as a healthy beef producer.[5]

The scale of the misperception nonetheless pushed Australian authorities into action to restore confidence. A rigorous on-farm testing regime was introduced in October. Any herds found to be affected were placed in immediate quarantine. After a few weeks the bans were lifted, although the USA held out for a month, perhaps in part because of greater sensitivity toward health scares. By February 1995 exports to Japan, the biggest market, had returned to normal levels, but other economic troubles plunged the sector back into crisis by September.

The legacy of the scare was remarkable but not untypical for a crisis provoked by a 'risky' product. CFZ created 'an astounding and unwarranted impact', noted an industry scientist.[6] The pesticide was not harmful to human health, yet the stubborn fear that somehow a risk *might* exist had done damage. Although the export bans had been shortlived, the main importers treated the product more cautiously over the next five months. Many Japanese and Taiwanese consumers continued to avoid Australian beef. South Korea banned Queensland and New South Wales beef producers from a major tender for its 1995 frozen beef, although Australian officials gave assurances that the situation was under control. The Australian Government paid over A$6 million (US $3.8m, 3.3m Euros) in compensation to farmers. Expensive 'reassurance campaigns' were planned for Japan and the USA; costs had been imposed by the new testing, by holding the product in warehouses and the dislocation to shipping. A A$125 million suit (US $79m, 68m Euros) was launched by beef farmers against government authorities and ICI, the maker of the ill-fated and officially harmless pesticide. The government minister responsible criticized the industry for being 'very patchy in recognizing the commercial imperative to address food safety issues'.[7] Then, as in every crisis, came the expensive task of recovery. 'The reality is', declared the chief executive of the Australian Meat and Livestock Corporation, 'we still have to work hard commercially again in regaining the confidence of our customers, our reputation, our standing in the international food community.'[8]

Can effective communication make a difference when faced by an irrational response to a 'threat', perhaps occurring on a global scale? What should go into a programme of issues management or risk communication? The next section describes operational necessities and tactical options.

Building a programme

Identify the perceived issue or risk

A crisis, risk or issue is rarely what the affected company thinks it to be once it enters the public domain and is exposed to the attitudes or agendas of other audiences. In spite of what a company may be doing internally to address a particular problem, the external view might persist that the business is dirty, greedy, dishonest or dangerous. Those public attitudes may represent old, outdated viewpoints, but nonetheless they will exist and persist. Identifying underlying fears or concerns obliges a company to treat a problem as something other than a matter to be resolved by technical or legal applications.

An issue or risk strategy must first research beyond a specific incident to seek those fears or concerns. For example:

Event	*Perceived issues/risks*
Racial, sexual or ethnic harassment	You tolerate abuses of power or position. You do not recognize the rights of minorities and genders. You are liars. You are not in control of your own company. Your employees live in fear.
Fraud/embezzlement	Your company does not have adequate financial controls in place. You do not care about your shareholders. You lied and covered up.
Aeroplane crash	You are unsafe. Your employees are badly trained. You do not care about the victims. You put profits before people. Your aircraft are underserviced.

Illness or harm caused by a product or service	You are unsafe.
	You have ignored dangers or safety needs.
	Profits are more important to you than people.
	You do not care about the weak, the vulnerable or your victims.
Hazardous or toxic emissions, spills or leaks	You put profits before people.
	You are unsafe.
	You do not care about the environment or the community.
	You have broken regulations or safety procedures.

You do not care; you are not safe; you neglect important problems until it is too late; you are greedy. If the event occurs abroad, the damaging words 'you are a foreign multinational' may also be pronounced to weight attitudes against your operations and management. If such perceptions are not addressed at the heart of a communications programme, they will harden into opinion.

Define the objective

The prime objective of communication – the shaping of opinions and attitudes to secure total acceptance of your point of view – is difficult to reach in societies where freedom of speech encourages constant competition between messages as well as products. Nonetheless, a few near-triumphs have occurred, usually at the expense of the business rather than its critics. The decline of the asbestos industry charted on page 23 owed much to a consistent failure by companies to respond to growing public concern about the risks inherent in the product; while the demonization of tobacco also owed a great deal to corporate inactivity in the face of mounting scientific evidence and expert lobbying from the 1960s until recent years.

The problems of asbestos and tobacco might be dismissed as inevitable; but it should be remembered that the asbestos industry comprised a series of large, confident blue-chip companies, and cigarettes were part of mainstream fashion rather than a subversive exercise in stress relief. Moreover, other hazardous products continue to exist and to prosper, and deal fairly and effectively with criticism. Why not asbestos or tobacco? Late and ineffective communication on risk contributed to their difficulties.

On the whole, however, ultimate and permanent victories of one view over another are rare and therefore the progress of a long programme of communication is hard to distill into concrete, measurable objectives, unlike other forms of business activity. Issues and risks are tied to ideas and perceptions and these, perhaps fortunately, are nebulous: shifting, constantly adapting, and resistant to easily quantifiable consumer-based strategies of 'hard sell'.

It is more helpful to examine the needs of specific audiences that are usually the same as those facing companies in a crisis. The objectives differ, and there is more time available to communicate.

- **Key influencers.** The individuals and groups seeking to drive and shape the debate around an issue; the experts whose opinions and research is sought; the civil servants and politicians whose decisions could have legislative impact; representatives of opposed or supportive interest groups.

  Objectives: to build firm and lasting contacts with your key influencers; to provide non-controversial platforms for discussion or to provide information on new developments; to become a credible, authoritative contributor to the issue under discussion.

- **The community.** The towns, villages or regions with a direct stake in the issue or risk; the families, local businesses, local politicians and media, voluntary organizations, schools and churches.

  Objectives: to be seen as a good neighbour. A participant in local activities, a contributor to local causes, an accessible source of information, open to dialogue, and as interested in improving and protecting the neighbourhood as any other resident.

- **The national and international media.** The correspondents specializing in your issue, region, or popular with key influencers.

  Objectives: to create authoritative platforms for communicating your key messages; to become a source of public comment on the issue or risk; to provide correspondents with the necessary ideas, news, resources and expertise to develop features or reports; to demonstrate impartiality by directing the media to independent experts and opinion.

- **Your 'general public'.** The *general* public does not exist. Save in the worst of controversies when literally everyone is interested, it is more usual for every issue and risk to have a *specific* public – the individuals or groups who are most affected, who are most likely to follow the issue closely and who become the *vox populi* in any form of public discussion: it might be the elderly, children (and by extension parents), community or religious leaders, women, or a particular profession.

Objectives: to demonstrate concern, commitment and compassion; to show that you fully understand the human side of the problem; to empathize with the emotions that lead public opinion; to put a face to the utterances of a faceless corporation; to demonstrate by words and deeds that you share their concerns and are equally committed to resolving them.

For specific issues, a critical step is to rate each audience on a plus or minus scale to decide their attitudes and thus their likely actions and response. A scaling might appear on these lines:

Financial Analysts
Local communities   **Industry experts**
Activists   **Researchers**   **Employees**
Extreme Negative   →   *Extreme Positive*

The strategy-building process then proceeds through:

- **What do our audiences think and feel now?** A thorough identification of their concerns.
- **What do we want them to think and feel?** The required messages and communications actions on our part break down into:
  1. supporting those on the positive end of the scale.
  2. encouraging those in the middle to move towards the positive end or at least stay in the centre.
  3. pulling as many of those on the negative side towards the middle and the positive end of the scale.
  4. if necessary, block those far out to the negative end of the attitude scale to minimize their influence on other audiences.
- **How do we tell them?** Coordinating overall message tracks or lists and communication actions to ensure consistency, coherence and effective reach.

Develop a message

Belief in a point of view is not for sale. Society does not buy ideas in the same way that it buys products. It does not want to feel that it has been led or bullied into agreement. Your messages – the essential expressions of your ideas – coordinated across the company carefully as in a crisis (see 'Build a tactical framework' on page 172), must take account of these obstacles. There is a further problem. Most people will not approach your evidence with an open mind. They will have been influenced by existing principles, experience, outlook on life or feelings on related topics. The technical, health or safety record of a product may be excellent, but because it frightens people or can be linked to other issues of concern the product may still be distrusted. Instead, outsiders may see the product's manufacturers as over-complex, speaking a highly specialized language which is subject to misunderstanding. Good issues and risk communications transform argument into clear, simple messages which can be handled easily by the media and consequently understood by the general public.

Messages are also distorted by time pressures. An issue generally revolves around a subject of universal concern such as discrimination or respect for the environment; the sense of a direct personal threat is less imminent. When a significant percentage of the audience feels *personally* threatened, the issue accelerates into a risk, and the scope for offering a logical, long explanation is constrained by increases in levels of personal emotion. That emotion is based on fear, and it has been shown that fear is hard to assuage by science.

For these reasons, a well-prepared and well-delivered message about an issue or risk does not give the impression of trying to change people's minds. Instead:

- it demonstrates how a certain point of view complements *existing* beliefs or hopes of your audiences;
- it aligns with a carefully identified emotion, and takes 'ownership' of it;
- it expresses the social, non-economic as well as economic benefits of your point of view;
- it takes extreme care to select the terms and phrases. Individual words such as 'hazardous', 'sludge' or 'toxic' pack a powerful punch, and will be used as emotional shorthand by the media and your critics. A more informed and responsible message sets aside loaded phrases, while showing you understand the product must be treated carefully. In issues management careful employment of specific words can help to convey that your much-criticized idea actually contains value. It is an old approach. Ivy Lee, a pioneer of twentieth-century public relations, advised the Standard Oil billionaire John D. Rockefeller to avoid using

'such loaded terms as trust, monopoly, oligopoly, or cartel when referring to Standard Oil' and 'speak instead of "cooperation"'.[9]

- it avoids technical explanation. As with crises, issues and risks must be explained in the language of your audiences.

Used to support an honestly held and legitimate view, these approaches are the stuff of free speech in our age of mass communication. Interest groups communicate in precisely this manner. 'Oligopoly' and 'cooperation' can be equally subjective: both are legitimately used to illustrate a particular belief. Corporations are not always able to grasp this point. They are more used to communicating commercially about products, or within an industry. Their usual audiences speak the same language. Financial analysts, industry experts, customers, the 'trade': all view the world within similar parameters. An issue throws up a series of audiences with little or no understanding of what a company does or any of the commercial pressures and conditions which govern how businesses run and make profits.

Lay strategic foundations

Problems charged with emotion are rarely solved by an aggressive corporate response. The corporation's task is not only to have its say, but to ensure that what it has to say is accepted. Companies usually have to overcome instinctive suspicion or cynicism toward their activities, and in consequence their communications should aim to shed light rather than add to the heat of debate.

If the statement above could only be applied to one industry, it would arguably be nuclear energy, responsible for about 17 per cent of the world's electricity. The massive scale of the controversy that dogged nuclear power in the 1970s and 1980s forced the industry into communicating on the risks of nuclear energy to non-technical external audiences. Many companies, like Scottish Nuclear Limited, offer real and virtual tours of its plants and briefings on sensitive issues like the transport of radioactive waste and global warming. The Uranium Information Centre in Melbourne, Australia created resource papers for schoolchildren such as 'Uranium = Energy = the ability to do the work' and advocacy papers setting out the case for nuclear power. In London, the Uranium Institute provides quiz questions on the industry ('How much coal does it take to give the same amount of electricity as you can get from one kilogram of uranium?') and reviews of scientific research into the environmental record of nuclear power. The Nuclear Energy Institute in Washington has an online 'store' selling print and electronic publications including short videos such as 'Transportation of Used Nuclear Fuel' with 'dramatic crash test footage', 'designed for policymakers and the general public alike', and another that presents the history of nuclear energy 'untainted by pro- or anti-nuclear bias and unfiltered by narration'.[10]

Whatever one's opinions about nuclear matters or the originality of some of the initiatives, it is clear that the industry has learnt from the activities of its opponents. A massive and partially coordinated vehicle for public advocacy and explanation is rolling forward. It is international in scope, with the goal of making technology comprehensible, safeguards credible and risks acceptable. The nuclear industry's non-adversarial approach invites consideration of the strategic principles guiding issues and risk communication in general. Those principles include:

- **Education.** Encouraging an audience to look at an existing problem in a new way, or to think about a subject that it had never previously considered by a non-patronizing presentation of information that does not shirk difficult questions.
- **Persuasion.** Repeating the advantages inherent in your point of view to the community, the environment or society at large. Effective persuasion demonstrates to audiences that a company is not blinded by profit, but like them is capable of seeing the bigger picture.

Even when the issue has generated two sides, persuasion should not if possible be allowed to degenerate into debate. Debate usually polarizes sides and hardens attitudes, and businesses usually enter such debates at a disadvantage since, as research suggests, they are ranked among the least trustworthy sources of information.[11] Acceptance of communications requires a degree of trust. If the audience does not know or trust your company they will fail to listen, let alone understand your point of view. The public does not care how much you 'comply' with existing regulations. Compliance is the way companies themselves are inclined to measure their effectiveness and how safety and health standards are benchmarked: it is not communications. The public cares that you show that you care. Shell was forced to change course over Brent Spar because certain audiences, particularly German consumers, believed what Greenpeace told them. They went on believing the interest group even when it was revealed that Greenpeace's original allegations on the level of contaminants in the legs of the platform were over-estimated; few observers accused them of using scare tactics.

- **Dialogue.** Discussion and negotiation are part and parcel of business life; but in issues management they have a separate communication value, and indicate that you are receptive and adaptable. Dialogue does not mean first arriving at a decision, then presenting it to the local community and finally inviting them to talk about what has already been decided. Calls for dialogue are less likely to succeed if the public is convinced that your mind is already made up. Dialogue means, ideally, raising a problem or proposal at the earliest stage, away from the media spotlight, and listening to and accommodating suggestions.

There is no guarantee that everyone will be receptive. Some groups or individuals will have their minds made up on the issue; others may be automatically biased against business of all kinds. Usually, though, it is possible to identify opinion-formers who are willing to join a mutual search for solutions.

Build a tactical framework

The strategic imperatives of education, persuasion and dialogue require a framework. It should include some or all of the following elements, whose dual purpose is to communicate and coordinate an organization's key messages and activities.

- **Coalition-building**

Coalition-building describes the idea of uniting an industry around a single purpose under an umbrella organization. The Nuclear Energy Institute, for example, includes companies that operate nuclear energy plants in the USA and elsewhere. A coalition is an effective base for the promotion of an issue.

A coalition provides distance. It can present outside points of view some way from its corporate members. Industry spokespeople, independent expert opinion, press statements, sponsored events and even stationery demonstrate that the organization does not speak for a particular person or company, but for a group of like-minded organizations.

A coalition is 'objective'. One company with a point of view is more vulnerable to accusations of bias than an industry organization presenting the same point of view. 'Bias' is a particularly sensitive problem in issues management, especially for business, which can always be accused of putting profits before conscience or ethics. A coalition, launched with a clear identity to monitor events and coordinate action through its own offices or a consultancy, can present its views to audiences as matters of general and legitimate concern to an industry. For example, patient groups are a device used by pharmaceutical and healthcare companies to keep interested parties together and ready to handle or counter issues related to a drug or therapeutic area. Likewise, patient groups can form around a particular issue where victims seek influence through numbers. It is fair to say that some coalition-building can appear less legitimate: the anti-smoking lobby describes the objective coalitions defending smokers' rights as 'astro-turf' organizations – fake, covertly funded versions of their genuine 'grassroots' opponents. However, it has also been claimed that genuine smokers' groups are forming without the initiation or assistance of the tobacco industry, in a backlash to stringent laws and regulation.

A coalition improves consistency. Consistency is as difficult a goal to achieve in issues management as in crisis. It is, though, equally important. Differences of opinion among businesses over an issue, and failure to respond quickly to new differences, will be exploited by others. A coalition helps like-minded organizations to coordinate resources and ideas.

- **The Position Paper**

The coalition's task of coordination can be focused by a Position Paper, the foundation on which a programme is erected. The Position Paper is a report that:

1. Surveys the scientific, technical, economic and social evidence on the issue.
2. Explores the main opposing evidence and arguments.
3. Develops the main arguments in favour of the organization's viewpoint.
4. Provides the messages that the organization uses to transmit those arguments.
5. Is subject to periodic reviews in order to remain relevant.

In other words, a Position Paper is a campaign document that sets out the position for all those responsible for its communication. The paper does not need to provide the details of a communication strategy – those are equally substantial matters, constantly subject to change and review, that are best reserved for a separate document.

- **Objective platforms for delivering messages to key opinion-formers**

Accusations of bias usually hurt corporations much more than their critics, yet few messages are objective. Ivy Lee once provocatively suggested that the only 'fact' is a mathematical equation: everything else is a point of view.[12] Nevertheless, when it comes to sensitive issues, some influential or informed audiences prefer to rise above the emotional currents driving the issue or risk, and must be communicated with in a dispassionate, technical, detailed, evenhanded fashion. This is true of opinion-formers such as scientists, politicians, civil servants and journalists specializing in technical and scientific subjects. Suitable platforms are used to reinforce that impression. They might include:

1. sponsored scientific conferences;
2. media briefings led by a panel of respected independent experts;
3. one-to-one meetings between ministers and officials.

*   **Community relations**

As with crisis, every issue or risk has its local, regional or cultural dimensions. The quality of community relations often spells the difference between success and failure. Companies entering a district for the first time have new opportunities to build messages into their communications, tailored to local needs, without having them filtered through the national media.

In Western societies, the notion of good community relations is closely tied to openness. Openness in turn is closely tied to the idea of full and frank disclosure. If, for example, a district is concerned about the health or environmental impacts of a proposed landfill or drilling operation, or, even more dramatically, a nuclear power station, a well-intentioned corporation will often attempt to build its credentials by stressing its commitment to public consultation. Hearings, inquiries and information sessions have their place, but the larger the issue, the more contentious they can become, since the very openness of the process can encourage public posturing rather than constructive discussion; the participants find themselves negotiating through the press instead of with each other; attitudes harden under the delays, distractions and distrust.

While such efforts have a part to play, it is instructive to note that other corporations believe that open and forthright community relations can also operate on a less charged level. Even when a sensitive issue or risk is involved, communications between a corporation and community need not revolve solely around the problem itself. Some cultures, particularly those more sensitive to the prospect of confrontation, lend themselves to a more tangential approach to an issue or risk. Community relations in Japan, the anthropologist Brian Moeran notes, is characterized by 'a network of obligation and debt, *giri* and *ninjo*, of "unrequited passive love" and "presumption upon" others', that works to head off the discomforts of conflict.[13]

This form of consensus-building was employed by Tokyo Electric to construct a nuclear power station. The company's most important need, observed its chief executive, was to build friendly relations rather than provide logical explanations about the planned facility. Japan's intensely structured system of family, community and nation encouraged a direct approach to local residents: Tokyo Electric tapped into the area network of 'obligation and debt'. Local wives, who controlled their family's purse strings, were taken on tours of the site. They were led by another local woman who helped promote the benefits of nuclear power among her peers. The construction workers themselves were also integrated into the process of building relations. Before their work day began around dawn, they would go to local farms to help with weeding. Inevitably, they would be invited in for tea, and a direct and personal relationship with the company was established, based on more trust than could possibly be forged by public hearings on the actual issue or risk.

A smaller-scale but nonetheless instructive and equally indirect approach to a 'risky product' and community relations was exhibited in 1988 by MSA Management, the operators of a mall in the Bible belt of Atlanta, Georgia. One of the mall's tenants, a cinema, was scheduled to run Martin Scorcese's controversial *Last Temptation of Christ*. The film's roster of temptations included a sexually charged scene between Christ and Mary Magdalene, and a moment when Christ tore his heart from his chest and presented it to the astonished disciples. Anti-*Temptation* protests at other cinemas across America had been loud, lengthy and at times violent. MSA chose to provide local demonstrators with all the necessary amenities: an area was reserved for their exclusive use, with a sound system and portable toilets. 'It's because we realize everyone in this issue has rights', said an MSA spokesman. The company's imaginative approach to the issue helped it to maintain relations with both its tenants and its local customers by meeting the needs of both, instead of being forced to choose between them.[14]

- **Corporate responsibility**

Shell Nigeria does not just drill and refine oil. Its website details other work with the people of the Ogoni region. Shell builds classrooms, funds scholarships, makes roads, lays on water and conducted a $4.5 million environmental survey of the Niger Delta. The company, in fact, is aware and fully concedes that it is under fire for its environmental and human-rights performance from networked Western interest groups. It wants to ensure that its record of corporate social responsibility is as widely known as possible. Shell Nigeria is prepared to divert large sums of money away from its primary purpose of oil production and into other commercially unprofitable areas in order to assist its issues communication strategy.

Issues communication and enlightened self-interest enjoy a close relationship: examples are legion for critics and captains of industry from alcohol companies who launch 'designated driver' campaigns in big cities each holiday season, to Odwalla's modest 'Web Activism and NGOs' site where the fruit juice company provides links to interest groups like Friends of the Earth and Rainforest Action. Odwalla's even more eclectic 'Research' link connects internet surfers to the US Food and Drug Administration, the International Bulldozer Blockade, and many points between. There is increasing emphasis on the yardstick of responsibility in public assessments of company perform-ances. More particularly corporate responsibility is now seen as a gauge of care, commitment and ethical standards as shown by senior management.

Corporate responsibility brings its own difficulties. A business naturally understands the need to be competitive more clearly than the need to show that it is being responsible. Business goals are generally hard, clear and eminently measurable. But when corporate responsibility is discussed, per-formance and quality of management is being assessed against a series of differing and often conflicting definitions and measurements. Furthermore, those factors are often judged by individuals and groups outside the busi-nesses. Even Odwalla's message of responsibility is defied by other web pages attacking its apple juice in the wake of the *e.coli* scare. The Body Shop in Australia sells armbands calling on the government to defend aboriginal land, but is criticized for its own dealings with indigenous peoples in Brazil.

Consider the various factors which contribute to corporate responsi-bility. Companies might be judged on some or any of the following:

1. environmental care
2. ethical operations
3. cultural sensitiveness
4. political awareness
5. ethical investment
6. political correctness.

Nebulous though the term is, the weight of public expectation ensures that corporate responsibility often has a role to play in issues management. It may be as large as Shell Nigeria's or as modest as Odwalla's, but if a company is held to be irresponsible over a particular issue or risk, is it not sensible for it to integrate responsibility into its reply? A successful version of corporate responsibility may be found at British Petroleum (BP) Chemicals in Port Talbot in South Wales. A teacher from a local school spends up to a year working with BP Chemicals. The result is that a trusted member of the local community learns at first hand about the health, safety and environment (HS&E) ethos which runs through BP's activities. His or her views will always carry more weight than all the corporate statements, brochures or advertising materials put out by the company.

Regular measurement

Effective evaluation is a challenge to public relations in general, and issues management in particular. No hard and fast measures exist to gauge the true effectiveness of a message. In issues management the path between communicating an issue and securing a company's objectives can wind somewhat confusingly for definitive measurement. Asked many years ago by a client to promote bacon, the famous public relations consultant Edward Bernays devised an issue-led campaign in which eminent doctors spoke about the benefits of a hearty breakfast. 'But', a journalist later questioned, 'does a hearty breakfast mean bacon? And does bacon mean his client's bacon?'[15] How, then, can you tell if an issues campaign has been worth it? Ineffective evaluation feeds corporate doubt about issues management and non-marketing public relations in general.

Despite all the obsessive technology now available for microscopically accurate measurement in many areas of human activity, communication remains hard to pin down. This is unsurprising: public relations, and especially programmes dealing with issues and risk, must encompass a broad and shifting horizon composed of needs, products, events, attitudes, expectations and comment. Nor do corporations and consultancies always focus on measurement, preferring to spend the money on the campaign itself.

In the final analysis, the methods of periodic evaluation must reflect specific, defined objectives, and not be satisfied with vagaries like 'our objective is to inform' or to 'raise awareness'. Are you positioning a company as a spokesperson for the industry? Are you trying to launch a product which could be perceived as risky? Do you want to generate interviews and socially responsible quotations for a chief executive? Do you have a point of view on an important issue that must reach a select few opinion-formers? How important is financial measurement – going over or under budget? As objectives differ, so must audiences, methods of communication, objectives and ultimately evaluation. Regular reviews of results play an essential part in issues management, followed by an update of all the communications that are needed to shape opinions or block opposition.

Effectiveness cannot be gauged by activity. Success does not equal the generation of news releases or staged events. A communication strategy succeeds because perceptions on audience maps, like the one described above, have moved in the desired direction. The proper task of measurement is to find and track those movements.

There are options to consider when putting an evaluation package together. What follows is a brief review of several of those options.

1. *Opinion polls and questionnaires.* How much has public awareness of the company shifted since the start of the campaign? Where do the audiences that matter most now stand? Try to visit fifteen or so of the key opinion leaders to find out how your communication looks from the receiving end.

2. *Focus groups.* These purely 'listening' sessions have a part to play at either end of an issues programme, in building strategy as well as evaluation of results. They provide an opportunity for a company and its consultants to hear unvarnished views about an issue or risk from target audiences, to develop new or confirm existing communication ideas, and to stabilize strategy. Smaller groups can consist of around half a dozen participants, often selected by research companies, in an hour-long session at the end of which the invigilator summarizes the trends of the discussion. The company, invigilator and consultants later sit down and evaluate the findings against strategy in a research summary. Larger sessions might last for up to two and a half hours and consist of around twenty people from a chosen audience, with several company and consultancy personnel blending in (where possible) unobtrusively with the audience to absorb revelatory murmurs and asides. To prevent the views of a few people dominating events, a session of this size is often hosted by outside specialists who warm up, form and reform the participants into smaller groups for questions before going back into a large session and then breaking up again.

3. *Collect press clippings and programme transcripts.* This is what companies often do when they measure results: the news, monitored and collected. If the clippings have a monumental bulkiness and a combined viewer/

listener/readership circulation of two hundred million, congratulations. But what does it all mean?

- Measure equivalent costs. How much would it have cost to advertise the same amount of space in the same publications? Did it save significant advertising costs? The same measurement applies to generating interest among selected targets – was it much cheaper to reach them with targeted messages rather than a largescale marketing and advertising effort?
- Measure what the clippings actually said. How often is your company mentioned? Your chief executive quoted? Your product described? How often do pictures or graphics accompany whatever was written?
- Who actually wrote about your organization? Was it covered by the journalists, editors and publications who matter most? If it was, what specifically is said by these opinion-leaders?
- Measure the volume and quality of personal contacts. Media coverage may be important but other vital platforms that deliver your message can be evaluated. The voluntary feedback, for instance. How many media inquiries did you receive? Who asked for copies of your speech, or visited your website, or your stand at the trade show? Who came to your reception and what did they think of it? Who do they represent? What did they ask? What did they take away with them? What happened when you followed up?
- What documentation is provided in support of the measurement claims? Does the company or its agency have the survey or interview results, lists of callers, clippings – perhaps even awards – to back up their assessments?[16]

Two issues campaigns: Comet and Ostmark

The scale of an issues or risk campaign partly depends on the time available. There may be very little time to address a highly charged issue before it warps into a fullscale crisis; or space for a response that educates target audiences about the full complexities of the issue. The size and duration of the programme is affected by:

- Whether there is a clear deadline (such as a legislative timetable, referendum or scheduled plant de-activation).
- The stage at which you have entered the discussion: is it a highly acrimonious, polarized issue, or one that is still fairly fluid?

- The size of the audiences and the number of locations where intervention is needed.
- The extent of existing contacts with opinion-formers. Are firm relationships with the political, media and community gatekeepers in place, or will they have to be built from scratch?
- A company's previous experience in managing issues and explaining risks.

It is possible to resolve sensitive issues rapidly. Comet, the British electrical goods retailer, was flexible enough to act with extreme speed to nip an incident in the bud in the vital few moments before it metamorphosed into a crisis. It did this by convincingly addressing the issues behind the incident which on the surface was damaging only for those directly involved. On the other hand Ostmark, a manufacturer, faced an issue involving multiple audiences in several countries, for which a longer and larger programme was required. The names involved in this particular programme have been changed, and several of the details adapted to illustrate the possibilities of long-term issues management.

Comet: a swift response to a sensitive issue

Issue: workplace harassment

Correct identification of the issue, followed by quick and public action, can forestall a crisis without threatening a company's reputation. The local Comet branch store at Llamselet, near Swansea in Wales, brought the giant UK retailers some unwanted attention in October 1995, when three store managers devised a small incentive scheme, to express their concern about the failure of staff members to meet their weekly quotas for warranty sales on electrical products. Employees were led to a storeroom. In it was a stepladder, which led to hangman's noose dangling from the ceiling. The four employees who missed their targets were told to step forward, and then to step up the ladder, and then to add an extra rung for every week of missed quotas.

Several employees complained to Comet's headquarters. Others complained to the press. 'Hanged if it's funny', said the *Yorkshire Post*. 'Sick', said the *Daily Mirror*. An anonymous employee described the episode as 'bizarre and humiliating'.[17]

This incident, apparently small but highly sensitive, contained several ingredients of a crisis in the making. Whether the matter grew any further depended heavily on Comet's corporate culture. The company might easily have treated it as an internal matter, and tried to brush off media inquiries.

Comet did not: instead, it publicly apologized 'for any distress this matter may have caused to any members of staff'. The company also explained that it had 'immediately implemented a thorough investigation into allegations regarding the pressure' at the store, and was satisfied that the incident was a prank that 'began in fun' but upset some of the staff members. Nevertheless, the three managers would be attending a disciplinary hearing. 'We accept the explanation that it was intended as a joke', said a spokeswoman, 'and because of this the managers will not be dismissed.'[18]

It is harder to spot an issue that has been contained before it bursts into a crisis. Comet dealt swiftly with a distracting and damaging issue of workplace harassment which had the potential to transcend the event and turn into a major embarrassment. The company managed this by:

- demonstrating publicly that it protected the rights of its employees
- showing that it was open, by explaining clearly what it was doing and following through its actions
- demonstrating it was a fair-minded organization by satisfactorily resolving the issue
- apologizing appropriately.

Comet's instant reaction revealed as much about its attitude to the underlying questions of fairness, control and trust as about the event itself, and helped prevent a crisis.

Ostmark: careful management of a major issue

Issue: environmental legislation

The European single market and increased awareness of environmental problems have tested the communication skills of many companies, large and small, and many industries. A number of companies, lacking knowledge of the demands made by risks and issues, have been caught by surprise. On the one side they face a tortuous, intricate process of legislation involving authorities that are themselves still learning the task of pan-European government, and on the other they must re-interpret a popular but dangerous agenda of clear and apparently manageable solutions to a serious global issue.

Here is a part-hypothetical, composite, issues management programme with something to say about effective management of a sensitive communication problem.

Background

Many companies lack the resources or the willpower to keep up with the ceaseless flow of European Union (EU) directives and the activities of the green lobby. Until recently, one of these companies was Ostmark, a multinational manufacturer of containers. There were several smaller competitors in the field, none of which offered a serious threat to Ostmark's position.

Ostmark made little effort to keep up with political affairs: its business was designing, making and selling containers. Anything else seemed to be a waste of resources, until, that is, the EU produced a proposal that the company could not ignore.

The proposed law was one of many designed to level the economic and social playing fields for citizens and companies in the member states – the 'Single Market'. Environmental legislation, being both social and economic in its implications, was a particularly sensitive area but not one that had up to then affected Ostmark. Now the EU needed to harmonize and 'green' the European packaging industry, which rough estimates held responsible for a third to a quarter of all solid waste. The proposal favoured a deposit system for refillable containers, a recovery system for recyclable packaging, and most controversially, established certain refilling and recycling targets that, if not reached, would be punished by increased taxation of the guilty containers to pay for the cost of disposal.

This was less of a problem for glass and aluminium containers, but a disaster for Ostmark. Its paperboard-based products were less widely used than glass or aluminium, and were simply not recyclable. Not surprisingly, perhaps, the larger glass and aluminium manufacturers had kept well abreast of the debate, and advised and consulted with officials from the earliest stages. Ostmark had not. The legislation as it stood would wipe out the company, and the industry.

Ostmark had to respond. The proposal had to pass on a lengthy legislative voyage through various EU institutions: the Commission, Council of Ministers, the European Social and Economic Committee, the European Parliament, and back to the Commission for final approval. Once it had achieved the status of a Directive, every member country had another two years to make its contents law in their own territories. The proposal was already in place; and an amendment would be harder to achieve than contributing to its original contents.

A further obstacle was that recycling, a clear measure of environment-friendliness, meant everything to the media, consumers and policy-makers. Ostmark's containers were sealed in plastic coatings and lined with a thin metallic interior to keep the food fresh and prevent leaks. The advantages of freshness and lightness were obtained at the cost of non-recyclability. To concede as much to the EU and to the media would raise even more questions about the industry. There was little public knowledge about Ostmark – it had no direct presence with consumers since its generic products bore the brand name of the companies who bought its containers. Nor did the public feel inclined to make a more sophisticated equation that balanced a product's green gains and losses at every stage from production to disposal. Environmental groups and politicians had for years used recyclability as a more convenient and easily understandable way to drive their message home to consumers. If Ostmark's message questioned the sanctity of recycling, the response might well be an attack on its product, followed by a movement of its business customers to glass and aluminium in response to public pressure. Somehow, Ostmark had to tackle the environmental issue credibly, responsibly and sensitively. An issues management programme was urgently needed to broaden the current environmental debate.

Objectives

Ostmark had two tasks. One involved lobbying, the other issues management.

- **Lobbying**: to convince EU bureaucrats and politicians that the proposal should be changed. This involved economic as well as environmental arguments, and employed the traditional paraphernalia: one-on-one meetings, memoranda, a thorough knowledge of the people whose influence on this issue counted the most, and detailed understanding of the EU legislative process.
- **Issues management**: to demonstrate to legislators that public opinion would accept a change permitting non-recyclable containers to continue production in the single market.

Issues management message

If its audiences could be encouraged to step back from seeing a company's environmental worth only in terms of recycling, Ostmark had a strong message to deliver. As with most issues management campaigns, it was almost too complex to communicate in its technical entirety without unworkably long messages. On the debit side, Ostmark's containers were – like glass bottles and metal containers – made in part from irreplaceable raw materials extracted from the earth. Furthermore, those materials were used as inner lining and were layered too thinly to separate from the rest of the container: another environmental loss. Until new technology was developed to perform the task of separation at a realistic cost, Ostmark's products would end their days in ugly landfill sites.

Ostmark's gains mounted at other stages of the product's life-cycle. The bulk of the product was woodchip, extracted from managed forests where trees were planted to replace those cut down. If there was no recycling at disposal, it did at least occur during production. Ostmark also believed its production process consumed less energy than was needed to melt and shape glass or metal. A further plus came during transportation of the finished products which, being square, could be stacked tightly together on transport trucks, allowing more to be transported at less cost to air pollution than rounded glass bottle or metal tins. Even after use, Ostmark's containers, buried in managed landfill sites, consumed less energy than would be required to recycle cans and reuse bottles. There was, in short, a case – albeit complicated – to be made.

Ostmark constructed an issues management programme designed to run for two years, based on two basic ideas. One recognized the need to broaden perceptions of what made a product 'green', and the other accepted the awkward fact that recycling had to be a central part of the strategy.

The programme

Ostmark knew that its environmental case had to be presented as impartially as possible in order to succeed with its audiences; it also had to demonstrate that the industry itself was investing time and resources in the search for recycling solutions.

- **Coalition-building**

The campaign was coordinated by the Environmental Containers Group (ECG). This was an industry association formed by Ostmark and its three smaller competitors. All communication in Brussels and elsewhere would be conducted under the group's aegis. The four companies each appointed a representative to the ECG from their own marketing and public relations departments. They met at a public relations consultancy in London and liaised regularly by electronic means. ECG stationery, business cards and news release paper were developed to help give the group an identity.

- **Independent experts**

The ECG's most persistent challenge was to ensure that its messages received a fair hearing among opinion-formers. It therefore identified and approached a group of academics and independent commentators who reviewed ECG's material favourably and provided valuable endorsements, as well as opening access to new political and environmental contacts.

- **The media**

The ECG's media relations typified many of the challenges that issues management regularly faces. A programme that educated science and environment correspondents was essential, but media opinion was so heavily disposed toward recycling that any attempt by the ECG to offer an alternative perspective ran the risk of being dismissed as commercial self-interest.

The ECG strengthened the impression of impartiality by:

1. Treating the subject as an environmental rather than a commercial issue.
2. Limiting its own role to that of facilitator.
3. Creating a panel of prominent independent experts who provided valuable third-party agreement that environmental costs and benefits cannot be restricted to recycling alone, using the food container as an example.
4. Creating a suitable vehicle to deliver the message: a portable 'seminar' held by the panel for invited journalists and moderated by a 'serious' television personality involved in education programming.
5. Holding the seminar across Europe in academic, professional settings such as universities, laboratories and museums, rather than the more usual hotel venues or corporate conference rooms.

- **Media tours**

The ECG invited correspondents to visit its production and extraction facilities in northern Europe. Journalists were able to follow the manufacturing process, ask questions and were provided with scientific information about the product's environmental impact.

- **Publicity**

The ECG became a source for industry news. Working through the public relations consultancy, the group disseminated news about environmental research underway in the industry, and new technology to address the problem of recycling. The focus was at all times on education and dialogue, not loud and defensive explanations of its position. The objective was to present the ECG as a responsible, believable association whose task was not propaganda, but the selective dissemination of information based on sound and clearly explained science.

- **The community**

As a small addition to the programme, the ECG created a roadshow of displays and interactive models that could be carried to communities across the EU. Talking directly with communities had several advantages: it side-stepped the media filter, forced the ECG to cut back on the scientific language which its members were accustomed to using and instead talk in more accessible terms; it dealt directly with the everyday local concerns like littering and waste disposal that in time would influence the political debate; and it helped to gel ECG's message about the environmental impact of its products into colourful and enjoyable activities. Recognizing the importance of communicating with future generations of consumers, the ECG prepared programmes with teachers in several countries that were designed for use in class or as extra-curricular activities.

Conclusion

A two-year programme was certainly necessary. The ECG faced a massive task. It had to work from a standing start to communicate about a complex issue before it grew into an irreversible crisis, build solid networks with journalists and experts, and bring its message home to consumers across the EU. Evaluation is further complicated because the programme is still in progress. Although the immediate objectives of the initiative were indeed realized: the ECG managed to delay the legislative process by a combination of lobbying and securing support from expert third-parties – the member companies realized that in order to prevent further surprises, a scaled-back programme would have to run beyond its allotted two-year time frame. Recycling has a strong hold on minds of consumers and activists, and adding a different perspective to the climate of opinion will take time and patience.

So far, however, the ECG has followed a coherent issues management strategy. It has:

- built stronger relationships with interested media.

- generated a good deal of local attention for its community initiatives.
- become a regular contributor to public discussion on waste disposal, recycling and green legislation at national and EU levels.

Issues and risks play by irregular and unpredictable rules. Like crises, they are heavily influenced by audiences outside a company. A company can use issues management and risk communication to take more control of its fate, before beliefs, perceptions and emotions collide with events to make a crisis in which the task of education becomes more difficult, and perhaps a matter of survival.

Summary

- Issues are shaped by 'social' concerns.
- Risks are shaped by personal fears.
- Risks are less rational than issues, because:
    1. fear is based on emotional responses
    2. fear cannot be dismissed; it will not go away
    3. the risk does not have to be real; it has only to be perceived
    4. fear has a massive influence on public attitudes and actions
    5. fear feeds crisis
    6. personal fear is a more powerful force than concern for others
    7. fear is countered by empathy, attentiveness and education.
- The longer a risk or issue is ignored, the greater its potential for damage.

An Issues or Risk Communication Programme must:

- Identify the perceived issue or risk.
- Define the objective by an examination of the needs of specific audiences.
- Create messages that:
    1. show how your point of view complements *existing* beliefs or hopes of your audiences
    2. take 'ownership' of a carefully identified emotion
    3. express the social, non-economic as well as economic benefits of your point of view
    4. take extreme care over words and phrases
    5. avoid technical explanation.

- Lay strategic foundations based on:
  1. education
  2. persuasion
  3. dialogue
- Develop a tactical framework, which includes:
  1. coalition-building
  2. a Position Paper
  3. objective platforms for delivering messages to key opinion-formers
  4. community relations
  5. corporate responsibility
- Measure the results periodically, and revise tactics as required.

Notes

1   Hunt, P., Public Affairs Manager, Shell UK. (1997) *Brent Spar: A Drop in the Ocean?* Business in the Community Occasional Paper 5. London: Shell.

2   'Japan: Murayama closes book on Minimata Disaster'. *Reuter News Service – Far East*, 15 December 1995.

3   Brogan, H. *The Longman History of the United States of America*. London: Longman, 1991, p. 467.

4   'Australian consumers shrug off beef chemical scare'. *Reuter News Service – Australia & New Zealand*, 23 November 1994.

5   *ibid.*

6   'Australia: Australian beef exports recovering after scare'. *Reuter News Service – Australia & New Zealand*, 13 December 1994.

7   'Australia: Beef marketing fund up 20pc'. *Australian Financial Review*, 15 February 1995.

8   'Australia: US calls for more tests on suspect meat'. *Sydney Morning Herald*, 23 November 1994.

9   Chernow, R. *Titan. The Life of John D. Rockefeller, Sr.* New York: Random House, 1998. p. xx.

10   'NEI store'. www.nei.org/store/other_pubs.html

11   Porter Novelli survey, August 1993. 'U.S. corporations lack credibility'. *Toronto Star*, 14 August 1993.

12   Lee, Ivy L. 'The problem of international propaganda: a new technique necessary in developing understanding between nations'. London: Occasional Papers 3, 3 July 1934. See also Lee, Ivy L. (1925). *Publicity: Some of the things it is and is not.* New York: Industries Publishing.

13   Moeran, B. *A Far Valley. Four Years in a Japanese Village.* Tokyo: Kodansha, 1998, p. 198.

14   'Protest of "Last Temptation" takes many forms across U.S.'. *St Petersburg Times*, 10 September 1988.

15   Gladwell, M. 'The spin myth. Are our spin meisters just spinning one another?'. *New Yorker*, 6 July 1998.

16   Numbered paragraphs '1' and '3' are taken from: Moore, Simon. 'Make your marketing measurable'. *Mass High Tech*, 20–6 April 1998.

17   ' "Hanging" bosses rapped; Comet store staff made to play sick hangman game if sales targets were not reached'. *Daily Mirror*, 18 October 1995.

18   *ibid.*

7 Crisis preparedness

It is clear that the information aspects need to be more fully incorporated at the earliest stages of planning.
Defence Committee inquiry into media handling during the Falklands crisis, April 1983

Crisis preparedness planning involves more than operational contingency plans. As we have seen in Chapter 4, crisis management demands simultaneously:

- solving the problem or issue (real or perceived)
- controlling and coordinating all internal and external communications
- running the rest of the business.

Preparedness plans must therefore assist and support management to anticipate and handle these demanding functions under crisis conditions. However good the extemporized actions and responses, corporate, management and product reputations can still be undermined, or even seriously damaged, if speculation and allegations are feeding internal and external audiences with negative information and rumours. Preparedness planning is a critical tool for wresting back and maintaining control over escalating crisis circumstances.

The value of advance preparation is now understood by many large corporations. The 1996–7 Infoplan survey, *Crisis Alert*, discovered that 75 per cent of 500 leading UK companies had already suffered what they believed to be a crisis. Most said that their crisis plan had worked successfully. 91 per cent of respondents felt 'prepared' for several potential crises, including blackmail, accidents, health and safety emergencies and product failures. 84 per cent had designated a senior director to take responsibility for crisis management. Two years earlier the figure had been 58 per cent.

A 1990 survey of the Fortune 1000 US companies by Boston-based crisis consultants Clarke found crisis plans had an average age of three years. This timespan is important: corporate structures, market spread, and product ranges are constantly changing, along with management positions, personalities, issues and telephone numbers; a periodically reviewed and updated plan is likelier to remain useful. Crisis preparedness plans should be revisited, re-tested and revised.

A preparedness plan is not foolproof. It can reduce but not eliminate risk. Placing extinguishers in rooms where there is a known fire hazard is a wise precaution, but there is always the chance that a fire will break out in another room. At such times it is useful to remember some words attributed to President and General Dwight D. Eisenhower: 'In preparing for battle I have always found that plans are useless but planning is essential.' Regardless of where disaster originates, planning prevents you from making the deadly mistake of splitting operational action from communication, trains you to shake off the personal shock and move quickly into action, and allows you to establish consistent, credible mechanisms and messages for response and recovery.

A preparedness plan is more than a traditional operational or emergency manual, because it recognizes that the outcome of your crisis hinges on what you say and how you say it as much as what you do. A programme to deliver a preparedness plan consists of six elements:

- An assessment of risks and threats.
- A risk audit of the company's operations.
- Strategic and tactical plans for operational handling of the identified risks and threats.
- A thorough understanding of the audiences that could be involved.
- A communication strategy that is closely integrated with operational decision-making.
- Simulation to test the integrity of the completed plan.

Crisis preparedness planning

The audit

The first task of a crisis preparedness plan is the confidential audit, a survey of the company's operations, with the aim of identifying vulnerabilities such as those described above. A wide-ranging audit sets the parameters for subsequent preparedness planning, and must cover as much of the company as possible, from headquarters to local facilities, from senior management to shop-floor employees, if possible. The audit should incorporate all aspects of production, quality control, supply and distribution, the existing communication capability of the company and its regular management structure. It should ask how things work, who makes them work and what keeps those people awake at night. The audit should also research trends in the relevant industry sector: what types of crisis have arisen in the past to trouble the industry?

The value of an audit may best be understood by selecting an hypothetical and unlikely candidate for a crisis preparedness plan: a small family firm of well-known Swiss chocolate manufacturers. While it may be disappointing at first not to be battling the high-profile excitements faced by a chemical multinational or a nuclear power plant, an audit would reveal that *chocolatiers* are not immune from crises common to the food industry in general. Product contamination, tampering and health scares present the most obvious threats.

The first stage of a full crisis preparedness planning programme is the detailed assessment of such threats, and likely 'blockages' in the process of response. Our chocolate makers would be peculiarly exposed to an attack on quality. The firm exports all over the world, and the attention paid to quality means it charges higher prices than local rivals. Customers tend to be well-off and relatively well-informed. A crisis could drive many of these people away and the media would readily target the company because it is known as an upmarket brand. Additionally, the firm's small size would prevent it from deploying the resources that an international crisis would demand. The company is careful and slow-moving. Conservatism is the very reason for its success, but would this culture be a help or a hindrance in a crisis? Other issues would also emerge: the European Union's minute regulations affecting descriptions of food, food quality and packaging could have a long-term impact on the company, and this area – if it is not watched – may generate an expensive legislative Ostmark-type crisis which the company, by itself, lacks resources or expertise to fight. It would be a wise and modest precaution to keep closer track of the legislative scene in Brussels.

What areas might be audited? These do not differ significantly in outline whether the company's business is chocolates or software:

- supplier profiles
- selecting, shipping and receiving of raw products and materials
- production and manufacturing processes
- quality control and quality assurance
- outward distribution of product
- customer profiles and priorities
- regulatory framework and relationships
- management and employees

- health and safety
- site security
- corporate management and head office
- communications systems and procedures
- past problems and current issues experienced by this company and its industry sector.

Examine the following issues (*inter alia*):

- **People.** From the decision-making process (how many layers of management stand between a decision and its execution? How centralized is responsibility for key decisions?) to the composition and morale of the workforce (part-time? full-time? franchized? unionized?)
- **Product life-cycle.** What procedures are taken to ensure health, safety, quality and delivery at each stage of the product's journey from raw material through production, distribution, use and disposal?
- **Corporate geography.** Is the company scattered across one country or several? How is communication between sites coordinated and conducted?
- **Documentation.** Are any emergency plans in place within the company? Do they include a detailed role for communication? Are there updated lists of people to contact? Is there a security policy? What has been done to communicate important issues such as health, safety or confidentiality to employees?
- **Regulatory framework and relationships.** How are regulatory changes monitored and analysed? Which national and international authorities are responsible for regulating the industry and related areas? What is the extent of the company's contact with officials and key politicians?
- **Current media relations.** Who does the company know already? What is the state of its relations with local, national, regional, web and trade media?
- **The extent and nature of contacts with other audiences.** Independent experts, trade unions, the neighbourhood, industry associations, interest groups.
- **Public reputation.** Who, if anyone, holds opinions about the company's products, people or operations? Retailers? Interest groups? Politicians? The media? The consumer? The industry? What views do these groups have of the industry sector?

Threat assessment

We have seen how certain incidents target certain industries. There is a close but not exclusive relationship between product recall and children's toys; environmental contamination and oil or chemicals; crashes and airlines. Other crises are more universal, for example massive litigation, fraud, extortion, large-scale redundancies or sexual harassment.

The potential risks can sometimes seem overwhelming, yet a solid plan should take pains to identify all those that appear to be substantive, and explain how they might emerge within the organization. Different threats will require different operational and communication handling, differently composed management teams, and will affect diverse audiences. The more comprehensive the assessment, the better prepared the company. Risks and threats need to be assessed and ranked or prioritized. One pharmaceutical multinational has 60–80 risks ranging from adverse drug reactions from hurricane to bursting dams near facilities to armed employees. Clearly, such a list must be fully assessed and ranked before realistic plans can be constructed.

The Y2K problem, in which everything that relies on a computer might fail to work because the year 2000 will be confused with 1900, has belatedly struck non-scientific humanity (a belatedness which itself represents a failure of issues management). At the risk of dating this chapter, Y2K will be used to illustrate the elements of a preparedness plan. In the most extreme version of the problem, it may be virtually impossible to communicate since – aside from couriers on bicycle or foot – our highways of information and transportation could be disabled. It would be prudent, though, and of more value for a general guide to preparedness, to assume that universal gridlock will not prevail.

Y2K is of peculiar interest. It turns one basic aspect of the crisis experience onto its head: the date for the crisis is set, but the exact problems that will be experienced are hard to predict, or even unknown.

The possibility of a significant 'Year 2000' crisis trails in Y2K's wake, which may prove larger than the technical difficulties created by the 'Bug' itself. In the last half of 1999 companies may be confronted with uncontrolled scenarios which seem likely to be driven and escalated by rumour, speculation, allegations and accusations. Consumers, employees, customers, suppliers, regulators, politicians, community leaders and journalists will become preoccupied with the unknown aspects of problems that could arise at the end of 1999. In the USA scared consumers are stockpiling food and fuel; there is talk of household shelters being required and even possible civil unrest. Other audiences will react to the issue in different ways, but unless rapid and coordinated measures are taken by corporate management to anticipate and handle such extreme reactions, concerns over the unknown will metamorphose into genuine and deep-rooted fears, which can only result in self-fulfilling prophecies. The necessary integrated operational and communications management schemes require strategic planning and corporate coordination with internal and external groups and individuals.

Paramex

Our imaginary company, Paramex, founded in 1974, is a medium-sized and successful exporter of high-precision computerized optical and temperature-monitoring equipment used in hospitals and supermarkets. We shall concentrate here on the Y2K aspects of the general Year 2000 problem, which is manageable within the context of this discussion.

What could possibly happen to Paramex at the stroke of midnight on 31 December 1999? The impact of Y2K on healthcare, as on so many other areas, cannot be exactly determined. The Chief Executive of the National Health Service Confederation in Britain has said, cautiously but publicly, that deaths as a result of Y2K are 'unlikely'. MPs on the House of Commons Public Accounts Committee have warned after hearing testimony from health managers that potential problems with medical equipment 'could be life threatening'.[1] Uncertainty is a rich breeding-ground for crises. Even if the actual problems are localized, hard questions might be asked by media, customers, victims or their families, and authorities. The topical nature of the Millennium Bug should not distract us from the universal principles that Paramex must apply. A confidential audit of the Y2K implications for this company might highlight two major threats:

- **Safety.** Malfunction or failure of optical tools used in certain surgical procedures; malfunction or failure of temperature control equipment in supermarket storage areas.
- **Systems breakdown.** Postponement of vital surgery in several North American and European hospitals. Failure of food refrigeration systems.

These are indirect crises, for Paramex is not liable to be the centre of public attention in the first instance. That privilege will fall to its customers: the hospitals, food retailers and airports that have purchased its systems. They will suffer the problems, and have publicly recognized names. The media will put Paramex's customers under pressure, at least to begin with. Nevertheless, we have indicated that a crisis can draw in more than one company, and the complexities of Y2K are an excellent example of how events may ripple outward and raise difficult questions for other organizations. The ripples of a Y2K crisis, like other crises, originate with an event that affects one organization and can spread out in the direction of the companies that supplied them with the faulty product, and out again towards the contractors that supplied parts for the faulty product. Manchester United's Munich disaster involved both the airline and, for a time, the engine manufacturers. *E.coli* at Jack In The Box damaged the franchisees, Foodmaker the parent company, and Vons, who supplied the meat. The Elk Test crash affected Daimler-Benz, who then publicly criticized the tyre, and by implication its makers. NASA reacted to the Hubble telescope's problems by placing responsibility on their contractors.

Audience identification

Monitoring, meetings and desk research can help pinpoint the external groups likely to react to specific crises. While Paramex's audiences are as generic as those described elsewhere, they must be refined to names, addresses and contact numbers for:

- Management and employees.
- Any suppliers or contractors involved in construction or installation of equipment.
- Customers and agents.
- Victims and their families.
- Regulatory authorities in the countries involved.
- Interest groups concerned with patient rights, food safety or Year 2000 and Y2K.
- Media (including hi-tech, healthcare, retail, consumers and local media in the vicinity of customer sites).
- Recognized independent Year 2000 and Y2K experts and consultants.

Success in crisis communications usually falls to companies who have committed time and management effort to building and maintaining relationships with these audiences in advance, reflecting the old adage that you make your own luck.

Define key messages

Before Paramex dives into the process of drafting holding statements, it should define responses and messages as discussed on page 110. The statements should be prepared as templates against identified crisis scenarios (which is the logical development of the ranked risks and threats listing process).

The key messages must form the core of everything the troubled company says and does. They should not be slogans, but convey important ideas about the sort of company that Paramex is, its priorities and its commitment to tackling the problem. For example:

- Our first responsibility is to the people who use our products.
- We are appalled at what has happened.
- We are working in cooperation with the regulatory authorities.
- We have committed all our resources to tackle the problem.
- We encourage questions and enquiries and have established facilities for people to contact us.
- We are a reliable and regular source of information on this issue.

Draft Initial Holding Statements

Draft statements should be developed to serve as templates in the event of particular crises. The detail must naturally change, but a draft has the advantage of clarifying the company's feelings and basic position in advance, without the pressures, distractions and temptations presented by actual events.

'Paramex Ltd. London.

[**Your location and date**: London: 2 January 2000, 4 p.m.] [**Describe the incident**: This afternoon, at 3 p.m. GMT, the BugEye Mark I, a high-precision Optical Device used in neurosurgery in hospitals around the world and manufactured by Paramex Ltd, malfunctioned during an operation at Holy Cross Children's Hospital, Seattle, USA.

[**Describe your feelings**: We are shocked and upset by this, and extend our deepest sympathies to the patient's family.] [**Give priorities and actions**: Our first priority is to patient safety and we will not rest until the cause of the malfunction has been found and corrected. As far as we are aware, this is the only incident of its kind to have occurred, and we have immediately contacted our customers and despatched teams to check, service and overhaul the BugEyes. All BugEyes have been withdrawn from service until we are satisfied that they are safe to use.]

[**Information and non-technical description of product**: At present there are 125 BugEye Mark I's in operation in 73 hospitals in Europe and North America. The model costs £10,000. It was first constructed in 1985, and resembles a human arm, double-jointed, plastic-coated, and ten feet in length. The BugEye is remote-controlled by a nurse. It is clamped on a power unit above the patient and relays colour images to a television monitor. By magnifying images up to 1000 times, the BugEye has helped surgeons to conduct intricate surgical procedures in once impossible-to-reach areas, including removal of tumours from the brain stem.]'

Background information

The most effective way of preparing detailed background information like the details noted in the last paragraph is to analyse and format it as if used as 'Notes to Editors'. This acid test ensures that jargon and technical language is cleaned out before it is used in communicating to non-technical, non-scientific or non-medical audiences.

Questions and responses

Prepare for questions by anticipating the worst that could be asked; they may present opportunities to deliver positive key messages styled for the spoken, not written word.

Q: Vital surgery is now being delayed in many hospitals because of your withdrawn equipment. Hundreds of waiting patients may die or be permanently damaged. Do you feel responsible?

R: We feel appalled at what happened. We're certainly not going to dodge responsibility if we find that our systems are at fault. That's why we're investigating this as a matter of extreme urgency. The BugEye won't be returned to service until we've confirmed it is completely safe.

Q: How long will that be?

R: The first checks will be completed today. If it is safe to do so, we will advise the hospitals that the equipment can be used immediately. The service teams will then move onto other hospitals. It's hard to say exactly at this stage, but we would like to have most equipment working as usual within five days.

Q: What happened?

R: We're reluctant to speculate. When we know for certain, we will tell you.

Q: What are you doing about this tragedy?

R: We've got six service teams of experts in the USA and Europe at work. The task for them is to visit every hospital that uses the BugEye and work with the local systems people to correct the problem. They were sent less than an hour after this tragedy occurred. So far – and I stress so far – nothing unusual has been reported.

Q: You are a successful hi-tech company. Why weren't you prepared for Y2K?

R: As I said, we don't want to dodge any share of the responsibility. We have had Y2K teams working with our customers for the last two years to iron out any possible problems. We of all people understand the risks, given the products we make. The process is complicated and vulnerable to a knock-on effect from problems elsewhere. It is very distressing to realize that we did not get it right, but we are working to isolate the problem and eliminate it.

Q: Did you make all the chips?

R: Yes.

or

R: No. The chips are made by a contractor, Miniprobe Systems. I want to stress that we're coordinating our efforts. We definitely don't want to go around blaming people. It's more constructive for all concerned if we can work together.

Q: The mother of the injured child has described you as incompetent and murderers. What do you have to say about that?

R: It's very sad and upsetting. This is a terrible thing. We're not in the business of being incompetent, so it's personally wrenching to hear those words. Of course, I can understand her anger. I'm angry too.

Q: Whose fault is it?

R: The most important thing for now is to get the system back to work to help those who urgently need it. We are investigating the source of the problem and when we discover what it is and how it happened, we'll comment and take any necessary action.

Q: The Health Ministry in the UK has launched its own investigation. How do you feel about that?

R: We are going to cooperate fully. Our company is as concerned as the Ministry in getting to the root of this problem.

Q: I understand that you also make equipment for supermarkets.

Are you satisfied that your other products are safe? What else could go wrong?

R: As well as the BugEye, we also manufacture equipment that monitors and controls refrigeration systems for several large food retailers. We have sent teams to check this equipment also. No problems have been discovered so far.

Appoint the Crisis Team

- **Core Crisis Management Team** (CCMT). These are the key figures who receive summaries of comment and activity, take strategic decisions and direct operational and communications activity. The CCMT must be limited to ten if it is to be effective. Typical membership in a manufacturing company would be:
    1. Chief executive – Team leader
    2. Chief finance officer
    3. Operational director
    4. Marketing/sales director(s)
    5. Corporate communications/affairs director (if the function exists at a sufficiently high level)
    6. Technical/engineering director
    7. Legal director/counsel
    8. Human resources/personnel director.
- **Support Management Team**. These are all the functions which have been identified during the audit as critical to possible risk or threat scenarios. Typically it would cover:
    1. Plant general managers.
    2. Security – for extortion, kidnap, product contamination.
    3. Quality control/assurance – usually the expert who has access to production records and quality checks and systems, and often reports to the Technical Director.
    4. Distribution/transportation, who can provide product tracing and distribution records and/or have access to a network of distributors or agents.
    5. Product managers of the most important items in the product range.
    6. Key account/customer managers for the biggest or most important customer accounts.
    7. Customer complaints manager.
    8. Managers with unique knowledge or technical expertise that could be required in a crisis (for example information technology or engineering managers/staff).

The critical points about all those nominated to either the CCMT or as Support Management are:

- They must all have nominated deputies or qualified alternatives (who should not be away at the same time where possible).
- Full details must be known of all their contact details at work and at home.

Any company must have a portfolio of spokespeople, comprising:

- Corporate spokesperson – who could be the lead spokesperson.
- A company spokesperson – probably a Public Relations/Public Affairs person who deals with the media on a day-to-day basis.
- Specialist or technical spokespeople – for example the technical director, medical director in a pharmaceutical company, marketing director, key product managers.

The portfolio of spokespeople are best placed under the coordination of the Public Relations/Public Affairs director/manager, who carries personal responsibility for keeping spokespeople trained, briefed and prepared to handle media contacts and interviews as agreed or directed by the CCMT. See page 102 for a survey of the CCMT's work programme in the midst of a crisis.

Logistics

- **Space.** Rooms must be dedicated for conversion into crisis control and media briefing centres at corporate headquarters, and where possible at the site of the incident. If the incident occurs in a single location or on company property this is easier to accomplish than multiple incidents occurring (as may be the case with Paramex) in customer sites across several countries. In that scenario, coordination with customers to develop or integrate onsite crisis management and communications will prove more productive than operating independently and wondering what the other team is doing about the problem or saying about you.
- **Comprehensive communication materials** should be available (and accessible via e-mail and the worldwide web) in whatever crisis room or communications centre will be used during a crisis:
    Call out and alert lists.

Key messages and response lists.

Standby statements.

Question and response lists.

Information sheets – configured for use in Notes to Editors (as discussed above) and by any other key groups/audiences (for instance, pharmaceutical companies must be ready to address physicians and pharmacists).

Product information and photos.

Contact details for all subsidiaries, facilities and corporate HQ(s).

Employee lists.

Supplier and contractor lists.

Customer lists.

External contact lists.

In the frenetic atmosphere generated by a high-profile incident, it is not advisable to spend precious time trying to gather together the tools for distributing messages on a large scale. A preparedness plan should set aside, as at Lockheed Martin (see page 124), the materials required to communicate fast and effectively to all your audiences. This includes stationery, pens and pencils, computers, printers, company letterhead and release papers. Pre-videotaped segments of production processes or workers in action should be prepared to help reporters understand and tell the story.[2] Arrangements should be made where necessary to ensure e-mail, pagers, fax, mobile and desktop telephones, teleconferencing and hotline capabilities. Information technology personnel should be identified to develop websites that carry news, updates and useful links with other sites.

Simulation – testing and validation

One of the starkest ways to demonstrate the impact of crisis is by simulation training. A company can be flung into a crisis with all its audiences baying for information, decisions, responses and action. Suddenly, executives will see how much they need to prepare. These simulation sessions can range all the way from desktop-management decision games to realistic simulations on company premises with full operational tests.[3] As a general principle, even traditional onsite emergency exercises should incorporate communication. The FBI's hostage-taking drills include press conferences to tackle media leaks as well as the actual business of retrieving the hostage.

Desktop exercises

The desktop or 'what if' format can be used to assess the effectiveness of plans and assist crisis management teams to work through the mechanics of simultaneously handling the operational and communications challenges and demands of crisis situations.

The goals for the session need to be clearly defined in advance to ensure that new crisis managers will be enabled to confront situations and problems with all the necessary experience and training.

Using scenarios drawn from the ranked list of risks and threats facing the company, crisis managers and communicators are presented with developing situations through written, verbal and audio-visual inputs. A session should be planned, managed and facilitated by an experienced crisis manager with training experience.

While a desktop exercise will be conducted under training conditions, pressure can be exerted on teams and systems by the regulation of the inflow of information and demands for decisions and actions from the players. In order to meet the objective of a session, at suitable points it will be necessary to interrupt the flow of the exercise to discuss issues or take corrective action when major problems arise. In all cases the participants should go away with a sound understanding of their roles within crisis procedures, systems and management teams. At the conclusion of a session a list of next steps should be agreed with responsibilities and timelines being assigned for taking agreed actions.

In many cases desktop exercises highlight wider training and briefing needs within the crisis management organization. Once this first process of validation has been completed, crisis managers and systems should be ready to undergo simulation tests.

Simulation test exercises

Once crisis preparedness plans and teams have undergone initial validation and specialist training, the next step is to subject plans, procedures and systems to testing through the use of simulation techniques.

Simulation uses telephone, audio-visual and role-playing techniques to create realistic depiction of crisis situations and scenarios. Carefully researched issues and problems are woven into a schedule of events which will face crisis managers with a series of real-life situations and crisis problems. While the prime objective is to let managers experience the pressures of working in the fishbowl environment of crises, it still remains important to ensure that a session highlights problems in teams and plans, while providing a teaching experience for the players.

In order to maintain the fine balance between injecting realistic pressure and tensions into the exercise and ensuring that everyone learns, a simulation session should be planned, coordinated and facilitated by a practical crisis manager who has had wide experience of this advanced training format. At the same time the risks of realistic simulation triggering a real crisis should never be ignored. All written and verbal communications before and during the event should be prefixed or marked with caveats to ensure recipients know they are dealing with a simulated exercise situation. At the same time non-participating managers should be told that a simulation exercise is underway. Care also needs to be taken when introducing surprise inputs (TV crews 'door-stepping' senior executives with demands for interviews, or role-playing journalists attempting to bluff their way into facilities, offices or meetings). It is advisable to warn security, reception and switchboard staff when such an exercise is due to take place.

Wherever possible, real communication channels and systems should be used during a simulation exercise. Where this is not possible, every effort must be made to ensure that exercise constraints do not force crisis managers to manage problems which become a burden additional to those imposed within the exercise scenarios.

Over the agreed period of the simulation exercise, the crisis managers should be confronted by an escalating series of situations. As the events unfold the problems should become more complex while timelines steadily reduce, mirroring the circumstances that could be faced under real crisis conditions.

The success of any simulation exercise will depend on three key factors:

- The schedule of exercise events should be researched in depth before being prepared by a multidisciplined team of managers, probably with call upon external experts and crisis specialists.
- All inputs to the exercise should be pre-prepared and rehearsed in advance. At the same time plans need to be made to ensure that the input team is capable of adapting their activities to respond to the actions and communications of the crisis management team(s).
- The simulation facilitator should be supported by observers with sufficient knowledge of company operations and experience to be able to assess the actions and reactions of the crisis managers.

The simulation exercise should be followed immediately by a 'hot washup' debrief, an immediate review of the exercise play while first impressions are fresh in the minds of players, observers and the input team. Subsequently a full report should be prepared for consideration by crisis managers to cover:

- observations and comments on the exercise play;
- record of comments and decisions taken during the hot washup debrief session(s);
- recommendations for future preparedness planning and training.

Special crisis training

As has been shown in this book, crisis demands special skills and capabilities from those managers likely to be faced by the demanding high-profile situations that could emerge and escalate into the public domain at any time. If companies are to be truly ready to anticipate and handle crises, in addition to the desktop and simulation testing and training discussed above, they may need to consider several other forms of special training for managers and employees.

As part of any preparedness programme, the following training could be included:

- Adverse media training for spokespeople. Using identified risk and threat scenarios, spokespeople should learn to handle aggressive and probing interviews with print, radio and TV journalists.
- Media handling for staff who could be required to handle calls from journalists in pursuit of a crisis story or scoop. Secretaries to key executives, switchboard operators, security staff and receptionists could all benefit.
- If a dedicated crisis media handling team is part of the plans, media handling training can be used to select and train personnel nominated for this important role.
- Training on crisis handling techniques for operators assigned to hotline, information lines or consumer/customers services. This training can be used to ensure that operators will be able to handle the pressures and demands of working for long hours under crisis conditions.

Trust and reputation management

It's clear many companies need to improve the way they communicate in order to maintain their most important asset – a good reputation.
Bob Druckenmiller, President, Porter Novelli Public Relations

Reputation depends on perception, and perception on communication. In early 1996 the non-profit consortium, Business for Social Responsibility, surveyed 25 American companies which enjoyed positive corporate reputations, and asked if they made a particular effort to nurture their good name. 'The answer', reported the consortium, 'was "yes", in their decision-making processes, their strategic planning . . . They do ongoing market research, in a sense . . . If we had done the survey five years ago, we would have drawn a blank.'[4]

Corporate reputation has been central to these pages. It is the heart of the crisis: the thing that critics wound, reporters dissect and managers must protect. This book exists because companies must on occasion take drastic steps to defend this valuable asset. In the information age, communication cannot be an afterthought in the management of corporate reputation. It is important to close this account by setting the emerging field of trust and reputation management alongside preparedness as a means of crisis prevention.

Reputation is not the commercial strength of a company's product. In February 1996 Shell Exploration and Production (Expro) appointed its first reputation manager. 'We realised', a Shell executive admitted, 'that all the work we had done on brand and reputation wasn't enough.'[5] It has been shown that the more a company succeeds in the world of commerce, the more it is judged on a set of shifting standards, set by external groups, organizations and individuals. Often those standards are defined by indistinct and emotive parameters, especially when something goes wrong.

The yardsticks for reputation are varied and often conflicting. At any moment a company and its management may be reviewed and judged against:

- Financial and product performances and returns.
- Legal and regulatory standards and regulations.
- Accepted and expected ethical behaviours.
- Environmental sensitivity of management or potential impact of operations.
- Cultural standards, in different markets and regions of the world.
- Depth of commitment to public health and safety.
- Personal and human rights of employees, consumers, suppliers and subcontractors.
- Requirements for political correctness.

At the same time those involved in the assessment and judgement of reputation will represent a bewildering array of groups varying from customers to employees, financial analysts to local communities, regulators to interest groups, ministers and politicians to the media.

When we come to consider the defence of corporate reputation, management has to accept that success and failure will be weighed in the same balance, albeit against differing standards. Success can be driven by the processes of normal business activity. However, when a serious problem thrusts a company into the public domain the stakes change, while the pressures and time frames are radically escalated.

Since many corporations operate across borders and undertake business in several markets simultaneously, the defence of reputation needs to be considered in a multinational context also. When a crisis strikes, three of its main characteristics, all international and multimarket in scope, impinge upon reputation:

- Since the sun never sets on international business, markets are always open somewhere in the world. Of particular importance is the rolling effect upon stock markets and political agendas.
- The media now provide 24-hour news services, which we have already noted means information is constantly being updated and disseminated around the world. The effect is that a serious issue or incident will be picked up and passed on, effectively feeding your crisis into the next set of deadlines – and headlines.
- International crisis management teams can never close up shop, since at any moment decision-making and communications control could be active in some part of the world.

This book has examined some of the factors which affect corporate reputation and how companies should defend this important asset. As any insurer or risk manager will know, a risk or threat to a company carries the potential to escalate to crisis proportions. In the world of global communications serious issues, incidents and emergencies can, and will, be picked up and hurled into the public domain. Today, transparent management has become accepted as one of the risks of doing business with the consequent need to strive to meet the demands of different groups that watch and judge our every commercial and operational activity and statement.

Reputation management treats communication as more than a disparate series of tasks from marketing to investor relations and employee communication. Its purpose is to integrate all communication activities to maintain a company's good name. A successful integration programme begs several large questions:

- Do our employees understand, via inhouse communication, the strategic importance of reputation management, especially those who deal most often with external audiences: salespeople, receptionists, telephone operators and customer service representatives? One consultant has warned: 'Every employee in the entire organization is a reputation manager, from the top down.'[6] Have our employees contributed to building a strategy for our reputation in interviews, surveys or focus groups?

- Does our Mission Statement, or (in the case of Johnson & Johnson) Credo really address the most relevant of those yardsticks on which a good reputation is built, or is it solely focused on production, price, orders, slogans and share value?

- If our Mission Statement does address those issues, does it make a positive contribution to our public reputation, as revealed by desk research and direct contact with our audiences?

- If our Mission Statement does address those issues, is it, as in the case of Johnson & Johnson, the guiding principle behind our response to a crisis, or is it treated as little more than a commercial tool to be forgotten when legal and operational realities get too tough?

- Do we monitor upswings and downswings in our reputation? Much of the North Sea oil industry ignored the slow decline in public understanding and perception until Greenpeace exposed its weakened position. Nike did not track the conversion of its image as feisty underdog to exploitative bully until it became the target of public protest over its Asian labour practices.

- Does research reveal whether our company is well-regarded or wanting in any of the important yardsticks noted above?

- Do we have existing initiatives in these areas that could make a positive contribution to our reputation?

- Does our research focus on marketing alone, or does it measure us against the perceptions and beliefs of all our important audiences, from investors to the local community and non-profit interest groups?

- Have we ever built alliances or at least developed contacts with erstwhile critics or allies in the media, universities, local community or interest groups, to discuss common concerns and explain our activities?

- Do we have a 'Spar Test'? – a committee and a mechanism for assessing whether new and important business decisions, a new facility, operations in new markets and cultures or a breakthrough in technology, for example, touch on public concerns that could affect our reputation?

- Do all people responsible for our company's communication – including investor relations, marketing, law, public relations, customer relations and inhouse communication – work as a single group to discuss their activities and the expectations of their particular audiences?
- Is reputation management the responsibility of a senior company officer?
- Is reputation management a topic for regular consideration at Board level?

Companies cannot be ready to face these challenges unless they constantly seek to understand who plays a role in bolstering or undermining perceptions of their company, and the logic and agendas which drive these differing audiences. Thereafter they need to prepare, plan and train to be able to anticipate and handle possible crises, clear in the knowledge that crisis management and the defence of corporate reputation must always be conducted under public pressure.

In our crowded world, we want things that are often messy to make. We expect all the benefits of industry without the costs of producing them. There are those among us who succumb to greed or who are scared, and turn a blind eye or arrogant gaze when something is plainly wrong. Such people are found everywhere, including corporations. Crises are inevitable so long as people make mistakes, or make moral judgements based on the power, volume and invasiveness of modern words and images; so long as we are able to contrast the televised face of an injured child with the features of a man in a grey suit delivering a carefully worded statement from an expensive office. For us, that picture is often the whole story. Should it be? Above all, crisis communication challenges the impulse to believe that what you immediately feel is somehow true. It exists for troubled organizations to tell their own story, which they have a right to do, so that fair and balanced judgements can be reached.

Summary

Crisis preparedness planning

- **Audit.** The first stage of a full crisis preparedness planning programme is an audit of the company to target risks and threats.
- **Threat assessment.** Identify substantive threats, and explain how they might emerge within the organization.
- **Audience identification.** Monitoring, meetings and desk research can help pinpoint the external groups likely to react to specific crises.

- **Define key messages.** These must form the core of everything the troubled company says and does. They should not be slogans, but convey important ideas.
- **Draft Initial Holding Statements.** These should be developed to serve as templates in the event of particular crises.
- **Background information.** Detailed papers written for key audiences in clear, non-technical terms.
- **Questions and responses.** Prepare for questions by anticipating the worst that could be asked; even such questions present opportunities to deliver positive messages styled for the spoken, not written word.
- **Appoint the Crisis Team.**
  Core Crisis Management Team (CCMT). These are the key figures who receive summaries of comment and activity, take strategic decisions and direct operational and communications activity.
  Support Management Team. These are all the functions which have been identified as critical to possible risk or threat scenarios.
  The company must also have a *portfolio of spokespeople*.
- **Logistics.** Rooms must be dedicated for conversion into crisis control and media briefing facilities, and communication materials should be available.

Testing and validation

Desktop exercises
- The goals for the session need to be clearly defined in advance.
- Use scenarios drawn from the ranked list of risks and threats facing the company.
- Interrupt the flow of the exercise to discuss issues or take corrective action when major problems arise.
- At the conclusion, list next steps with responsibilities and timelines.

Simulation test exercises
- In-depth research by a multidisciplined team of managers, probably with external experts and crisis specialists.
- All inputs to the exercise should be pre-prepared and rehearsed in advance.
- The simulation should be supported by observers able to assess the actions and reactions of the crisis managers.
- The simulation exercise should be followed immediately by a debrief.

Special crisis training

- Adverse media training for spokespeople.
- Media handling for staff who could be required to handle calls from journalists.
- Training on crisis handling techniques for operators assigned to hotline, information lines or consumer/customers services.

Trust and reputation management

- Do our employees understand, via inhouse communication and participation, the strategic importance of reputation management?
- Does our Mission Statement address the yardsticks on which a good reputation is built?
- Is our Mission Statement the guiding principle behind our response to a crisis, or is it a disposable commercial tool?
- Do we monitor upswings and downswings in our reputation?
- Does research reveal whether our company is well-regarded or wanting in any of the important yardsticks noted above?
- Do we have existing initiatives in these areas that could make a positive contribution to our reputation?
- Does our research focus on marketing alone, or does it measure us against the perceptions and beliefs of all our important audiences?
- Have we ever built alliances with external groups to explain our activities?
- Do we have a 'Spar Test?'
- Do all people responsible for our company's communication work as a single group to discuss their activities and the expectations of their particular audiences?
- Is reputation management the responsibility of a senior company officer?
- Is reputation management a topic for regular consideration at Board level?

Notes

1   '"Lives at risk" from Millennium Bug'. 19 August 1998. http://news.bbc.co.uk/hi/english/health/newsid_153000/153975.stm
2   'Reputation management: How to handle the media during a crisis'. *Risk Management*, March 1995.
3   Interview with Mike Seymour. 'Who you gonna call?', *Management Review*, February 1995.

4   Ettorre, Barbara. 'The care and feeding of a corporate reputation'. *Management Review*, June 1996.
5   'In pursuit of repute'. *Utility Week*, 15 August 1997.
6   Ettorre, Barbara. *op. cit.*

Case study: Bluepage

It had gone well, on the whole. Jennifer Stone pottered around her flat, savouring the silence and looking forward to her first quiet evening in precisely fourteen days.

The whole thing had subsided as quickly as it emerged when it was discovered, and swiftly announced, that Mrs Hill's alarm had been damaged in her fall. At least Turnbull had been right about that: there was nothing wrong with their alarms. Now Bluepage was working with Synex on a more robust model in case of outdoor accidents.

To Jennifer's surprise, her CEO Bob Wallace had been an excellent spokesperson. Empathetic, clear and calm. A fatherly, even grandfatherly figure for the media from that first, nerve-wracking and hostile news conference, through the recall decision and the host of interviews up to the announcement about what really happened to Mrs Hill's alarm.

Jennifer thought that she now knew Mrs Hill better than she had ever known anyone in her life.

There had been some awkward moments: threats of group actions; a stern warning from a junior health minister with responsibility for the elderly; some nasty criticism from Age Watch. She had not enjoyed being in their sights. After all, they had got what they wanted – publicity – by bringing the company to its knees. Any expansion plans were out of the question for at least the next two quarters while Bluepage recovered the costs of the crisis, and sought to win back customer confidence.

Most of all perhaps, Jennifer Stone had surprised herself. The crisis consultant had been impressed with her ability to handle difficult messages for the news-hungry media. Together, they had crafted communications to journalists, investors and customers. There had been mistakes, but once the crisis team began working to a regular routine, with the consultant and with Bob Wallace, the decisions flowed more smoothly, and more sensibly.

At the end of the day, the crisis turned out to be less important that it felt. It was a tempest in a teapot. She felt sudden anger. What a waste of her life! A draft relaunch plan lay on the counter top. She eyed the document resentfully, and then thoughtfully as she pondered the opportunities that the relaunch might bring. Perhaps that is one of the most important things for her, and for Bluepage, to learn. Not that people get things absurdly out of proportion, but that every crisis, however trivial the cause, needed to be treated seriously. Jennifer switched off the light, and left the room.

Bibliography

Books

Albrecht, Steven (1994) *Fraud: Bringing Light to the Dark Side of Business.* Burr Ridge, IL: Irwin.

Albrecht, Steven (1996) *Crisis Management for Corporate Self-defense: How to Protect Your Organization in a Crisis . . . How to Stop a Crisis before It Starts.* New York: AMACOM, American Management Association.

Barton, Laurence (1993) *Crisis in Organizations: Managing and Communicating in the Heat of Chaos.* Cincinnati: College Division South-Western Publishing Co.

Bate, Roger (1997) *What Risk?* Oxford: Butterworth-Heinemann.

Branch, Melville C. (1994) *Telepower, Planning and Society.* Westport, CT: Praeger.

Fink, Steven (1986) *Crisis Management: Planning for the Inevitable.* New York: American Management Association.

Flin, Rhona (1996) *Sitting in the Hot Seat: Leaders and Teams for Critical Incident Management.* Chichester: John Wiley & Sons.

Gottschalk, Jack A. (ed.) (1993) *Crisis Response: Inside Stories on Managing Image under Siege.* Detroit: Visible Ink Press.

Green, Peter Sheldon (1994) *Reputation Is Everything.* Burr Ridge, IL: Irwin.

Marconi, Joe (1992) *Crisis Marketing: When Bad Things Happen to Good Companies.* Chicago: American Marketing Association; Cambridge: Probus.

Meyers, Gerald C. (1986) *When It Hits the Fan: Managing the Nine Crises of Business.* Boston: Houghton Mifflin.

Mitroff, Ian I. and Pearson, Christine M. (1993) *Crisis Management: A Diagnostic Guide for Improving your Organization's Crisis-Preparedness.* San Francisco: Jossey-Bass.

Pinsdorf, Marion K. (1987) *Communicating when Your Company Is Under Siege: Surviving Public Crisis.* Lexington, MA: Lexington Books.

Regester, Mike and Larkin, Judy (1997) *Risk, Issues and Crisis Management. A Casebook of Best Practice.* London: Kogan Page.

Sethi, S. Prakash (1994) *Multinational Corporation and the Impact of Public Advocacy on Corporate Strategy.* Hingham, MA: Kluever.

Woolfson, Charles, Foster, John and Beck, Matthias (1997), *Paying for the Piper: Capital and Labour in Britain's Offshore Oil Industry.* London: Mansell.

Articles

Andsager, Julie and Smiley, Leiott. 'Evaluating the public information: shaping news coverage of the silicone implant controversy'. *Public Relations Review*, 22 June 1998, no. 2, vol. 24, p. 183.

Benoit, William L. 'Image repair discourse and crisis communication'. *Public Relations Review*, 22 June 1997, no. 2, vol. 23, p. 177.

Dwyer, Steve. ' "Hudson, we have a problem!" Hudson Foods' inability to handle a crisis management program'. *Prepared Foods*, May 1998, no. 5, vol. 167, p. 14.

Fisher, Rick. 'Control construct design in evaluating campaigns'. *Public Relations Review*, 22 March 1995, no. 1, vol. 21, p. 45.

Gorski, Thomas A. 'A blueprint for crisis management: Understanding what it takes to weather the inevitable storm'. *Association Management*, January 1998, no. 1, vol. 50, p. 78.

Holding, Robert F. 'The day Inside Edition called'. *Association Management*, February 1998, no. 2, vol. 50, p. 34.

Kearns, P.M. 'Protect your company's image; includes related articles on crisis communication'. *Communication World*, 18 August 1998, no. 7, vol. 15, p. 41.

Kim, Irene and Wilson, Steve (eds). 'Crisis management'. *Chemical Engineering*, January 1998, vol. 105, no. 1, p. 123.

Lauzen, Martha M. 'Public relations practitioner role enactment in issues management'. *Journalism Quarterly*, vol. 71, no. 2, p. 356.

Morrison, J. Ian. 'The future tool kit'. *Across the Board*, vol. 31, no. 1, p. 19.

Pearson, Christine M., Rondinelli, Dennis A. and Robertiello, Jack. 'Crisis management in Central European firms'. *Business Horizons*, 15 May 1998, no. 3, vol. 41, p. 50.

Rosen, Sheri. 'Crisis in context; Digital Knowledge; use of Internet in public relations and crisis communications.' *Communication World*, December 1998, no. 1, vol. 16, p. 34.

Unattributed. 'Managing environmental information and crises is called the environmental challenge of the 90s'. *Supervision*, March 1993, vol. 54, no. 3, p. 6.

Williams, David E. and Olaniran, Bolanle A. 'Expanding the crisis planning function: Introducing elements of risk communication to crisis communication practice'. *Public Relations Review*, 22 September 1998, no. 3, vol. 24, p. 387.

Index